T0176861

Implementing Cryptography Using Python®

Shannon W. Bray

WILEY

Published by
John Wiley & Sons, Inc.
10475 Crosspoint Boulevard
Indianapolis, IN 46256
www.wiley.com

Copyright © 2020 by John Wiley & Sons, Inc., Indianapolis, Indiana
Published simultaneously in Canada

ISBN: 978-1-119-61220-9

ISBN: 978-1-119-61222-3 (ebk)

ISBN: 978-1-119-61545-3 (ebk)

Manufactured in the United States of America

No part of this publication may be reproduced, stored in a retrieval system or transmitted in any form or by any means, electronic, mechanical, photocopying, recording, scanning or otherwise, except as permitted under Sections 107 or 108 of the 1976 United States Copyright Act, without either the prior written permission of the Publisher, or authorization through payment of the appropriate per-copy fee to the Copyright Clearance Center, 222 Rosewood Drive, Danvers, MA 01923, (978) 750-8400, fax (978) 646-8600. Requests to the Publisher for permission should be addressed to the Permissions Department, John Wiley & Sons, Inc., 111 River Street, Hoboken, NJ 07030, (201) 748-6011, fax (201) 748-6008, or online at http://www.wiley.com/go/permissions.

Limit of Liability/Disclaimer of Warranty: The publisher and the author make no representations or warranties with respect to the accuracy or completeness of the contents of this work and specifically disclaim all warranties, including without limitation warranties of fitness for a particular purpose. No warranty may be created or extended by sales or promotional materials. The advice and strategies contained herein may not be suitable for every situation. This work is sold with the understanding that the publisher is not engaged in rendering legal, accounting, or other professional services. If professional assistance is required, the services of a competent professional person should be sought. Neither the publisher nor the author shall be liable for damages arising herefrom. The fact that an organization or Web site is referred to in this work as a citation and/or a potential source of further information does not mean that the author or the publisher endorses the information the organization or website may provide or recommendations it may make. Further, readers should be aware that Internet websites listed in this work may have changed or disappeared between when this work was written and when it is read.

For general information on our other products and services please contact our Customer Care Department within the United States at (877) 762-2974, outside the United States at (317) 572-3993 or fax (317) 572-4002.

Wiley publishes in a variety of print and electronic formats and by print-on-demand. Some material included with standard print versions of this book may not be included in e-books or in print-on-demand. If this book refers to media such as a CD or DVD that is not included in the version you purchased, you may download this material at http://booksupport.wiley.com. For more information about Wiley products, visit www.wiley.com.

Library of Congress Control Number: 2020940306

Trademarks: Wiley and the Wiley logo are trademarks or registered trademarks of John Wiley & Sons, Inc. and/or its affiliates, in the United States and other countries, and may not be used without written permission. Python is a registered trademark of Python Software Foundation. All other trademarks are the property of their respective owners. John Wiley & Sons, Inc. is not associated with any product or vendor mentioned in this book.

V10019736_071020

To Stephanie, Eden, Hayden, and Kenna,
with all my love, for making each and every day special.

About the Author

Shannon W. Bray started his career in information technology in 1997 after being honorably discharged from the United States Navy. He started his IT career working on programmable logic controllers out in the Gulf of Mexico and then started writing business applications using various technologies until 2000 when .NET was first released; since then, the languages of choice have been C++, C#, Windows PowerShell, and Python. From there, Shannon worked on writing software until he started working with Microsoft SharePoint. The Microsoft stack of technologies forced Shannon out of just writing code into building large secure solutions. Shannon's career has taken him to engagements all over the world where he has worked with a number of U.S. government agencies. Shannon became interested in cryptography while pursuing a master's degree in cybersecurity, and he has continued to research cryptography and cybersecurity as he pursues a PhD in computer science.

Shannon has earned the following certifications: Microsoft Certified Master, Microsoft Certified Solutions Master, Certified Information Security Manager (CISM), Security+ (Plus), the CompTIA Advanced Security Practitioner (CASP+), and a number of other industry certifications. In addition to writing, Shannon speaks nationally at technology conventions and works as a mentor teaching technology to youth programs.

Shannon lives in the Raleigh, North Carolina, area with his wife, Stephanie, two daughters, Eden and Kenna, and son, Hayden. During the dive season, Shannon enjoys diving off the coast of North Carolina. During the rest of the year, Shannon works on IT projects around the house that utilize single-board computers and, most often, propellers. He is currently building a home security system that uses Python, cryptography, and drones. As of the release of this book, Shannon is currently running for the U.S. Senate for the state of North Carolina to help bring cybersecurity issues to the mainstream and to help people understand the importance of end-to-end encryption.

Shannon can be contacted through LinkedIn at `www.linkedin.com/in/shannonbray`.

Acknowledgments

While this is my third book, every book comes with its own set of challenges. Completing a book is not always a fun project but does become a labor of love. As soon as you start, life has a way of throwing changes at you, and it seems that you never have the time that you thought you would have. Shortly after starting this book, I started a PhD program with the Missouri University of Science and Technology and transitioned through a number of government contracts, ran for political office, and then became a work-from-home teacher as the world battled a global pandemic. I knew that the editing team would be earning their pay with whatever I put together. That team has been wonderful with their feedback and responsiveness. Specifically, I'd like to thank the following people on the Wiley team: Barath Kumar Rajasekaran, production editor; Jim Minatel, acquisitions editor; Pete Gaughan, content enablement manager; Brent Cook and James Langbridge, technical editors, and, most importantly, Kim Wimpsett, the project editor. Kim did her best to keep me on schedule, but I found new ways to miss a few deadlines.

Contents at a Glance

Contents

Introduction

I initiated my journey into cryptography while studying for my undergrad. Most of the cryptography concepts I learned were based on what one would need for their CISSP or Security+ exams. Most of my understanding was at a high level, and it was difficult to remember the more intricate aspects until cryptography became a primary focus.

It wasn't until I started my master's in cybersecurity that I began applying cryptographic features within a scripting environment. The concepts in this book will help you advance your knowledge and experience as you dig deeper into understanding the use of cryptography in Python.

Over the past few years, several governments have discussed legislation that will ensure that any form of communication, whether it's an email, text message, or video chat, can always be read by the police or intelligence services if they have a warrant. Governments are putting pressure on technology companies to give them backdoor access or the keys to the kingdom so that they can keep the country safe.

The fight between lawmakers and encrypted messaging platforms has entered new territory. Imagine a world where the government has seized the opportunity to scan every electronic message by government-approved scanning software. The privacy and security of all users will suffer if law enforcement agencies achieve their dream of breaking cryptosystems. Proponents of end-to-end encryption, like Microsoft, Facebook, and Google, may lose their campaign to maintain user security as a priority.

We have all heard of times when it would be beneficial for encrypted data to magically become readable; this is often related to criminal cases. Should criminals be allowed to plot their plans in secret? Where does the right to our privacy start? In reality, there are technical and legal issues with allowing governments to do this; this of course will be strongly opposed by technology and privacy advocates. The world is at war on what can be encrypted, what should be encrypted, and who should have the keys to unlock someone else's encryption.

Whether you agree or disagree with what powers a nation-state should have over encrypted communications in their country, you should understand what encryption is, how to apply it when needed, and how to ensure that the data you are receiving is authentic and confidential. Over the course of this book, you will get a basic understanding of how to cryptographically secure your messages, files, or Internet traffic using easy-to-understand Python recipes that have been created or updated to support Python 3.

What This Book Covers

This book focuses on helping you pick the right Python environment for your needs so that you can hit the ground running. You will get an understanding of what algorithms are and explore the basics of Python.

Once you have an idea of where you are starting from, you will get an overview of what cryptography is, what perfect secrecy means, and the history of cryptography and how its use changed our world.

To get a full understanding of some of the cryptographic concepts, a little math is needed. You will get an understanding of how prime numbers, basic group theory, and pseudorandom number generators help build cryptographic solutions. This will build the foundation for understanding various stream and block ciphers and highlight some of their encryption modes and weaknesses.

Every cryptographic discussion is better with pictures, so we will spend a chapter focusing on how image cryptography and steganography work. We'll also highlight a few issues that you will need to be aware of while dealing with images.

Message integrity is just as important as message secrecy. Knowing who sent the message to you directly relates to whether the message is credible. You will learn how to generate message authentication codes to ensure integrity during transit.

The strength of encryption will be shown at the end of the book when you will learn about PKI schemes and explore how to implement elliptic curve cryptography in an application. The application you build will exchange data in a highly secure format over an unsecure channel, thus ensuring that you are able to control your own end-to-end encryption scheme that no one will be able to decrypt without the keys you create. I hope you find the journey as fun as I did.

What You Need to Know

This book assumes that you are fairly new to cryptography. While there is a brief introduction to how to set up and use Python, you will get the most out of the book if you have experience in another programming or scripting language.

What You Need to Have

The concepts presented in this book can be executed on Microsoft Windows, Linux, Chromebook, or iOS. Your choice of editor will most likely depend on the underlying operating system, although most of the Python recipes presented here will execute in online editors as well as most shells that are using a Python interpreter that is 3.0 or greater.

How to Use This Book

The topics in this book get more advanced as you progress through it, so you can work through the material from front to back and build your skills as you go. You can also use this book as a reference that you can consult when you need help with the following situations:

- You're stuck while trying to figure out how to secure your data.
- You need to do something using cryptography that you've never done before.
- You have some time on your hands, and you're interested in learning something new about Python and cryptography.

The index is comprehensive, and each chapter typically focuses on a single broad topic. Don't be discouraged if some of the material is over your head. As you work through the coding samples and build out the final solution, the concepts should become easier to understand.

What's on the Website

Nearly everything discussed in this book has examples with it. You can (and should) download the many useful examples included with this book. We have verified that each file will run in environments that are Python version 3.0 and higher.

The files are located at `github.com/braycrypto/cryptography`, as well as at `www.wiley.com/go/cryptographywithpython`.

Introduction to Cryptography and Python

Cryptography is one of the most important tools we have at our disposal as information security professionals. It provides us with the ability to protect sensitive information from unauthorized disclosure through encryption. Cryptography is the use of mathematical algorithms that can be used to transform data either into an encrypted form (ciphertext) or into its decrypted form (plaintext). The purpose of these algorithms can be quite complicated. The goal of this book is to help simplify the use of cryptography using the available libraries in Python, so you will begin your journey into cryptography by setting up a Python environment. You'll also get a review of using Python, and then you'll write your first cipher using Python. Specifically, you'll do the following:

- Gain an understanding of algorithms
- Explore various Python installations
- Set up Python 3 on various machines
- Explore the basics of the Python language
- Write your first cipher using Python

Exploring Algorithms

The algorithms you will explore in this book can be quite sophisticated, but most of the logic is encapsulated into little black boxes that allow you to interface with the algorithms using functions. In the programming or mathematical world, a function is merely a way to enter values and receive output. When using algorithms in cryptography, we generally have two inputs for encryption and two inputs for decryption:

- The encryption process will take the *plaintext message* (P) along with an *encryption key* (K) and then run the plaintext through encryption algorithms, which will return *ciphertext* (C).

- On the decryption side, the ciphertext (C) will be supplied along with the encryption key (K), which will produce the plaintext (P) message.

As you study various encryption themes throughout this book, you will find that they are described by three algorithms: *GEN* for key generation, *ENC* for the encryption algorithm, and *DEC* for the decryption algorithm. You'll revisit this concept at the end of this chapter when you learn how to create a Python function.

GEN: choose a random key uniformly from $\{0,1\}^{\ell}$ $\{0,1\}^{\ell}$ (the set of binary strings of length ℓ ℓ)
ENC: given $k \in \{0,1\}^{\ell}$ $k \in \{0,1\}^{\ell}$ and $m \in \{0,1\}^{\ell}$ $m \in \{0,1\}^{\ell}$ then output is $c := k \oplus m$ $c := k \oplus m$
DEC: given $k \in \{0,1\}^{\ell}$ $k \in \{0,1\}^{\ell}$ and $c \in \{0,1\}^{\ell}$ $c \in \{0,1\}^{\ell}$, the output message is $m := k \oplus c$ $m := k \oplus c$.

Why Use Python?

Using Python for cryptography is simpler than using languages such as C or C++; while free libraries such as OpenSSL are available, their use can be quite complex. Python removes these complexities with many built-in libraries that aid in cryptography scripting. It is also a great choice because Python is free in terms of license. Python can be described as an open-source, general-purpose language that is object oriented, functional, and procedural, and it allows for the interface with C/ObjC/Java/Fortran and even .NET. A number of versions are available, from 2.5.*x* through 3.*x*. Currently, 3.*x* is becoming more popular as new libraries are introduced. Python comes preinstalled with Linux and macOS, and you can install it on Windows as well. You will learn how to install Python in each of these environments later in this chapter.

Because Python is available for Windows, Linux/Unix, Mac, and Chromebooks, among others, the lessons you learn here will be portable to several environments. Python has proven to be quite powerful in information security and can be used to quickly script solutions to help you become a better security practitioner. If you are using Ubuntu Linux, every command you see in this book will work. If you are on a Mac, you can use the Terminal app found inside the Utilities folder. On a Windows machine, you have several options as well: you can install a number of tools such as Cygwin, Visual Studio, or PyCharm; use the Windows 10 Linux subsystem; or just install Ubuntu Linux from the Microsoft Store. If you are new to Linux, I recommend practicing your command-line skills a bit to help get you comfortable.

When you start the Python shell (by typing `python` or `python3` at the command line), you will see the version and the date associated with the version. For instance, if you install and run Python in a Linux environment, you should see something similar to the following:

```
Python 3.7.4+ (default, Sep  4 2019, 08:03:05)
[GCC 9.2.1 20190827] on linux
Type "help", "copyright", "credits" or "license" for more information.
>>>
```

The majority of Python interpreters use >>> as a prompt to accept user input; one notable exception is IPython, which is discussed briefly in a moment. Once you are in a Python shell, exit by pressing CTRL+D or typing `exit()`. Python files use a .py extension, and we start their execution in Linux environments by typing `python3 filename.py;` (keep in mind that you still need to chmod +x the file).

NOTE   In Unix-like operating systems, the chmod **command sets the permissions of files or directories.**

As you will learn later in this chapter, a large number of modules are available for Python, many of which we will use along your journey of learning cryptography. One of the more notable modules you will learn more about is NumPy. NumPy offers numerical operations to Python, including fast multi-dimensional array operations, random number generation, and linear algebra. Another module that you will be introduced to is Matplotlib, which is an excellent library for plotting. In Chapter 6, you will learn more about PyFITS, which is a module that provides access to Flexible Image Transport System (FITS) files. FITS is a portable file standard that is widely used throughout the astronomy community to store images and tables. We will be combining it with our cryptography techniques to encrypt and decrypt image files.

Downloading and Installing Python

You can download the Python interpreter from www.python.org/python, where you'll find versions for Ubuntu, macOS, and Windows. Be sure to download version 3.7 or higher, since Python 2 is now unsupported.

Installing Pip, NumPy, and Matplotlib

Ensure you are in a command shell environment with a prompt. In the following example installation, you will get an update to the packages that come with your Python version.

Pip, or Pip3 in this case, is the package management system for Python; it is used to install and manage software packages written in Python. Pip is similar to tools like Bundle, NPM, and Composer in other programming languages. NumPy, which stands for Numerical Python, is a Python package that is the core library for scientific computing. It contains a powerful n-dimensional array object, and provides tools for integrating C, C++, and many other languages. Matplotlib is an excellent solution for scientific plotting; it has the ability to be automated and produce a wide variety of customizable high-quality plots.

Once the shell is open, type the following commands:

```
~$ sudo apt-get update
~$ sudo apt install python-pip
~$ pip3 install numpy
~$ pip3 install matplotlib

~$ $ python3 -c "import numpy as np; import matplotlib.pyplot as plt; x
= np.linspace(0, 2 * np.pi); y = np.sin(x); plt.plot(x, y); plt.show()"
```

NOTE   Depending on your environment, you may need to install `python3-pip` to get Pip3 to work. On installs such as Ubuntu 16.04 on Windows, you will not be able to install version 3 when you install `python-pip`.

To start the Python 3 shell, type the following:

```
~$ python3
```

You should see something similar to the following depending on the version that is installed:

```
Python 3.X.X (default, date)
[GCC 6.3.0 20170516] on linux
Type "help", "copyright", "credits" or "license" for more information.
>>>
```

To test whether you have the additional packages installed correctly, open your favorite Python editor. If you don't have one, you can elect to use Nano in a Linux environment or even Notepad in a Windows environment. Type the following:

```
#!/usr/bin/env python

import numpy as np
```

```
import matplotlib.mlab as mlab
import matplotlib.pyplot as plt
mu, sigma = 100, 15
x = mu + sigma*np.random.randn(10000)
# the histogram of the data
n, bins, patches = plt.hist(x, 50, normed=1, facecolor='green',
alpha=0.75)
# add a 'best fit' line
y = mlab.normpdf( bins, mu, sigma)
l = plt.plot(bins, y, 'r--', linewidth=1)
plt.xlabel('Smarts')
plt.ylabel('Probability')
plt.title(r'$\mathrm{Histogram\ of\ IQ:}\ \mu=100,\ \sigma=15$')
plt.axis([40, 160, 0, 0.03])
plt.grid(True)
plt.show()
```

Save the file as matplot.py and execute the file. The preceding Python recipe will generate a plot using NumPy and the Matplotlib library (see Figure 1.2).

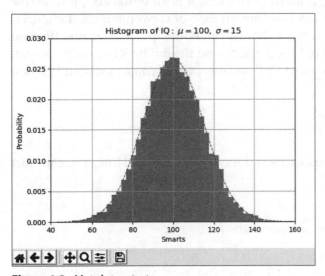

Figure 1.2: Matplot.py test

Installing the Cryptography Package

Python has a Cryptography package that provides cryptographic recipes and primitives to Python developers. It is designed to be your "cryptographic standard library." As of this writing, it supports Python 2.7, Python 3.4+, and PyPy 5.4+. You can install the Cryptography package by using Pip3. The syntax is as follows:

```
$ pip3 install cryptography
```

The Cryptography package includes both high-level recipes and low-level interfaces to common cryptographic algorithms such as symmetric ciphers, message digests, and key derivation functions. For example, to encrypt something with Cryptography's high-level symmetric encryption recipe, use this:

```
>>> from cryptography.fernet import Fernet
>>> # Put this somewhere safe!
>>> key = Fernet.generate_key()
>>> f = Fernet(key)
>>> token = f.encrypt(b"A really secret message. Not for prying eyes.")
>>> token
'...'
>>> f.decrypt(token)
'A really secret message. Not for prying eyes.'
```

Installing Additional Packages

IPython is available through many providers; it is an enhanced, interactive version of Python. IPython offers a combination of convenient shell features, special commands, and a history mechanism for both input and output. IPython offers a vastly improved set of functionality and flexibility; it is a fully compatible replacement for the standard Python interpreter. You can install IPython by typing the following:

```
sudo  apt install IPython3
apt-get install python3-IPython
```

To use IPython, type **IPython3** **-h** at the system command line. You can start the shell by typing this:

```
~$ IPython3
```

You should see something similar to the following:

```
Python 3.5.3 (default, Sep 27 2018, 17:25:39)
Type "copyright", "credits" or "license" for more information.

IPython 5.1.0 -- An enhanced Interactive Python

In [1]:
```

Please note that you will need to pay attention to the version of Python; this example is using Python 3.5.3, but you may see something like Python 2.*x* if you did not specify IPython3. When Python 3 first came out, many libraries didn't exist, so many people stayed with 2.*x*. Python 3 has caught up and is now a great language. There are, however, a few differences between Python 2.*x* and Python 3, so if you find that some of your scripts fail, try running them using an alternate version.

Testing Your Install

Once you have selected the platform of your choice, open the Python IDE. Find the Python console panel and type the following:

```
>>> print('Hello World')
Hello World
>>> x = 100
>>> x*(1 + 0.5)**10
5766.50390625
>>> import math
>>> math.sqrt(49)
7.0
```

If everything goes as expected, you should see the output shown in Figure 1.3.

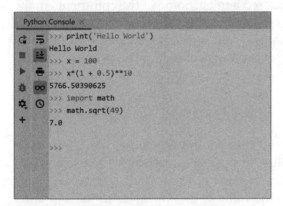

Figure 1.3: Python installed successfully

Diving into Python Basics

Prior to getting into the variables, spacing, strings, and loops, I will cover a few of the basics you will need to know. Names in Python are case sensitive and cannot start with a number. They can contain letters, numbers, and underscores. Some examples include:

- ▪ `alice`
- ▪ `Alice`
- ▪ `_alice`
- ▪ `_2_alice_`
- ▪ `alice_2`

The language includes a number of reserved words, such as `and`, `assert`, `break`, `class`, `continue`, `def`, `del`, `elif`, `else`, `except`, `exec`, `finally`, `for`, `from`, `global`, `if`, `import`, `in`, `is`, `lambda`, `not`, `or`, `pass`, `print`, `raise`, `return`, `try`, `while`.

The goal of this book is not to teach Python from the ground up; it is, however, logical that you may be coming from another scripting or programming language and may need a brief overview of the nuances of Python. While keeping it as short as possible, in this section I discuss variables, operators, strings, loops, and files. The hope is to give you enough information that you can debug your Python code in the case of a typo.

One major difference between Python and many other languages is that whitespace is meaningful, and many of your early errors probably will be a result of indentation being misused. A newline in Python ends the line of code unless you use the backslash (\) character. You will find that you need to use consistent indentation throughout your code. The first line of code with less indentation is outside a code block, whereas the lines with more indentation start a nested block.

As with other languages, Python allows you to comment your code. Commenting your code should be considered a must. Some of the comments in the code used in this book have been removed to shorten the code examples, but you will be well-served by comments as you revisit previously written code. In Python, comments start with #; everything following the pound sign will be ignored.

Using Variables

The programs you write throughout this book will need to store values so they can be used at a later time. Values are stored in variables; the use of a variable is signified by the = sign, which is also known as the *assignment operator*. For example, if you wanted to store the value 21 in a variable named `age`, enter **age = 21** into the shell:

```
>>> age = 21
```

Variables can be overwritten or used in calculations. Explore the following by typing it into your shell:

```
>>> age + 9
30
>>> age
21
>>> age = age + 9
>>> age
30
```

Python doesn't enforce any variable naming conventions, but you should use names that reflect the type of data that is being stored. It is important to know that in Python, variable names are case sensitive, so age and Age represent two different variables. This overview shows the use of variables with numbers; we will examine the use of variables and strings next.

Using Strings

Strings allow you to use text in programming languages. In cryptography, you use strings a great deal to convert plaintext to ciphertext and back. These values are stored in variables much like the numeric examples used in the preceding section. Strings in Python are stored using the single quote (') or double quote ("); it does not matter which quote you use as long as they are matching. To see an example, type the following into the shell:

```
>>> name = 'John'
>>> name
'John'
```

The single quotes are not part of the string value. Python only evaluates the data between the quotes. If you wanted to set a variable to an empty string, you would use the following:

```
>>> name = ''
```

In Python, you can concatenate multiple strings together by using the plus (+) operator. See the following example:

```
>>> first = 'John'
>>> last = 'Doe'
>>> name = first + last
>>> name
'JohnDoe'
```

Notice that the strings concatenate exactly the way they store values; if you need a word separation, plan for the use of spaces.

Introducing Operators

You have now seen the + operator used in both numeric and string variables. Other operators can be broken down into the following categories: arithmetic, comparison, logical, assignment, bitwise, membership, and identity.

Understanding Arithmetic Operators

Arithmetic operators perform mathematical calculations (see Table 1.1).

Table 1.1: Arithmetic Operators

OPERATOR	DESCRIPTION	EXAMPLE
+	Addition	10 + 20 will give 30
–	Subtraction	10 - 5 will give 5
*	Multiplication	10 * 10 will give 100
/	Division	10 / 2 will give 5
%	Modulus	20 % 10 will give 0
**	Exponent	10**2 will give 100
//	Floor Division	9//2 is equal to 4 and 9.0//2.0 is equal to 4.0

Most of these operators work precisely the way you expect from other programming languages. It is critical to our exploration to examine modular (%) arithmetic in detail as it plays an essential role in cryptography. We write things like 28≡2(mod26), which is read out loud as "28 is equivalent to 2 mod 26." While not entirely accurate, modular arithmetic focuses on the remainder. In our example, 26 divides into 28 one time with two remaining, or x(mod p) as the remainder when x divides into p. We can say that a≡b(mod q) when a–b is a multiple of q. So 123≡13(mod 11) because 123–13=110=11·10. Now I've heard folks describe the remainder of x mod p, which does refer to the unique number between 0 and p–1, which is equivalent to x. An infinite sequence of numbers are equivalent to 53(mod13), but out of that continuous sequence, there is precisely one number that is positive and smaller than 13. In this case, it's 1. In a math setting , I would call 1 the canonical representative of the equivalence class containing 53 modulo 13.

Table 1.2 shows some examples to help you wrap your head around the concepts; they will be presented again when you examine ciphers and explore finding the modular inverse in cryptographic math.

Table 1.2: Arithmetic Operator Examples

EXPRESSION	DESCRIPTION	SYNTAX
28 (mod 26)	28 is equivalent to 2 mod 26	28 % 26
29 (mod 26)	29 is equivalent to 3 mod 26	29 % 26
30 (mod 26)	30 is equivalent to 4 mod 26	30 % 26

One additional feature of Python is the use of the multiplication operator with strings. The feature can be advantageous when you need to create specifically formatted strings that may be used in some attacks such as buffer overflows. One example can be examined using the print function, as shown here:

```
>>> # Python 2.7
>>> print 'a' * 25
aaaaaaaaaaaaaaaaaaaaaaaaa

>>> # Python 3.5
>>> print ('a' * 25)
aaaaaaaaaaaaaaaaaaaaaaaaa
```

NOTE   Python 3 and higher require you to use Print() as a function. You must include the parentheses.

Understanding Comparison Operators

The comparison operators, also known as *relational operators*, compare the operands (values) on either side and return true or false based on the condition (see Table 1.3).

Table 1.3: Comparison Operators

OPERATOR	DESCRIPTION	EXAMPLE
==	Compares two operands to see if they are equal; if the values are equal, it returns true.	(10 == 20) is not true
!=	Compares two operands to see if they are not equal; if the values are not equal, it returns true.	(10 != 20) is true
<>	Compares two operands to see if they are not equal; if the values are not equal, it returns true.	(10 <> 20) is true
>	If the operand on the left is greater than the operand on the right, the operation returns true.	(10 > 5) is true
<	If the operand on the right is greater than the operand on the left, the operation returns true.	(10 < 20) is true
>=	If the operand on the right is equal to or less than the value on the left, the condition returns true.	(10 >= 5) is true
<=	If the operand on the left is equal to or less than the value on the right, the condition returns true.	(5 <= 10) is true

Understanding Logical Operators

The logical operators include and, or, and not (see Table 1.4).

Table 1.4: Logical Operators

OPERATOR	DESCRIPTION	EXAMPLE
and (logical AND)	If both the operands evaluate to true, then condition becomes true.	(a and b) is true.
or (logical OR)	If any of the two operands are non-zero, then condition becomes true.	(a or b) is true.
not (logical NOT)	Used to reverse the logical state of its operand.	Not(a and b) is false.

Understanding Assignment Operators

You first explored the assignment operators when we covered variables. In addition to using the equal sign, Python offers many assignments that work as a shorthand for more extended tasks. To get an understanding of how this works, examine Table 1.5.

Table 1.5: Assignment Operators

OPERATOR	DESCRIPTION	EXAMPLE
=	Assigns values from right-side operands to left-side operands.	c = a + b assigns value of a + b into c
+= (add AND)	Adds the right operand to the left operand and assigns the result to the left operand.	c += a is equivalent to c = c + a
-= (subtract AND)	Subtracts the right operand from the left operand and assigns the result to the left operand.	c -= a is equivalent to c = c - a
*= (multiply AND)	Multiplies the right operand with the left operand and assigns the result to the left operand.	c *= a is equivalent to c = c * a
/= (divide AND)	Divides the left operand with the right operand and assigns the result to the left operand.	c /= a is equivalent to c = c /
%= (modulus AND)	Takes modulus using two operands and assigns the result to the left operand.	c %= a is equivalent to c = c % a
**= (exponent AND)	Performs exponential (power) calculation on operators and assigns the value to the left operand.	c **= a is equivalent to c = c ** a
//= (floor division)	Performs floor division on operators and assigns the value to the left operand.	c //= a is equivalent to c = c // a

Understanding Bitwise Operators

The bitwise operators work on bits and perform bit-by-bit operations (see Table 1.6). Assuming a = 60 and b = 13, the binary format of a and b will be as follows:

a = 0011 1100

b = 0000 1101

Table 1.6: Bitwise Operators

OPERATOR	DESCRIPTION	EXAMPLE
& (binary AND)	Copies a bit to the result if it exists in both operands.	(a & b) (means 0000 1100)
| (binary OR)	Copies a bit if it exists in either operand.	(a | b) = 61 (means 0011 1101)
^ (binary XOR)	Copies the bit if it is set in one operand but not both.	(a ^ b) = 49 (means 0011 0001)
~ (binary One Complement)	This operator is unary and has the effect of "flipping" bits.	(~a) =-61 (means 1100 0011 in two's complement form due to a signed binary number.
<< (binary Left Shift)	The left operand's value is moved left by the number of bits specified by the right operand.	a << 2 = 240 (means 1111 0000)
>> (binary Right Shift)	The left operand's value is moved right by the number of bits specified by the right operand.	a >> 2 = 15 (means 0000 1111)

Understanding Membership Operators

Membership operators test for membership in a sequence, such as strings, lists, or tuples. There are two membership operators, in and not in, as shown in Table 1.7.

Table 1.7: Membership Operators

OPERATOR	DESCRIPTION	EXAMPLE
in	Evaluates to true if it finds a variable in the specified sequence and false otherwise.	x in y; here in results in a 1 if x is a member of sequence y.
not in	Evaluates to true if it does not find a variable in the specified sequence and false otherwise.	x not in y; here not in results in a 1 if x is not a member of sequence y.

Understanding Identity Operators

Identity operators compare the memory locations of two objects. There are two identity operators, is and is not, as shown in Table 1.8.

Table 1.8: Identity Operators

OPERATOR	DESCRIPTION	EXAMPLE
is	Evaluates to true if the variables on either side of the operator point to the same object and false otherwise.	x is y; here is results in 1 if id(x) equals id(y).
is not	Evaluates to false if the variables on either side of the operator point to the same object and true otherwise.	x is not y; here is not results in 1 if id(x) is not equal to id(y).

Using Conditionals

You will need to evaluate various conditions as you are writing your code; conditional statements in Python perform different actions or computations and decide whether a condition evaluates to true or false. We use the IF statement for our Boolean test. The syntax is as follows:

```
If expression
    Statement
Else
    Statement
```

To use it in an actual program, type the following:

```
>>> # Python 3.5
>>> for i in range(1,5):
>>>     if i == 2:
>>>         print ('I found two')
>>>     print (i)
```

In addition to the IF statement, Python also makes use of ELSE and ELIF. ELSE will capture the execution if the condition is false. ELIF stands for else if; this gives us a way to chain several conditions together. Examine the following:

```
>>> # Python 3.5
>>> for i in range(1,5):
>>>     if i == 1:
>>>         print ('I found one')
>>>     elif i == 2:
>>>         print ('I found two')
>>>     elif i == 3:
```

ile loop is used to execute a block of statements while a condition is true. th the for loop, the block of statements may be one or more lines. The ation of the following lines defines the block. Once a condition becomes he execution exits the loop and continues. Before printing the final state- the following snippet prints 0, 1, 2, 3, 4:

```
# Python 3.5
count = 0
while (count < 5):
    print count
    count = count + 1
print ("The loop has finished.")
```

ue

ntinue statement is used to tell Python to skip the remaining statements current loop block and continue to the next iteration. The following snip- ll produce an output of 1, 3, 4. The continue statement skips printing . equals 2:

```
# Python 3.5
for i in range(1,5):
    if i == 2:
        continue
    print (i)
```

ak statement exits out from a loop. The following snippet produces an of 1, 2, 3, 4, 5, 6, 7, 8, 9, 10, 11. Once i = 12, the loop is abandoned:

```
Python 3.5
or i in range(1,15):
    if i == 12:
        break
    print (i)
```

use the else statement in conjunction with the for and while loops to nditions that fail either of the loops. Notice that since the count variable 0 in the following example, the while loop does not execute. You should the two final print messages:

```
Python 3.5
unt = 10
```

```
>>>         Print ('I found three')
>>>     else
>>>         Print ('I found a number higher than
>>>     print (i)
```

Using Loops

When you use scripting or programming language
statements in multiple repetitions. Loops give us th
specific condition is met. For the sake of what you u
shows the for loop, the while loop, the continue stat
and the else statement. Unlike other programming la
of the loop by using keywords or brackets, Python
need to focus on how your syntax is spaced when wi

for

The for loop is used to iterate over a set of stateme
n number of times. The for statement can be used
range of numbers. The following syntax prints out t

```
>>> # Python 3.5
>>> for i in range(1, 10):
>>>     print (i)
```

The for loop can also execute against the num
Examine the following snippet, which produces tl

```
>>> # Python 3.5
>>> numbers = [1, 5, 10, 15, 20, 25]
>>> total = 0
>>> for number in numbers:
>>>     total = total + number
>>> print (total)
```

As with numbers, the same technique is usef
following outputs three names—Eden, Hayden, i

```
>>> # Python 3.5
>>> all_kids = ["Eden&", "Hayden&", "Kenna&"]
>>> for kid in all_kids:
>>>     print kid
Eden
Hayden
Kenna
```

while

The w
As w
inder
false,
ment,

```
>>>
>>>
>>>
>>>
>>>
>>>
```

contir

The cc
in the
pet w
when

```
>>>
>>>
>>>
>>>
>>>
```

break

The br
output

```
>>>
>>>
>>>
>>>
>>>
```

else

You ca
catch c
equals
only se

```
>>> }
>>> c
```

```
>>> while (count < 5):
>>>     print (count)
>>>     count = count + 1
>>> else:
>>>     print ("The count is greater than 5")
>>> print ("The loop has finished.")
```

Using Files

In this book, we will be using external files to both read and write. We will be using the `file` function, which takes the file location and then performs an operation. Table 1.9 shows the operations available.

Table 1.9: File Operations

OPERATOR	DESCRIPTION
R	Open text file for reading. The stream is positioned at the beginning of the file.
r+	Open for reading and writing. The stream is positioned at the beginning of the file.
W	Truncate file to zero length or create text file for writing. The stream is positioned at the beginning of the file.
w+	Open for reading and writing. The file is created if it does not exist, otherwise it is truncated. The stream is positioned at the beginning of the file.
Append	Open for writing/appending to the file. The file is created if it does not exist. The stream is positioned at the end of the file. Subsequent writes to the file will always end up at the current end of file.
a+	Open for reading and writing. The file is created if it does not exist. The stream is positioned at the end of the file. Subsequent writes to the file will always end up at the current end of file.

An example we will be using later in this chapter is the following:

```
>>> # Python 2.7
>>> f=file('dictionary.txt', 'r')
>>> words = [word.strip() for word in f]
>>> f.close()

>>> # Python 3.5
>>> f = open('dictionary.txt', 'r')
>>> words = [word.strip() for word in f]
>>> f.close()
```

Understanding Python Semantics

Assume you have assigned y an object. Examine the following:

x = y does not make a copy of the object y references.

x = y creates a reference to the object that y references.

This may be confusing but it is an important concept, so let's look at an example:

```
>>> # Python 3.5
>>> a = [1, 2, 3]      # a is a reference to the list [1, 2, 3]
>>> b = a         # b now references a
>>> a.append(4)     # appends the number 4 to the list a references
>>> print (b)        # print what b references
[1, 2, 3, 4]
```

Why does this happen? When you type a command such as x = 3, an integer is created and stored in memory. A variable named x is created and references the memory location storing the value, which in this case is 3. When you say that the value of x is 3, what you are really saying is that x now refers to the integer 3 at a specific memory location. The data type that is created when you assign the reference to x is of type integer.

In Python, the data types include integer, float, and string (and tuple) and are immutable. You can change the value that is referenced by the memory location. Here is an example:

```
>>> # Python 3.5
>>> x = 4
>>> x = x + 1
>>> print x
5
```

In the preceding example, when you increment x, you are actually looking up the reference of the name x and the value that it references is retrieved. When you add 1 to the value, you are producing a new data element 5, which is assigned to a fresh memory location with a new reference. The name x is then changed to point to the new reference. The old data, which contained 4, is then garbage collected if no name refers to it.

Sequence Types

Python has a number of sequence types. These include str, Unicode, list, tuple, buffer, and xrange. You were previously introduced to string literals, so let's examine the other ones. Unicode strings are similar to strings but are indicated in the syntax using a preceding "u" character: u'abc', u"def". Lists are assembled with square brackets, separating list items with commas: [1, 2, 3]. Tuples are constructed with the comma operator (not within square brackets), with or without enclosing parentheses, but an empty tuple must have the enclosing parentheses, such as a, b, c or (). A single-item tuple must have a trailing comma, such as (d,). A tuple is a simple immutable ordered sequence of items that can be of mixed types. An immutable object is an object that often represents a single logical structure of data. Lists in Python are a mutable ordered sequence of list items that can be of mixed types as well. Mutable objects are those that allow their state (i.e., data that the variable holds) to change. In Python, only dictionaries and lists are mutable objects.

Buffer objects are not directly supported by Python syntax, but can be created by calling the built-in function buffer(). They don't support concatenation or repetition.

Xrange objects are similar to buffers in that there is no specific syntax to create them, but they are created using the xrange() function. They don't support slicing, concatenation, or repetition, and using in, not in, min(), or max() on them is inefficient.

Most sequence types support the following operations. The in and not in operations have the same priorities as the comparison operations. The + and * operations have the same priority as the corresponding numeric operations:

- Tuples are defined using parentheses (and commas):

  ```
  >>> tu = (23, 'abc', 4.56, (2,3), 'def')
  ```

- Lists are defined using square brackets (and commas):

  ```
  >>> li = ["abc", 34, 4.34, 23]
  ```

- Strings are defined using quotes (", ', or """):

  ```
  >>> st = "Hello World"
  >>> st = 'Hello World'
  >>> st = """This is a multi-line
  string that uses triple quotes."""
  ```

You can access individual members of a tuple, list, or string using square bracket "array" notation. All of the objects are zero-based, which means that the first element in the group is in the zero position:

```
>>> tu = (23, 'abc', 4.56, (2,3), 'def')
>>> tu[1] # Second item in the tuple.
'abc'
>>> li = ["abc", 34, 4.34, 23]
>>> li[1] # Second item in the list.
34
>>> st = "Hello World"
>>> st[1] # Second character in string.
'e'
```

One of the most interesting operations in Python that we will make use of is how the indices work. You can use both positive and negative indices to work with the element you need:

```
>>> t = (23, 'abc', 3.14, (2,3), 'def')
```

With a positive index, you count from the left, starting with 0:

```
>>> t[1]
'abc'
```

With a negative index, you count from the right, starting with –1. Examine the t assignment shown previously. You will notice that 3.14 is in the 3rd position on the right. Using the negative number, you are able to start with the right side and work your way left. Examine how the -3 works next:

```
>>> t[-3]
3.14
```

You can use a similar technique to parse a range of data:

```
>>> t = (23, 'abc', 4.56, (2,3), 'def')
```

Return a copy of the container with a subset of the original members. Start copying at the first index, and stop copying before the second index:

```
>>> t[1:4]
('abc', 4.56, (2,3))
```

You can also use negative indices when slicing:

```
>>> t[1:-1]
('abc', 4.56, (2,3))
```

You can omit the first index to make a copy starting from the beginning of the container:

```
>>> t[:2]
(23, 'abc')
```

You can omit the second index to make a copy starting at the first index and going to the end of the container:

```
>>> t[2:]
(4.56, (2,3), 'def')
```

To make a copy of an entire sequence, you can use [:]:

```
>>> t[:]
(23, 'abc', 4.56, (2,3), 'def')
```

Note the difference between these two lines for mutable sequences:

```
>>> list2 = list1       # 2 names refer to 1 ref
                        # Changing one affects both
>>> list2 = list1[:]    # Two independent copies, two refs
```

To examine the content within lists, you use the in operator. Some examples include the following:

- Boolean test whether a value is inside a container:

```
>>> t = [1, 2, 4, 5]
>>> 3 in t
False
>>> 4 in t
True
>>> 4 not in t
False
```

- For strings, tests for substrings:

```
>>> a = 'abcde'
>>> 'c' in a
True
>>> 'cd' in a
True
>>> 'ac' in a
False
```

- Be careful: the in keyword is also used in the syntax of for loops and list comprehensions.

The + operator produces a new tuple, list, or string whose value is the concatenation of its arguments:

```
>>> (1, 2, 3) + (4, 5, 6)
(1, 2, 3, 4, 5, 6)
>>> [1, 2, 3] + [4, 5, 6]
[1, 2, 3, 4, 5, 6]
>>> "Hello" + " " + "World"
'Hello World'
```

The * operator produces a new tuple, list, or string that repeats the original content:

```
>>> (1, 2, 3) * 3
(1, 2, 3, 1, 2, 3, 1, 2, 3)
>>> [1, 2, 3] * 3
[1, 2, 3, 1, 2, 3, 1, 2, 3]
>>> "Hello" * 3
'HelloHelloHello'
```

We will now take another look at tuples. As stated previously, tuples are *immutable,* which means you cannot change them. You can only make a fresh tuple and assign its reference to a previously used name:

```
>>> t = (23, 'abc', 4.56, (2,3), 'def')
>>> t[2] = 3.14

Traceback (most recent call last):
File "<pyshell#75>", line 1, in -topleveltu[
2] = 3.14
TypeError: object doesn't support item assignment

>>> t = (23, 'abc', 3.14, (2,3), 'def')
```

Lists, on the other hand, are *mutable*; this means we can change the lists without having to reassign them. The variable will continue to point to the same memory reference when the assignment is complete. The downside is that lists are not as fast as tuples:

```
>>> li = ['abc', 23, 4.34, 23]
>>> li[1] = 45
>>> li
['abc', 45, 4.34, 23]
```

The following examples are operations that only apply to list objects:

```
>>> li = [1, 11, 3, 4, 5]
>>> li.append('a') # Our first exposure to method syntax
>>> li
[1, 11, 3, 4, 5, 'a']
>>> li.insert(2, 'i')
>>>li
[1, 11, 'i', 3, 4, 5, 'a']
```

Python has an extend() method that operates on lists in place; this operation is different than the plus (+) operator, which creates a fresh list with a new memory reference.

```
>>> li.extend([9, 8, 7])
>>>li
[1, 2, 'i', 3, 4, 5, 'a', 9, 8, 7]
```

You may find this a bit confusing as the extend() method takes a list as an argument, whereas the append() method takes a singleton as an argument:

```
>>> li.append([10, 11, 12])
>>> li
[1, 2, 'i', 3, 4, 5, 'a', 9, 8, 7, [10, 11, 12]]
```

Additionally, Python list objects can also use the `index()`, `count()`, `remove()`, `reverse()`, and `sort()` methods as shown here:

```
>>> li = ['a', 'b', 'c', 'b']
>>> li.index('b') # index of first occurrence
1
>>> li.count('b') # number of occurrences
2
>>> li.remove('b') # remove first occurrence
>>> li
['a', 'c', 'b']

>>> li = [5, 2, 6, 8]
>>> li.reverse() # reverse the list *in place*
>>> li
[8, 6, 2, 5]
>>> li.sort() # sort the list *in place*
>>> li
[2, 5, 6, 8]
>>> li.sort(some_function) # sort in place using user-defined comparison
```

One thing to keep in mind when you are debating between using tuples versus lists is that the list objects are slower but are more powerful than tuples. Lists can be modified and have many operations that can be used on them. You can convert between tuples and lists by using the `list()` and `tuple()` functions, as shown here:

```
li = list(tu)
tu = tuple(li)
```

Dictionaries provide a way to store a mapping between a set of keys and a set of values. The keys can be any immutable type, whereas the values can be any type. A single dictionary can store a range of different types and allow you to define, modify, view, look up, and delete a key-value pair within the dictionary. Here is an example of a dictionary:

```
>>> d = {'user':'bozo', 'pswd':1234}
>>> d['user']
'bozo'
>>> d['pswd']
1234
>>> d['bozo']
Traceback (innermost last):
File '<interactive input>' line 1, in ?
KeyError: bozo
>>> d = {'user':'bozo', 'pswd':1234}
```

```
>>> d['user'] = 'clown'
>>> d
{'user':'clown', 'pswd':1234}
>>> d['id'] = 45
>>> d
{'user':'clown', 'id':45, 'pswd':1234}

>>> d = {'user':'bozo', 'p':1234, 'i':34}
>>> del d['user'] # Remove one.
>>> d
{'p':1234, 'i':34}
>>> d.clear() # Remove all.
>>> d
{}
>>> d = {'user':'bozo', 'p':1234, 'i':34}
>>> d.keys() # List of keys.
['user', 'p', 'i']
>>> d.values() # List of values.
['bozo', 1234, 34]
>>> d.items() # List of item tuples.
[('user','bozo'), ('p',1234), ('i',34)]
Introducing Python Functions
```

Introducing Custom Functions

Now that you understand strings, let's examine reusable code. In Python, you create a new function and assign it a name by using the def keyword. All functions in Python return results to the calling statement. Arguments are passed by assignment, and arguments and return types are not declared. When you pass arguments to a function, the values are assigned to locally scoped names. The assignment to argument names will not affect the caller since they are passed by assignment and not by reference. You will, however, affect the caller if you change a mutable argument.

Create a new file in your editor of choice and type the following:

```
def myEnc(plaintext, key):
    return "ciphertext"
```

Save the file as MyFunctions.py. In the command line, type **MyFunctions.py**. You should notice that nothing happens. Now type the following:

```
myEnc('hello','secret key')
```

The output should be ciphertext.

The script you created is an example of a function. The def keyword is used to define the function; as you might have guessed, myEnc is the name of the function. It takes two parameters or inputs and returns an output. We use functions to build logic we intend to use multiple times. The benefit of using functions is that if you decide you need to change the script, you can change it in one place and not have to search for other areas in which you performed the same logic. This will help in both troubleshooting and code maintenance. We will be using functions quite a bit throughout this book.

In Python, you can declare some arguments as optional. Examine the following segment of code, paying attention to the third and fourth arguments:

```
def func(a, b, c=10, d=100):
! print (a, b, c, d)
>>> func(1,2)
1 2 10 100
>>> func(1,2,3,4)
1,2,3,4
```

Something to watch out for is that all functions have a return value even if you do not provide a return line inside the code. Functions that do not provide a return line will return the special value of None. Note also that, unlike other languages, Python does not provide a way to overload a method, so you are not allowed to have two different functions with the same name and a different list of arguments. Some benefits to functions include that they can be used as arguments to functions, return values of functions, and be assigned to variables, and may contain parts of tuples, lists, and other objects.

Downloading Files Using Python

You can download files and content in Python in a number of ways. One of the preferred ways in Python 3 is to use the requests module. The get method of the requests module is used to download the file contents in binary format. You can then use the open method to open a file on your system. Here's an example of downloading files using the requests module:

```
>>> import requests
>>> print('Beginning file download with requests')
>>> url = 'https://raw.githubusercontent.com/noidentity29/
AppliedCryptoPython/master/secret.txt'
>>> r = requests.get(url)
>>>
>>> # Windows Path - C:\Users\ShannonBray\Downloads\
>>> with open('/Users/ShannonBray/Downloads/secrets.txt', 'wb') as f:
>>>     f.write(r.content)
>>>
>>> # Retrieve HTTP meta-data
>>> print(r.status_code)
>>> print(r.headers['content-type'])
>>> print(r.encoding)
>>>
```

```
>>> url = 'https://raw.githubusercontent.com/noidentity29/
AppliedCryptoPython/master/dictionary.txt'
>>> r = requests.get(url)
>>> with open('/Users/ShannonBray/Downloads/dictionary.txt', 'wb') as f:
>>>     f.write(r.content)
>>>
>>> # Retrieve HTTP meta-data
>>> print(r.status_code)
>>> print(r.headers['content-type'])
>>> print(r.encoding)
```

In this script, the `open` method is used once again to write binary data to a local file. If you execute the script and go to your `Downloads` directory, you should see your newly downloaded text file named `secrets.txt`.

Utilizing the `requests` module, you can also easily retrieve relevant metadata about your request, including the status code, headers, and much more. In the preceding script, you can see how we access some of this metadata.

You can also elect to use the `curl` bash command, such as in the following example:

```
curl -O https://raw.githubusercontent.com/noidentity29/AppliedCryptoPython/
master/secret.txt
curl -O https://raw.githubusercontent.com/noidentity29/AppliedCryptoPython/
master/dictionary.txt
```

Introducing Python Modules

Python *modules* are special packages that extend the language. You saw your first module when you used the `import math` call shown previously. You can examine the modules that are loaded by typing **dir()**. As shown with the math module, when a module is preinstalled, we can use the `import` command to upload it. To examine the modules that are preinstalled on your system, type the following:

```
>>> help()
help> modules
help> modules hashlib
q
```

The `hashlib` is a built-in module that is preinstalled that will allow you to run hash functions. We will discuss hashing in detail throughout this book, but for now, we will explore the use of `hashlib` as a module. Type **import hashlib**, then in the terminal type **hashlib.** (enter the dot after `hashlib`), and press the Tab key. You should see a list of methods, as shown in Figure 1.4. You can explore these methods by typing the module and method followed by a question mark, such as `hashlib.sha256?`.

```
IPython 1.2.1 -- An enhanced Interactive Python.
?         -> Introduction and overview of IPython's features.
%quickref -> Quick reference.
help      -> Python's own help system.
object?   -> Details about 'object', use 'object??' for extra details.

In [1]: import hashlib

In [2]: hashlib.
hashlib.algorithms  hashlib.md5    hashlib.new    hashlib.sha1    hashlib.sha224    hashlib.sha256    hashlib.sha384    hashlib.sha512
```

Figure 1.4: Module methods

Now that you understand the importance of Python modules, let's import the `hashlib` library and then use the MD5 and SHA message digests. Type the following in Python:

```
>>> import hashlib
>>> hashlib.md5('hello world'.encode()).hexdigest()
'5eb63bbbe01eeed093cb22bb8f5acdc3'
>>> hashlib.sha512('hello world'.encode()).hexdigest()
'309ecc489c12d6eb4cc40f50c902f2b4d0ed77ee511a7c7a9bcd3ca86d4cd86f
989dd35bc5ff499670da34255b45b0cfd830e81f605dcf7dc5542e93ae9cd76f'
```

NOTE Python 3 and higher require that Unicode objects be encoded before they are hashed.

Creating a Reverse Cipher

For this next exercise, we build on what we have learned in this chapter by creating a function named `reverseCipher` that accepts one parameter: `plaintext`. We can then call our function and pass the plaintext into it and print out the return ciphertext. Our method modifies the plaintext so that the ciphertext is the complete reverse:

```
def reverseCipher(plaintext):
    ciphertext = ''
    i = len(plaintext) - 1
    while i >= 0:
        ciphertext = ciphertext + plaintext[i]
        i = i - 1
    return ciphertext
plaintext = 'If you want to keep a secret, you must also hide it from
yourself.'
ciphertext = reverseCipher (plaintext)
print(ciphertext)
```

This code should produce the following result:

```
.flesruoy morf ti edih osla tsum uoy ,terces a peek ot tnaw uoy fI
```

Summary

In this chapter, you were introduced to the use of cryptographic algorithms. Most of the functions that you will construct throughout the course of this book will follow the format of having functions to GEN (generate a key), ENC (encrypt plaintext to ciphertext), and DEC (decrypt ciphertext to plaintext). This chapter also offered a few options on building your Python. You also were given an overview of the Python concepts that you will need to know prior to taking on complicated applications. The chapter concluded with you writing your first cipher code that took plaintext and returned the reverse.

## CHAPTER 2

Cryptographic Protocols and Perfect Secrecy

Cryptography has been used since 1900 BC to ensure message secrecy. Up until the 1970s, the use of cryptography was primarily found in government and military applications; the use expanded to telecommunication and financial industries over the following decade. In today's world, we find cryptography in cell phones, emails, web browsers, and bank cards. Over the next few years, we can expect cryptography to play a role in how we communicate with our refrigerators, cars, and other devices connected through the Internet of Things.

It is important to ensure the use of strong encryption of sensitive data and that we provide integrity and confidentiality of the data. In this chapter, we will look at the study of cryptology and its components and then dive into perfect secrecy. Claude Shannon, often regarded as the father of information theory, defined perfect secrecy for secret-key systems and showed that perfect secrecy exists. Basically, perfect secrecy is the idea that no matter how much ciphertext you have, it will not convey anything about the contents of the plaintext or key. It can be proved that any such scheme must use at least as much key material as there is plaintext to encrypt. In terms of probabilities, this means that the probability distribution of the possible plaintexts is independent of the ciphertext.

In this chapter, you will continue your journey into understanding the importance of message perfect secrecy. Specifically, you will do the following:

- Gain an understanding of cryptology and the various attack methods
- Explore key lengths and their importance for long-term security

- Gain an understanding of the one-time pad
- Create message secrecy using the binary XOR operator
- Gain an understanding of cryptographic hashes
- Explore the basics of Claude Shannon's theorem
- Explore the concepts of perfect forward secrecy

The Study of Cryptology

The term *cryptology*, which was first used in 1844, means the study of codes and the practice or art of writing or solving them. The word originates from the Greek words *kryptós*, meaning "hidden secret"; *graphein*, meaning "to write"; and *logia*, meaning "to study." It has become a much-researched field that focuses on techniques for securing communications from eavesdroppers.

Cryptology's focus is in the construction and analysis of protocols that prevent any person or system from decrypting messages without authorization. Cryptology helps ensure the core tenets of cybersecurity by providing confidentiality, integrity, authentication, and nonrepudiation. We will explore how we use cryptology for each of these using Python as we move through this book. For now, the important takeaway is that the study of cryptology is broken down into two fields: cryptography and cryptanalysis.

Understanding Cryptography

Specifically, cryptography is the science of secret writing with the goal of hiding the meaning of the message. Cryptography is further broken down into cryptographic protocols, symmetric algorithms, and asymmetric (or public-key) algorithms.

Cryptographic protocols, also known as security or encryption protocols, consist of a well-defined series of steps and message exchanges between several entities in order to achieve a specific security objective. Cryptographic protocols should encapsulate a number of properties in order to be viable:

- The protocol must be known by each party involved, and each party must know the well-defined steps to follow in advance of the protocol's use.

- The protocol must be unambiguous; every step is well-defined and easy to understand.

- The protocol must be followed by each party involved.

- The protocol must also be complete.

- The protocol must not give away any details about the message.

Cryptographic protocols are used in secure application-level data transport such as Transport Layer Security (TLS), which is used to secure HTTPS web connections. Another protocol that we will explore later in the chapter is the Diffie-Hellman key exchange, which is also used by TLS in its secure communications. Other applications include secret splitting, secret sharing, time-stamping, key escrow, zero-knowledge proofs, blind signatures, electronic money, and securing elections. The data integrity of the message exchange process is a critical aspect of the selected protocols; data integrity is a building block for cryptographic protocols.

Cryptography's Famous Family: Alice and Bob

Alice and Bob are the world's most famous cryptographic couple; you will see references to the dynamic couple through a wide variety of examples inside this book (see Figure 2.1). Since their inception in 1978, Alice and Bob have at once been called "inseparable" and been subject of numerous travels, torments, and even divorces. In the ensuing years, other characters have joined their cryptographic family. There's Eve, the passive and submissive eavesdropper; Mallory, the malicious attacker; and Trent, trusted by all, just to name a few. Alice and Bob, along with their extended family, were first used to explain how cryptography works but now have become widely used across engineering and scientific domains. Alice and Bob have become an archetype of digital exchange and a lens through which to view broader digital culture.

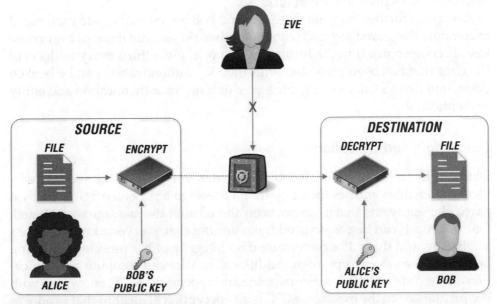

Figure 2.1: Alice and Bob

Alice and Bob are fictional characters originally invented to make research in cryptology easier to understand. In a now-famous paper ("A method for obtaining digital signatures and public key cryptosystems"), authors Ron Rivest, Adi Shamir, and Leonard Adleman described exchanges between a sender and receiver of information as follows: "For our scenarios we suppose that A and B (also known as Alice and Bob) are two users of a public key cryptosystem." In that instant, Alice and Bob were born.

Diffie-Hellman

One of the most critical aspects of cryptography is safely exchanging secret keys without being compromised. During the 1960s, key exchange was costing the government, banks, and big businesses a fortune as they exchanged keys using heavily guarded couriers who traveled around in person to deliver cryptographic keys. Fortunately, the Diffie-Hellman protocol was introduced to handle the growing issues with key exchange.

As with any other protocol that only covers key exchange, the Diffie-Hellman protocol does not perform any authentication. Therefore, neither Alice nor Bob knows with whom they are exchanging the message after the protocol is run. The Diffie-Hellman exchange cannot guarantee the privacy of a communication following the exchange; it has to be combined with an authentication mechanism. The protocol design does offer an advantage, however; it allows the protocol to guarantee the property of perfect forward secrecy (PFS), which protects the message from a compromise of any data that has been protected with other keys prior to the compromise.

To explain further, imagine that Alice and Bob both sign the data exchanged to compute the shared key (SK) with their private keys. Even if one of the private keys is compromised in the future, it will not allow a third party to decrypt the data that has been protected with the SK. Authentication can be broken down into two security service categories: data origin authentication and entity authentication.

Data Origin Authentication

Data origin authentication, also known as data integrity, is the security service that enables entities to verify that a message has been originated by a particular entity and that it has not been altered after the message was created. One approach can be conjectured by assuming that everyone knows Alice's public key, and that Alice can ensure data integrity of her messages by using her private key to encrypt them. Additionally, Alice can compute a modification digest code (MDC) over her message and append the MDC encrypted with her private key to the message. MDC is an encryption algorithm that produces a one-way cryptographic function. With message integrity being critical to message security, cryptographic protocols often provide data origin authentication services as a building block of the protocols.

Entity Authentication

Entity authentication is a security service that is used between peer entities to verify the identity of each party involved. Each application that contains sensitive information should be built around entity authentication and verify the entity; authentication is typically performed using various means, such as:

- Something you know (e.g., passwords)
- Something you have (e.g., physical keys, cards, or tokens)
- Something you are (e.g., biometric properties such as fingerprint or retinal scans)
- Someplace you are (e.g., geolocation)

Entity authentication is more than an exchange of messages. It must also provide timeliness. One cannot guarantee that any party involved in the message exchange is actively participating at the specific moment the message is received. Most authentication protocols establish a secret session key for security of the session following the authentication exchange. Two main categories of protocols are used for entity authentication:

- **Arbitrated authentication:** A trusted third party (TTP), also known as an arbiter, is directly involved in every authentication exchange. The primary advantage is that it allows two parties (Alice and Bob) to authenticate to each other without knowing any pre-established secret. Even if Alice and Bob do not know each other, the same cryptographic key can be used. This type of key is known as a *symmetric key*. One disadvantage of arbitrated authentication is that the TTP can become a bottleneck to the process, therefore violating the availability of the CIA Triad. Another disadvantage is that the TTP can monitor all authentication activity.

- **Direct authentication:** Alice and Bob directly authenticate to each other. The primary advantage is that no online participation of a third party is required; therefore, the two drawbacks mentioned in arbitrated authentication do not apply. The major drawback is that it requires asymmetric cryptography or pre-established secret keys.

NOTE The CIA Triad is the implementation of confidentiality, integrity, and availability, which are important aspects to how we view the security of our solutions. The security model is designed to guide policies for information within our systems, solutions, and applications. You may also see the model referred to as the AIC Triad (availability, integrity, and confidentiality) to avoid confusion with the United States Central Intelligence Agency. The three elements of the triad are considered the most crucial components of security, although you may see other elements introduced. The CIA Triad, in this context, defines confidentiality as a set of rules that limit who has access to information, integrity as the assurance that the information is accurate and trustworthy, and availability as the guarantee that the data can be reliably accessed when needed by authorized personnel or systems.

Symmetric Algorithms

Symmetric algorithms are the simplest and fastest way to encrypt and decrypt messages. They typically involve two parties, with each member having an identical key. As a memory mnemonic, think of the "S" in symmetric as the word *same*.

We will be diving into many of the symmetric key algorithms such as DES, 3DES, IDEA, Blowfish, Skipjack, and AES in Chapter 6, but we mention them now to help prepare you for our discussion on historical ciphers later in this chapter. Other examples of symmetric algorithms include IPSec, Kerberos, and Point to Point.

Asymmetric Algorithms

Asymmetric algorithms are more complex and typically slower. In fact, many systems use asymmetric algorithms simply to swap symmetric keys and then use symmetric algorithms for the rest of the encryption operation. The key point to take away for now is that the asymmetric algorithm requires the use of two different keys: one public and one private. Messages that are encrypted with one key can only be decrypted with the other. This offers many advantages, such as nonrepudiation and the use of digital certificates.

We will explore asymmetric algorithms and the use of public and private keys using Python in Chapter 7. An example of an asymmetric encryption algorithm is ElGamal, which is used in OpenPGP. Other examples include Elliptic curve cryptography, RSA, Diffie-Hellman key exchange, and DSA.

The Needham-Schroeder Protocols

In 1978, Roger Needham and Michael Schroeder invented two protocols. The first is their symmetric key protocol, which later formed the basis for the Kerberos protocol invented by MIT. This protocol aims to establish a session key between two parties on a network to protect communications.

The second protocol was their public-key protocol, which is based on public-key cryptography. The goal of the second Needham-Schroeder protocol is to establish mutual authentication between two parties, A and B; the protocol assumes that an adversary may intercept, delay, read, copy, or forge the message in transit. The protocol also assumes that each party (Alice and Bob) has received secret keys from a trusted third party (TTP). The protocol uses shared keys for both the encryption and decryption process.

Use Table 2.1 to analyze the following exchange:

Let us assume that Alice needs to send a communication to Bob. Alice will need to generate a random number R_A and send a message to the TTP: A➜ TTP(A, B, r_A)

The TTP generates a session key $K_{A,B}$ for secure communications between Alice and Bob and responds to Alice: TTP ➜ A: $\{r_A, B, K_{A,B}, \{K_{A,B}, A\}_{KB, TTP}\}_{KA, TTP}$

Alice decrypts the message and extracts $K_{A,B}$. She confirms that r_A is identical to the number generated by her in the first step; this informs her that the reply from the TTP is fresh.

Alice sends the message to Bob: A➜B: $\{K_{A,B}, A\}_{KB, TTP}$

Bob decrypts the message and obtains $K_{A,B}$. He then generates a random number r_B and replies to Alice: B ➜ A: $\{r_B\}_{KA,B}$

Alice decrypts the message and verifies that it contains r_B-1.

Table 2.1: Notation of Cryptographic Protocols

NOTATION	MEANING
A	Name of A, analogous to B, E, TTP, CA
CA_A^-	The certification authority for A
R_A	A random value chosen by A
t_A	The timestamp generated by A
$(m_1,...,m_n)$	The concatenation of messages $m_1,..., m_n$
A ➜ B: m	A sends message m to B
$K_{A,B}$	The secret key, only known to A and B
$+K_A$	The public key of A
$-K_A$	The private key of A
$\{m\}_K$	The message m encrypted with the key K, synonym for E(K, m)
H(m)	Modification detection code (MDC) over message m, computed with function H
A[m]	Shorthand notation for (m, $\{H(m)\}_{-KA}$)
Cert $_{-CK CA}(+K_A)$	The certification authority certificate for public key $+K_A$ of A, signed with the private certification key $-CK_{CA}$
CA<<A>>	Shorthand notation for Cert $_{-CK CA}(+K_A)$

The protocol exchanges r_B and r_B-1 in an effort to ensure that an attacker, Eve, cannot impersonate Bob by replaying messages from Alice. However, as old session keys $K_{A,B}$ remain valid, Eve may manage to get to a known session key $K_{A,B}$ and impersonate Alice:

E ➔ B: $\{K_{A,B}, A\}_{KB, TTP}$

B ➔ A: $\{r_B\}_{K(A, B)}$ *Eve has to intercept this message

E ➔ B: $\{r_B\text{-}1\}_{K(A, B)}$

In short, even if Eve does not know $K_{A,TTP}$ or $K_{B, TTP}$, she can impersonate Alice.

The Otway-Rees Protocol

The Needham and Schroeder public-key solution has a number of similarities to a protocol proposed by Otway and Rees. Use Table 2.1 to analyze the following exchange:

Alice generates a message containing an index number i_A, her name (A), and Bob's name (B), plus an additional random number R_A encrypted with the key $K_{A, TTP}$ she shares with the TTP, and sends the following message to Bob:

A➔B: $(i_A, A, B, \{r_A, i_A, A, B\}_{K(A,TTP)})$

Bob generates a random number, r_B, and uses it to encrypt i_A, A, and B using the key $K_{B, TTP}$. Bob shares the message with the TTP:

B ➔ TTP$(i_A, A, B, \{r_A, i_A, A, B\}_{K(A,TTP)}, \{r_B, i_A, A, B\}_{K(B,TTP)})$

The TTP generates a new session key $K_{A,B}$ and creates two encrypted messages, one for Alice and one for Bob. The TTP sends them both to Bob:

TTP ➔ B: $(i_A, \{r_A, K_{A,B}\}K_{A,TTP}, \{r_B, K_{A,B}\}_{K(B,TTP)})$

Bob then decrypts his part of the message and verifies R_B. Bob sends part of the message to Alice:

B ➔ A: $(i_A, \{r_A, K_{A,B}\}_{K(A, TTP)})$

Alice decrypts the message and checks i_A and R_A to verify that they have not been modified since the message exchange started. If they have not changed, she can be sure that the TTP has sent her a fresh session key $K_{A,B}$ for communications with Bob. If she uses the key in an encrypted communication with Bob, she can be sure of his authenticity.

A benefit of the Otway-Rees protocol is that the index number, i_A, further protects against replay attacks. However, this requires that the TTP checks if i_A is bigger than the last i_A he received from Alice. The TTP will generate the two messages if both parts of the message contain the same index number i_A and names A, B. If both are true, then Alice and Bob can be sure that they have authenticated to the TTP during the encrypted communication.

Kerberos

Kerberos, an open-source security protocol developed by MIT in the late 1980s, is an authentication and access control service for workstation clustering. Its design goals include security, reliability, transparency, and scalability. The underlying cryptographic primitive of Kerberos is symmetric encryption; Kerberos V4 uses DES, while V5 allows for other algorithms.

Assume that Alice wants to access one or more different services that are provided by different servers: Server 1, Server 2, etc. Each server is connected over an insecure network. The Kerberos protocol will handle the authentication, access control, and key exchange:

- **Authentication:** Alice will authenticate to an authentication server, which will provide a temporary permit to demand access for services. The permit is called a Ticket-Granting ticket (Ticket$_{TGS}$); the ticket can be thought of like a temporary passport.

- **Access Control:** Alice is able to present her ticket (Ticket$_{TGS}$) to a Ticket Granting Server (TGS) to obtain access for a service provided by a specific server; in this example, we will call it Server 1. The TGS decides if the access will be permitted and answers Alice with a ticket for Server 1, Ticket$_{S1}$.

- **Key Exchange:** The authentication server provides a session key for communication between Alice and the TGS; the TGS will provide a session key for communication between Alice and Server 1. The session key also serves Alice for authentication purposes.

Alice begins the process by logging in to her workstation and requests access to a service. The first message is sent to the authentication server AS, containing her name, the name of the appropriate Ticket Granting Server TGS, and a timestamp t_A:

$$A \rightarrow AS: (A, TGS, t_A)$$

The authentication server verifies that Alice may authenticate to access services, generates the key K_A out of Alice's password (which is known to the AS), extracts the workstation address Addr$_A$ from the request, creates a Ticket Granting Ticket Ticket$_{TGS}$ and a session key $K_{A, TGS}$, and sends the following message to Alice:

$$AS \rightarrow A: \{K_{A, TGS}, TGS, t_{AS}, LifetimeTicket_{TGS}, Ticket_{TGS}\}_{KA} \text{ with } Ticket_{TGS} = \{K_{A, TGS}, A, Addr_A, TGS, t_{AS}, LifetimeTicket_{TGS}\}_{K_{AS, TGS}}$$

Once the workstation receives the message, it will ask Alice to type in her password. The workstation will compute the key K_A and use this key to decrypt the message. If Alice does not provide her correct password, the extracted values will be garbage and the rest of the protocol will fail.

Alice creates an authenticator and sends it together with the Ticket Granting Ticket and the name of the server to TGS:

A → TGS: (S1, Ticket$_{TGS}$, Authenticator$_{A, TGS}$) with Authenticator$_{A, TGS}$ = {A, Addr$_A$, t$_A$}$_{KA, TGS}$

Once the TGS receives the message, it will decrypt Ticket$_{TGS}$, extract the key K$_{A, TGS}$ from the message, and use the key to decrypt Authenticator$_{A, TGS}$. If the name, ticket, and address of the authenticator matches, the TGS will ensure the timestamp is still valid, check if Alice may access the service S1, and create the following message:

TGS → A: {K$_{A, S1}$}, S1, t$_{TGS}$, LifetimeTicket$_{S1}$}$_{KA, TGS}$ with Ticket$_{S1}$ = {K$_{A, S1}$, A, Addr$_A$, S1, t$_{TGS}$, LifetimeTicket$_{S1}$}$_{KTGS, S1}$

Alice decrypts the message and holds a session key for secure communication between her and S1. She sends a message to S1 to show her ticket and a new authenticator:

A → S1: (Ticket$_{S1}$, Authenticator$_{A, S1}$) with Authenticator$_{A,S1}$ = {A, Addr$_A$, t$_A$}$_{KA, S1}$

Once the ticket from Alice is received by Server 1, the server decrypts the ticket with the key K$_{TGS, S1}$ and shares with TGS the session key K$_{A, S1}$ for secure communication with A. Using the obtained key, the S1 checks the authenticator and responds to A:

S1 → A: {t$_A$ + 1}$_{KA, S1}$

Alice is able to verify that she is communicating with S1 and only S1 and the TGS knows the key K$_{TGS, S1}$ to decrypt Ticket$_{S1}$, which contains the session key K$_{A, S1}$ and so only S1 is able to decrypt Authenticator$_{A, S1}$ and to answer with t$_A$+1 encrypted with K$_{A, S1}$.

Multiple-Domain Kerberos

In many environments, an organization may be required to establish secure communications with a service that is located inside another domain. If both locations use their own Kerberos servers and user databases, then there are in fact two different domains; in this context, we will refer to them as *realms* to keep consistent with Kerberos terminology.

In an effort to avoid user duplication in both domains, Kerberos allows you to perform an inter-realm authentication. Inter-realm authentication requires that the Ticket Granting Servers of both domains share a secret key K$_{TGS1, TGS2}$. The basic concept that is presented is that the TGS service of another realm (domain) can be viewed as a normal server for which the TGS of the local realm can hand out a ticket.

After obtaining the ticket from the remote realm, Alice requests a service granting ticket from the remote TGS. This sets up a dependency that the remote realm must trust the Kerberos authentication service of the home domain of a "visiting" user. Scalability becomes a problem as n realms require $n \times (n-1) / 2$ secret keys. The message exchange in a multiple domain protocol run would look as follows:

A ➜ AS1: (A, TGS1, t_A)

AS1 ➜ A: {$K_{A, TGS1}$, TGS1, t_{AS}, LifetimeTicket$_{TGS1}$, Ticket$_{TGS1}$}$_{KA}$ with Ticket$_{TGS1}$ = {$K_{A, TGS1}$, A, Addr$_A$, TGS1, t_{AS}, LifetimeTicket $_{TGS1}$}$_{KAS, TGS1}$

A ➜ TGS1: (TGS2, Ticket$_{TGS1}$, Authenticator$_{A, TGS1}$) with Authenticator$_{A, TGS1}$ = {}A, Addr$_A$, t`$_A$}$_{KA, TGS1}$

TGS1 ➜ A:{$K_{A, TGS2}$, TGS2, t_{TGS1}, Ticket$_{TGS2}$}$_{KA, TGS1}$ with Ticket$_{TGS2}$ = {$K_{A, TGS2}$,A, Addr$_A$, TGS2, t_{TGS1}, LifetimeTicket$_{TGS2}$} $_{KTGS1, TGS2}$

A ➜ TGS2: (S2, Ticket$_{TGS2}$, Authenticator$_{A, TGS2}$) with Authenticator$_{A, TGS2}$ = {A, Addr$_A$, t``$_A$}$_{KA,TGS2}$

TGS2 ➜ A: {$K_{A,S2}$, S2, t_{TGS2}, Ticket$_{S2}$}$_{KA,TGS2}$ with Ticket$_{S2}$ = {$K_{A,S2}$, A, Addr$_A$, S2, t_{TGS2}, LifetimeTicket$_{S2}$}$_{KTGS2,S1}$

A ➜ S2: (Ticket$_{S2}$, Authenticator$_{A,S2}$) with Authenticator$_{A,S2}$ = {A, Addr$_A$, t```$_A$}$_{KA,S2}$

S1 ➜ A: {t```$_A$ + 1}$_{KA,S1}$

X.509

X.509 is an international recommendation of ITU-T and is part of the X.500-series defining directory services. It is the standard that defines the format of the public-key certificate. The X.509 certificates are used in many internet protocols that include TLS/SSL. The X.509 certificates are also used in offline applications such as electronic signatures. The certificate contains a public key and an identity (server name, host name, organization, or individual) and is either signed by a certificate authority (CA) or self-signed using an internal process.

The first version of X.509 was standardized in 1988. The second version, which resolved several security concerns, was standardized in 1993. The third version was drafted in 1995. When a certificate is signed by a trusted CA or validated by other processes, someone holding the certificate can be assured that the public key can establish a secure communication session with another party or validate documents that are digitally signed by the corresponding private key.

X.509 defines a framework for the provisioning of authentication services that comprise the certification of public keys and certificate holding and three different dialogues for direct authentication. The certification of public keys and certificate handling include processes that define the certificate format, the certificate hierarchy, and the certificate revocation lists. The three dialogues that are provided for direct authentication include:

- **One-way authentication:** Requires synchronized clocks
- **Two-way mutual authentication:** Also requires synchronized clocks
- **Three-way mutual authentication:** Based on random numbers

> **NOTE**   Clock synchronization on a network is important to a number of technologies, including Kerberos and X.509 certificates. The maximum tolerance for computer clocks should be 5 minutes. This helps limit that amount of time that a replay attack can happen. The most common way to synchronize clocks automatically is to use the Network Time Protocol (NTP). NTP is a hierarchical protocol. The source clock is called Stratum 1. Clocks that synchronize from the original source are called Stratum 2. Clocks that synchronize from Stratum 2 are called Stratum 3, and so on.

Public-Key Certificates

Public-key certificates essentially act as a passport that certifies that a public-key belongs to a specific name or organization. Certificates are issued by certificate authorities, more commonly known as CAs. One of the properties of using public-key certificates is that they allow all users to know without question that the public-key of the CA can be checked by each user. In addition, certificates do not require the online participation of a TTP. One thing that you must remember is that the security of the private key is crucial to the security of all users. The following represents the notation of a certificate binding a public key +KA to user A issued by a certificate authority CA using its private key -CKCA:

Cert-CKCA(+KA) = CA[V, SN, AI, CA, TCA, A, +KA] where:
    V = version number
    SN = serial number
    AI = algorithm identifier of signature algorithm used
    CA = name of certification authority
    TCA = period of validity of this certificate
    A = name to which the public key in this certificate is bound
    +KA = public to be bound to a name

Certificate Chains and Certificate Hierarchy

Consider communication between our two users: Alice and Bob. Each user lives geographically apart. Each user may have public keys from different CAs. For simplicity, designate Alice's certificate authority as CA_A and Bob's certificate authority as CA$_B$. If Alice does not know or trust CA$_B$, then Bob's certificate is useless to her; the same will hold true for Bob and his knowledge or trust of Alice's CA$_A$. In order to provide a solution to this issue, you can construct a certificate chain. If CA$_A$ certifies CA$_B$ with a certificate CA$_A$<<CA$_B$>> and CA$_B$ certifies CA$_A$'s public key with a certificate CA$_B$<<CA$_A$>>, then both Alice and Bob can check their certificates by checking a certificate chain. Assume Alice is presented with CA$_B$<<Bob>> and attempts to look up if there is a certificate CA$_A$<<CA$_B$>>. She checks the chain: CA$_A$<<CA$_B$>>, CA$_B$<<Bob>>. Certificate chains are not limited to just the two certificates.

You can use Python to create X.509 certificates. The following code will generate two certificates: `rsakey.pem` and `csr.pen`. The `rsakey.pem` is a private key that is encrypted using the super-secret password Ilik32Cod3 and will then use the private key to generate a public key. We then generate a certificate signing request (CSR) using a number of custom attributes. Feel free to change these up as they will not affect the example.

```
from cryptography.hazmat.backends import default_backend
from cryptography.hazmat.primitives import serialization
from cryptography.hazmat.primitives.asymmetric import rsa
from cryptography import x509
from cryptography.x509.oid import NameOID
from cryptography.hazmat.primitives import hashes
#Generate Key (RSA,DSA,EC)
encryptedpass = b"Ilik32Cod3"
key = rsa.generate_private_key(
public_exponent=65537,
key_size=2048,
backend=default_backend()
)
with open("rsakey.pem", "wb") as f:
    f.write(key.private_bytes(
    encoding=serialization.Encoding.PEM,
    format=serialization.PrivateFormat.TraditionalOpenSSL,
    encryption_algorithm=serialization.BestAvailableEncryption(encrypted
pass),
))
# Generate CSR
csr = x509.CertificateSigningRequestBuilder().subject_name(x509.Name([
x509.NameAttribute(NameOID.COUNTRY_NAME, u"US"),
x509.NameAttribute(NameOID.STATE_OR_PROVINCE_NAME, u"NC"),
x509.NameAttribute(NameOID.LOCALITY_NAME, u"Raleigh"),
x509.NameAttribute(NameOID.ORGANIZATION_NAME, u"Python Cryptography"),
x509.NameAttribute(NameOID.COMMON_NAME, u"shannonbray.us"),
])).add_extension(
x509.SubjectAlternativeName([
x509.DNSName(u"shannonbray.us"),
]),
critical=False,
```

```
# Sign the CSR with our private key.
).sign(key, hashes.SHA256(), default_backend())
with open("csr.pem", "wb") as f:
    f.write(csr.public_bytes(serialization.Encoding.PEM))
print('Operateion Completed.')
```

Certificate Revocation

If we continue to examine the situation presented, you can see that communications between Alice and Bob rely on the trust of the certificate authority and each party must keep their private key secure. Should one of their keys become compromised, the certificate needs to be nullified or revoked. If Alice's key was compromised in an attack, the attacker (Trent) can continue to impersonate Alice up to the end of the certificate's validity period. If Alice detects the compromise, she can ask for revocation of the corresponding public-key certificate. Certificate revocation is performed by maintaining a list of compromised certificates; these lists are known as certificate revocation lists, or CRLs. CRLs are stored in the X.500 directory; when a user or process is checking a certificate, it must not only confirm that the certificate exists but also make sure the certificate is not on a CRL. The certificate revocation process is quite slow and can be costly and ineffective.

If you've used the previous example to generate a key, you will be able to load it using the following code. Examine the use of `load_pem_private_key()`, as shown here:

```
from cryptography.hazmat.backends import default_backend
from cryptography.hazmat.primitives import serialization
from cryptography import x509
from cryptography.x509.oid import NameOID
from cryptography.hazmat.primitives import hashes
from cryptography.hazmat.primitives.serialization import load_pem_
private_key
encryptedpass = b"Ilik32Cod3"
key = load_pem_private_key(open('rsakey.pem', 'rb').read(),encryptedpass,
default_backend())
# Generate CSR
csr = x509.CertificateSigningRequestBuilder().subject_name(x509.Name([
x509.NameAttribute(NameOID.COUNTRY_NAME, u"US"),
x509.NameAttribute(NameOID.STATE_OR_PROVINCE_NAME, u"CA"),
x509.NameAttribute(NameOID.LOCALITY_NAME, u"San Francisco"),
x509.NameAttribute(NameOID.ORGANIZATION_NAME, u"Python Cryptography"),
x509.NameAttribute(NameOID.COMMON_NAME, u"8gwifi.org"),
])).add_extension(
x509.SubjectAlternativeName([
x509.DNSName(u"mysite.com"),
]),
```

```
critical=False,
# Sign the CSR with our private key.
).sign(key, hashes.SHA256(), default_backend())
with open("csr.pem", "wb") as f:
    f.write(csr.public_bytes(serialization.Encoding.PEM))
```

You can use the `openssl` command to view the CSR, as shown here:

```
$ openssl req -text -in csr.pem
```

```
Certificate Request: Data: Version: 0 (0x0) Subject: C=US, ST=CA,
L=San Francisco, O=Python Cryptography, CN=8gwifi.org Subject Public
Key Info: Public Key Algorithm: rsaEncryption RSA Public Key: (2048
bit) Modulus (2048 bit): Encrypted RSA key generated with the code
$ cat /tmp/rsakey.pem -----BEGIN RSA PRIVATE KEY----- Proc-Type:
4,ENCRYPTED DEK-Info: AES-256-CBC,EA2EB61CCC7A2FFD9D83D9D103B74F69
nuslMfQNj17cAdwCKWtWhcXCtOqpk6ii0SmxcuUgJWg5iUujN4p6LYHbWkalUTvi
...... -----END RSA PRIVATE KEY----- Generated CSR in the PEM
format $ cat /tmp/csr.pem -----BEGIN CERTIFICATE REQUEST-----
MIIC0jCCAboCAQAwZTELMAkGA1UEBhMCVVMxCzAJBgNVBAgMAkNBMRYwFAYDVQQH
DA1TYW4gRnJhbmNpc2NvMRwwGgYDVQQKDBNQeXRob24gQ3J5cHRvZ3JhcGh5MRMw
EQYDVQQDDAo4Z3dpZmkub3JnMIIBIjANBgkqhkiG9w0BAQEFAAOCAQ8AMIIBCgKC
.................... -----END CERTIFICATE REQUEST-----
```

Generating a Self-Signed Certificate

In cryptography and computer security, a self-signed certificate is an identity certificate that is signed by the same entity whose identity it certifies.

Examine the following Python code. In the example, you will create a self-signed certificate named `certificate.pem`. When generating the self-signed certificates, the issuer and the signer are the same:

```
from cryptography.hazmat.backends import default_backend
from cryptography.hazmat.primitives import serialization
from cryptography.hazmat.primitives.asymmetric import rsa
from cryptography import x509
from cryptography.x509.oid import NameOID
from cryptography.hazmat.primitives import hashes
import datetime

# Generate Key (RSA,DSA,EC)
encryptedpass = b"Ilik32Cod3"
key = rsa.generate_private_key( public_exponent=65537, key_size=2048,
backend=default_backend() )
```

```
with open("rsakey.pem", "wb") as f:
    f.write(key.private_bytes( encoding=serialization.Encoding.PEM,
        format=serialization.PrivateFormat.TraditionalOpenSSL,
        encryption_algorithm=serialization.BestAvailableEncryption(encryp
tedpass), ))

# In Self Signed Certificate Issuer and Signer are Same
subject = issuer = x509.Name([ x509.NameAttribute(NameOID.COUNTRY_NAME,
u"US"),
    x509.NameAttribute(NameOID.STATE_OR_PROVINCE_NAME, u"NC"),
    x509.NameAttribute(NameOID.LOCALITY_NAME, u"Apex"),
    x509.NameAttribute(NameOID.ORGANIZATION_NAME, u"Python Cryptography"),
    x509.NameAttribute(NameOID.COMMON_NAME, u"shannonbray.us"), ])

cert = x509.CertificateBuilder().subject_name(
        subject
    ).issuer_name(
        issuer
    ).public_key(
        key.public_key()
    ).serial_number(
        x509.random_serial_number()
    ).not_valid_before(
        datetime.datetime.utcnow()
    ).not_valid_after(
        datetime.datetime.utcnow() + datetime.timedelta(days=10)
    ).add_extension(
        x509.SubjectAlternativeName([x509.DNSName(u"localhost")]),
critical=False,
    ).sign(key, hashes.SHA256(), default_backend())

with open("certificate.pem", "wb") as f:
    f.write(cert.public_bytes(serialization.Encoding.PEM))
```

Formal Validation of Cryptographic Protocols

There are several formal validation methods for cryptographic protocols; these include expert system-based approaches, algebraic approaches, and special logic-based approaches:

- **Expert system-based approaches:** The knowledge of experts is formalized into deductive rules that can be used by a protocol designer to investigate different scenarios. The main drawback is that it is not well suited for finding flaws in cryptographic protocols that are based on unknown attacking techniques.

- **Algebraic approaches:** Cryptographic protocols are specified as algebraic systems. The analysis is generally conducted by examining algebraic term-rewriting properties of the model; the approaches then inspect if the model can attain certain wanted or undesirable states.

■ **Specific logic-based approaches:** These approaches define a set of pred-icates and provide a mapping of messages exchanged during a protocol run into a set of formulas. A generic set of rules allows them to analyze the knowledge and understand that it is obtained by the peer entities of a cryptographic protocol during a protocol run.

Configuring Your First Cryptographic Library

You will create your own code in many areas of this book, but you will also learn about a number of Python libraries that will help you get an understanding of cryptography by using their code that is encapsulated in defined methods.

In this section, you will install the pyca/cryptography library. The cryptog-raphy library includes both a high-level set of recipes and a low-level set of interfaces that will help with many cryptographic algorithms such as message digests, symmetric ciphers, and key derivation functions. You will need this library to examine the X.509 certificate code studied later in this chapter. You can install the cryptography library using pip. Type the following in your shell:

```
pip3 install cryptography
```

Understanding Cryptanalysis

Cryptanalysis is the study of restoring an encrypted message back to plaintext. Cryptanalysis is a critical aspect of cryptography as it helps ensure that current cryptography schemes are secure. We will be performing cryptanalysis on sev-eral of the historical ciphers presented in this chapter to show how encryption schemes once thought secure are now breakable with just a little effort.

Brute-Force Attacks

In a brute-force attack, the advisory attempts to decrypt the ciphertext by using every possible key. If the key is small enough, a brute-force attack can be suc-cessful in a matter of minutes. In fact, if the keys are around 2^{22}, we can write a Python script to crack the password utilizing brute force. For your estimation purposes, when it comes to brute-force attacks, the following helps you ballpark the amount of security you get for various size problems:

■ A key space/message space of 2^{64} is enough for a couple hours of security.

■ A key space/message space of 2^{128} is enough for several decades of pre-quantum security.

■ A key space/message space of 2^{256} is enough for several decades of post-quantum security.

The following is an example of code that will generate a four-digit PIN and then loop through the iterations using brute force to determine the password:

```
import random
# generate a password
generated_password = str(random.randint(0,9999))

# check values 0 - 9999
for i in range(10000):
    Trial = str(i)
    if Trial == generated_password:
        print('Found password: ' + generated_password)
```

Side-Channel Attacks

A side-channel attack is performed when the advisory has awareness of the physical implementation of the code to leak information. This could be done by observing the power usage of the CPU during the encryption or decryption process, or examining the amount of shared memory consumption of processes in virtual machines that are encrypting or decrypting messages.

Social Engineering

Social engineering is a nontechnical attack that is often quite successful. It relies on exploiting people with human interactions and often involves tricking people into breaking normal security procedures. Some common social engineering attacks include phishing, pretexting, baiting, quid pro quo, tailgating, or shoulder surfing.

Analytical Attacks

Analytical attacks in cryptography are attacks against the underlying encryption scheme to find weaknesses that can be exploited. This will be the cornerstone of our examination of many of the historical ciphers introduced in the previous sections.

Frequency Analysis

Frequency analysis will be a critical aspect of our ability to break ciphers using Python. Frequency analysis is the study of the frequency with which letters or groups of letters appear in ciphertext. In examining the English language, the most common letters are E, T, A, and O. In addition to examining single letters, we also examine common pairs of letters, which are referred to as digraphs. Examples of digraphs in the English language include TH, ER, ON, and AN.

There are also letters that are often repeated, which include SS, EE, TT, and FF. In addition, the sum of the frequencies squared is always going to be near .065 when the text has the same distribution as most English language text. So, if you check for that squared sum on the frequencies of characters in encrypted text, you'll know if your text has been substituted in some way or another.

Attack Models

No matter what type of encryption you choose, encryption ciphers are functions that require you to enter a message along with a secret key to produce the ciphertext. In symmetric encryption, each party uses the same key. In asymmetric encryption, one party uses a public key while the other uses a private key. The term *message space* is used to describe all possible messages that might have produced a specific ciphertext. The term *key space* is used to refer to all sets of possible permutations of a secret key. Finally, the term *cipher space* refers to all possible encrypted texts that were created. Typically, with cryptographic hashes the size of the cipher space is the number that matters the most for security; once the attacker can find a second input that matches the hash of a password, the identity of the account is compromised. When analyzing a brute-force attack, you need to estimate the number of inputs that have to be checked to reverse the output.

In the case of a hash function there is no secret key. Everyone needs to be able to verify that the same string hashes to the same value. A brute-force attack on a hash function requires trying every considered input, while a brute-force decryption requires trying every possible key. For your estimation purposes when it comes to brute-force attacks, you can use the following to ballpark the amount of security you get for various size problems:

- A key space/message space of 2^{64} is enough for a couple hours of security.

- A key space/message space of 2^{128} is enough for several decades of pre-quantum security.

- A key space/message space of 2^{256} is enough for several decades of post-quantum security.

Several common attack models can be used for cryptanalysis; each requires a different portion of the message. The common attack models include the following:

- Ciphertext Only (COA) is used when the malicious user only has access to the ciphertexts and does not have access to the plaintext prior to encryption. Frequency analysis is critical when using COA.

- Known-Plaintext (KPA) is used when the malicious user has access to both the plaintext and its encrypted version (ciphertext). Historical ciphers were very susceptible to this type of attack.

- Chosen-Plaintext (CPA) is an attack that occurs when the malicious users are able to define their own plaintext and have it encrypted, resulting in ciphertext that can be analyzed to determine how to decrypt other messages. A good example is the attacks on the German Enigma machine; once the Allies captured an Enigma machine, the CPA was used to determine how the encryption scheme worked.

- Chosen-Ciphertext (CCA) is an attack used where the cryptanalyst can gather information by obtaining the decryptions of chosen ciphertexts. One way to think about this type of attack is that you can test a slightly adjusted encryption. Change a bit and see if the decrypted message turns to gibberish. For instance, if you are a server on the internet and you change an encrypted packet in some way, you can see how the target reacts to your change when they go to decrypt.

Shannon's Theorem

Claude Shannon (1916–2001) was often regarded as the father of modern cryptology and information theory. After receiving his Ph.D. in mathematics, Shannon contributed to the field of cryptanalysis for national defense during World War II. He is also credited for the founding of digital circuit design theory in 1937. He published a paper in 1949 entitled "Communication Theory and Secrecy Systems." In this revolutionary paper, Shannon defines perfect secrecy for secret-key systems and shows that they exist. A secret-key cipher obtains perfect secrecy if for all plaintexts x and all ciphertexts y, it holds that $\Pr(x) = \Pr(x|y)$. In other words, a ciphertext y gives no information about the plaintext. Shannon's principle states, "The enemy knows the system."

Known as the gold standard of security in cryptography, "perfect security" is a special case of information-theoretic security wherein for an encryption algorithm, if there is ciphertext produced that uses it, no information about the message is provided without knowledge of the key. Examine the definition of perfect security as defined by Shannon.

Let $\varepsilon = (E,D)$ be a Shannon cipher defined over (K,M,C). Consider a probabilistic experiment in which the random variable k is uniformly distributed over K. If for all $m_0, m_1 \in$ M, and all $c \in$ C, we have: $\Pr[E(k, m_0) = c] = \Pr[E(k, m_1) = c]$; then we say that ε is a perfectly secure Shannon cipher.

To explain the definition in words, if the probability that a ciphertext c is m_0 is the same as the probability that the same ciphertext c is m_1, then the cipher ε is a perfectly secure Shannon cipher. That is, the perfectly secure Shannon cipher ε has produced a ciphertext that has equal probability of being any message, i.e., the ciphertext c gives no information about the plaintext m.

We will explore perfect security more as we explore the one-time pad in the next section.

One-Time Pad

Perfect secrecy is the concept that given a ciphertext (an encrypted message) from a cipher or perfectly secure encryption system, nothing will be revealed about the plaintext (unencrypted message) by the ciphertext.

A perfectly secret cipher has a couple of other equivalent properties:

- There is a key that encrypts every possible plaintext to every possible ciphertext (perfect key ambiguity). However, this is true only if the keys used are the same size as the messages.

- Even if given a choice of two plaintexts, one the real one, for a ciphertext, you cannot distinguish which plaintext is the real one (perfect message indistinguishability).

What perfect secrecy means in practice is that no amount of computation applied to the ciphertext will give you any advantage in knowing anything about the plaintext or key. This is obviously a desirable property of a cipher, and perfectly secret ciphers do exist. For example, a one-time pad (OTP) is a perfectly secret cipher.

When you examine the OTP, you may decide that it is the basis of modern cryptography or you may determine it does not accomplish what we need. Still, it is important that you understand the scheme and its subtleties. In this section, you will gain a formal description of the algorithm and will explore the OTP from Python; the goal is to show that it can be broken when used in a repetitive scenario.

XOR, AND, and OR

The bitwise operators work on bits and perform bit-by-bit operations. Assume $a = 60$ and $b = 13$. The binary format of a and b will be as follows:

$a = 0011\ 1100$

$b = 0000\ 1101$

Table 2.2 explains each bitwise operator and gives an example.

Table 2.2: Bitwise Operators

OPERATOR	DESCRIPTION	EXAMPLE
& (Binary AND)	Operator copies a bit to the result if it exists in both operands.	(a & b) (means 0000 1100)
| (Binary OR)	Operator copies a bit if it exists in either operand.	(a | b) = 61 (means 0011 1101)
^ (Binary XOR)	Operator copies the bit if it is set in one operand but not both.	(a ^ b) = 49 (means 0011 0001)
~ (Binary Ones Complement)	Operator is unary and has the effect of "flipping" bits.	(~a) = -61 (means 1100 0011 in 2's complement form due to a signed binary number)
<< (Binary Left Shift)	The left operand's value is moved left by the number of bits specified by the right operand.	a << 2 = 240 (means 1111 0000)
>> (Binary Right Shift)	The left operand's value is moved right by the number of bits specified by the right operand.	a >> 2 = 15 (means 0000 1111)

The `bin()` function in Python can be used to convert our integers 60 and 13 to their binary format. Type the following into the Python shell:

```
>>> a = 60
>>> b = 13

>>> print (bin(a))
0b111100
>>> print (bin(b))
0b1101
>>> print (bin(a & b))
0b1100
>>> print (bin(a | b))
0b111101
>>> print (bin(a ^ b))
0b110001
>>> print (bin(~a))
-0b111101
>>> print (bin(a<<2))
0b11110000
>>> print (bin(a>>2))
0b1111
```

Each value maps as shown. Alphanumeric characters, such as A, B, C, can also be converted to a binary format. The use of the ordinal function, `ord()`, will give a numerical value to an ASCII letter. Examine the following example:

```
>>> print (ord('A'))
65
>>> print (bin(ord('A')))
0b1000001
```

You will find that the use of XOR is critical to cryptography. The power of XOR is that it is self-decrypting. If you encrypt a value using XOR, you can easily reverse it with the same operation. We will show this with a simple integer solution first by typing the following into the shell. The following code takes two integers (240, 115) and gets their XOR value (131). You can then XOR 131 with either 240 or 115 and get the other value:

```
>>> x = 240
>>> y = 115
>>> z = (x ^ y) #131

>>> print (z ^ 115)
240
>>> print (z ^ 240)
115
```

To XOR a whole string with another string, we should convert plaintext into an integer, then XOR the integer and reverse that. The print() function will work in either scope. One of the biggest differences between the two code samples is the way we encode and decode hexadecimal values.

The following example shows how the encode method is used on the string:

```
def text2int(msg):
    print (msg)

    # convert string to hex
    hexstr = msg.encode('hex')
    print (hexstr)

    # convert hex to integer
    integer_m = int(hexstr, 16)
    print (integer_m)

    # convert integer back to hex
    back2hex = format(integer_m, 'x')
    print (back2hex)

    # convert back to string
    evenpad = ('0' * (len(back2hex) % 2)) + back2hex
    plaintext = evenpad.decode('hex')
    print (plaintext)

text2int("Hello World")
```

```
Hello World
48656c6c6f20576f726c64
8752161808888253379211 5812
48656c6c6f20576f726c64
Hello World
```

While examining the following code, notice the use of `binascii` along with the `hexlify()` and `unhexlify()` methods. The `hexlify()` method returns the hexadecimal representation of binary data. Each byte of the data is converted into a two-digit hex representation. The resulting output will be twice as long as the length of the data. The `unhexlify()` method returns the binary representation of the data. As you may have guessed, the `unhexlify()` method is the inverse of the `hexlify()` method:

```python
import binascii

def text2int(msg):
    print (msg)

    # convert string to hex
    #hexstr = msg.encode('hex')
    msg = msg.encode()
    hexstr = binascii.hexlify(msg)
    print (hexstr)

    # convert hex to integer
    integer_m = int(hexstr, 16)
    print (integer_m)

    # convert integer back to hex
    back2hex = format(integer_m, 'x')
    print (back2hex)

    # convert back to string
    evenpad = ('0' * (len(back2hex) % 2)) + back2hex
    #plaintext = evenpad.decode('hex')
    plaintext = binascii.unhexlify(evenpad)

    print (plaintext)

text2int("Hello World")
```

```
Hello World
b'48656c6c6f20576f726c64'
8752161808888253379211 5812
48656c6c6f20576f726c64
b'Hello World'
```

Armed with this information, you can now encrypt plaintext to an encrypted value and retrieve it only with a secret password, as shown here:

```python
import binascii

def xorKey(secret):
    secret = secret.encode()
    hexstr = binascii.hexlify(secret)
    key = int(hexstr, 16)
    print ("key: ", key)
    return key


def xorEnc(msg, key):
    msg = msg.encode()
    hexstr = binascii.hexlify(msg)
    print ("hexstr: ", hexstr)
    ciphertext = int(hexstr, 16) ^ key
    print ("ciphertext: ", ciphertext)
    return ciphertext

def xorDec(msg, key):
    xorMsgKey = msg ^ key
    back2hex = format(xorMsgKey, 'x')
    print ("back2hex: ", back2hex)
    evenpad = ('0' * (len(back2hex) % 2)) + back2hex
    plaintext = binascii.unhexlify(evenpad)
    print ("plaintext: ", plaintext)
    return plaintext


key = xorKey("mysecret")
key2 = xorKey("wrongpass")
cipher = xorEnc('Hello world',key)
plain = xorDec(cipher,key)
wrongplain = xorDec(cipher, key2)
```

As you can see, only using the right key will result in the correct message. The preceding should return the following:

```
key:  7888463101613466996
key:  2203408475604721431411
hexstr:  48656c6c6f20776f726c64
ciphertext:  8752161035372447587841051
back2hex:  48656c6c6f20776f726c64
plaintext:  Hello world
back2hex:  48651b73793d757c617a63
plaintext:  Hey=u|azc
```

One-Time Pad Function

Now that you have seen how XOR works, it will be easier to understand the one-time pad. OTP takes a random sequence of 0s and 1s as the secret key and will then XOR the key with your plaintext message to produce the ciphertext:

> GEN: choose a random key uniformly from $\{0,1\}^{\ell}$ $\{0,1\}^{\ell}$ (the set of binary strings of length $\ell\ell$)

> ENC: given $k \in \{0,1\}^{\ell}$ $k \in \{0,1\}^{\ell}$ and $m \in \{0,1\}^{\ell}$ $m \in \{0,1\}\ell$ then output is $c := k \oplus m$ $c := k \oplus m$

> DEC: given $k \in \{0,1\}^{\ell}$ $k \in \{0,1\}\ell$ and $c \in \{0,1\}^{\ell}$ $c \in \{0,1\}^{\ell}$, the output message is $m := k \oplus c$ $m := k \oplus c$

The output given by the OTP satisfies Claude Shannon's notion of perfect secrecy (see "Shannon's Theorem"). Imagine all possible messages, all possible keys, and all possible ciphertexts. For every message and ciphertext pair, there is one key that causes that message to encrypt to that ciphertext. This is really saying that each key gives you a one-to-one mapping from messages to ciphertexts, and changing the key shuffles the mapping without ever repeating a pair.

The OTP remains unbreakable as long as the key meets the following criteria:

- The key is truly random.
- The key the same length as the encrypted message.
- The key is used only once!

When the key is the same length as the encrypted message, each plaintext letter's subkey is unique, meaning that each plaintext letter could be encrypted to any ciphertext letter with equal probability. This removes the ability to use frequency analysis against the encrypted text to learn anything about the cipher. Brute-forcing the OTP would take an incredible amount of time and would be computationally unfeasible, as the number of keys would equal 26 raised to the power of the total number of letters in the message. In Python 3.6 and later, you will have the option to use the secrets module, which will allow you to generate random numbers. The function `secrets.randbelow()` will return random numbers between zero and the argument passed to it:

```
>>> import secrets
>>> secrets.randbelow(10)
3
>>> secrets.randbelow(10)
1
>>> secrets.randbelow(10)
7
```

You can generate a key equal to the length of the message using the following in the Python shell:

```
>>> msg = "helloworldthisistheonetimepad"
>>> key = ''
>>> for i in range(len(msg)):
>>>     key += secrets.choice('ABCDEFGHIJKLMNOPQRSTUVWZYZ')

>>> print (key)
CDHHCYIINAQHKMVOVAAYDPELIRNRU
```

In some ciphers, you can use language detectors. When the OTP is constructed properly, there may be a condition that the wrong key will produce English text, so there is no guarantee that using a language detector will offer the original message. The next example demonstrates that two possible messages may occur: Attack at Midnight! or Retreat Do Not Attack.

If you use the correct key, you will see the real message, while using the decoy key will present the other. If an attacker is trying to brute-force this scheme, it is possible they will find the wrong message.

The following code recipe introduces using `from ... import`. To refer to items from a module within your program's namespace, you can use the `from ... import` statement. When you import modules this way, you can refer to the functions by name rather than through dot notation. Using the `from ... import` construction allows us to reference the defined elements of a module within our program's namespace, letting us avoid dot notation. In this case, we use `hexlify` and `unhexlify`:

```python
from binascii import hexlify, unhexlify

def otpSuperMsg(msg1, msg2):
    hex1 = hexlify(msg1)
    hex2 = hexlify(msg2)
    cipher1 = int(hex1, 16)
    cipher2 = int(hex2, 16)
    msg = cipher1 ^ cipher2
    return msg

def otpEnc(msg, key):
    superKey = int(msg, 16) ^ key
    return superKey

def otpDec(msg, key):
    xorMsgKey = msg ^ key
    back2hex = format(xorMsgKey, 'x')
    evenpad = ('0' * (len(back2hex) % 2)) + back2hex
    plaintext = unhexlify(evenpad)
    return plaintext

realMessage = b"attackthematmidnight!"
decoyMessage= b"retreatanddonotattack"
msg = otpSuperMsg(realMessage, decoyMessage)
```

```
realMsg = hexlify(realMessage)
decoyMsg = hexlify(decoyMessage)
realKey = int(realMsg, 16) ^ msg
decoyKey = int(decoyMsg, 16) ^ msg

print ("The secret message is: ", msg)
print ("The real key is: ", realKey)
print ("The decoy key is: ", decoyKey)
print ()
# choose either the decoy key or the real key
key = realKey
plain = otpDec(msg, key)
print (plain)
print ()
key = decoyKey
plain = otpDec(msg, key)
print ()
print (plain)
```

The output using the keys should resemble the following:

```
The secret message is:  2786558560957958008612612925069442314935232105546
The real key is:  16719039157531782469730156535980050177335322118641
The decoy key is:  1424304971206786995281607951258238534864460563384
```

```
attackthematmidnight!
```

```
retreatanddonotattack
```

Once you use the same key more than once, you open the key to vulnerabilities as now the same key will convert more than one ciphertext to plaintext. Since there is most likely only one key that will decrypt two different messages, the key would be compromised. Using the real key in the preceding example again would tip the advisories of your encryption methods.

One-Way Hashes

You were briefly introduced to hashes in the previous chapter. As a reminder, a *hash function* is an algorithm that changes the input or changes the data of an arbitrary or random length into a fixed-sized output.

In our previous example, you saw passwords that were hashed using the SHA-512 algorithm. Storing passwords as hashes provides a level of security in the event that the password storage database is compromised. Hashes can be used as a more advanced version of checksums. When we move a file from one drive to another, we have a checksum on frames called a Frame Check

Sequence (FCS). It is important to note that not all hash algorithms are suitable for cryptography; those that are, are referred to as *cryptographic hash functions*.

Cryptographic One-Way Hashes

For a one-way hash to be used in cryptographic systems, the algorithm must provide preimage resistance, secondary resistance, and collision resistance:

- *Preimage resistance* means that an attempt to find the original message that produces a hash is computationally unrealistic or for a given h in the output space of the hash function, it is hard to find any message x with $H(x) = h$.

- *Secondary resistance* means that an attempt to find a second message that produces the same hash is computationally unrealistic or for a given message $x2 \neq x1$ with $H(x1)=H(x2)$.

- *Collision resistance* means that finding any two messages that will produce the same hash is computationally unrealistic for the message pair or s $x1 \neq x2$ with $H(x1)=H(x2)$.

In examining the rules, while the secondary resistance and collision resistance may appear very similar, they are slightly different. From a (second) preimage attack we also get a collision attack. The other direction doesn't work as easily, though some collision attacks on broken hash functions seem to be extensible to be almost as useful as second preimage attacks (i.e., we find collisions where most parts of the message can be arbitrarily fixed by the attacker).

The strength of the hash function does not equal the hash length. The strength of the hash is about half the length of the hash due to the probability produced by the birthday attack. The birthday attack exploits the mathematics behind the birthday problem in probability theory. Consider the scenario in which a teacher with a class of 30 students ($n = 30$) asks for everybody's birthday to determine whether any two students have the same birthday. The birthday attack treats our birthdays as uniformly distributed values out of 365 days. The general intuition is that it takes $\sqrt{N}$ samples from a space of size N to have 50% chance of collision. Imagine selecting some value (k) at random from N. Then out of the k values you picked there are $k(k-1)/2$ pairs. For any given pair there is a $1/N$ chance of collision. This gives $k(k-1)/2N$ chance of collision. Therefore, k ~$\sqrt{N}$ will lead to around 50% chance of collision.

The birthday attack relies on any match coming from within a set and not a specific match to a specific value. That intuition should guide us as we approach Message Authentication Codes (MACs). This birthday attack gives us a generic approach for finding two messages that hash to the same value in far less time than brute force. The size that matters is the output size of the hash function, too.

Message Authentication Codes

Hash-based Message Authentication Code (HMAC) is a key-based message digest algorithm that can be used for verifying the integrity of the message, to verify the authenticity of the sender of the message, or both. HMAC has been widely adopted for use in various systems and domains, such as server-to-server communications, Web Service APIs, etc. A well-known use of HMAC is in Amazon's AWS API calls where the signature is generated using HMAC.

HMAC can use a variety of hashing algorithms, like MD5, SHA1, SHA256, etc. The HMAC function is not process intensive, so it has been widely accepted, and it is easy to implement in mobile and embedded devices while maintaining decent security. The following code example shows how to generate an HMAC-MD5 digest with Python:

```
import hmac
from hashlib import md5

key = b'DECLARATION'

h = hmac.new(key,b'',md5)

# add content
h.update('We hold these truths to be self-evident, that all men are
created equal')

# print the HMAC digest
print (h.hexdigest())
```

Perfect Forward Secrecy

In our exploration of cryptography, perfect forward secrecy (PFS), also known as forward secrecy (FS), is a set of key agreement protocols that gives the participants in the message exchange assurances that their session keys will not be compromised even if the private key of the server is compromised. PFS protects past cryptographic sessions against future compromises of passwords or secret keys. The compromise of a single session key will not affect any data other than that exchanged in the particular session by generating a unique session key for each individual session; PFS further protects data on the transport layer of a network that uses common SSL/TLS protocols such as OpenSSL. In the past, OpenSSL was affected by the Heartbleed exploit. If PFS is used, encrypted communications and sessions recorded that may have become compromised cannot be used to decrypt future communications.

A public-key system has the property of PFS if it generates one random secrecy key per session to complete a key agreement, without using a deterministic algorithm. In essence, this guarantees that the compromise of one session cannot compromise others in the future. To examine an example, let us assume that Alice and Bob each generate a pair of long-term asymmetric private and public keys; they then verify the public-key fingerprints in person or out of band using an authenticated channel. The only thing the keys will be used for is authentication; these keys will not be used for encryption. Alice and Bob use the Diffie-Hellman key exchange algorithm to securely agree on an ephemeral session key. Alice sends Bob a message, encrypting it with a symmetric cipher. Bob decrypts Alice's message using the key negotiated previously. The process repeats for each message sent between the two parties.

PFS is designed to prevent the compromise of a long-term secret key from affecting the confidentiality of past conversations. PFS cannot defend against a successful cryptanalysis of the underlying ciphers being used, since a cryptanalysis consists of finding a way to decrypt an encrypted message without the key, and PFS only protects keys, not the ciphers themselves. If an attacker can capture a conversation whose confidentiality is protected through the use of public-key cryptography and wait until the underlying cipher is broken, this would allow the recovery of old plaintexts even if a system is employing PFS.

PFS is present in a number of protocol implementations such as IPSec (optional), SSH, STARTTLS, ATS, and Off-the-Record Messaging. Off-the-Record Messaging is a cryptographic protocol that is used for instant-messaging clients. PFS is a significant security used by several large internet information providers such as Google. Since late 2011, Google provided forward secrecy with TLS by default to users of its Gmail service, Google Docs service, and encrypted search services. Facebook, as of May 2014, supports STARTTLS. TLS 2.4 (released in August 2018) dropped support for ciphers that did not support PFS. ATS, which stands for App Transport Security, is a security that is used by Apple on iOS apps; it became mandatory on all its iOS devices after January 1, 2017.

We will explore PFS in more detail as we dig into the Diffie-Hellman key exchange and elliptic curve Diffie-Hellman in Chapter 8.

Published and Proprietary Encryption Algorithms

In the late 19th century, Auguste Kerckhoffs stated:

> **The cipher method must not be required to be secret, and it must be able to fall into the hands of the enemy without inconvenience.**
>
> **Security must rely solely on secrecy of the key.**

In today's age, keeping one's proprietary algorithm secret would be almost impossible. Information about the algorithm could be leaked by a disgruntled employee or obtained by an attacker and then reverse-engineered. In general, it is much easier for two parties to change their shared secret as opposed to having to re-create new cryptographic algorithms. For enterprise deployments, it would be much easier for all systems to use a standardized, well-proven cryptographic scheme.

Kerckhoffs' principle is accepted industry wide by making cryptographic schemes completely public as opposed to hoping systems stay secure by keeping the algorithms secret or "security by obscurity." It can be quite costly to an organization to create its own algorithms that may be broken without the organization ever finding out about it. The encryption schemes used publicly have all been publicly scrutinized, and studied, and have no known weaknesses.

Summary

Cryptology is broken down into the two fields of cryptography and cryptanalysis. Cryptography is the science of secret writing with the goal of hiding the meaning of the message. Cryptography is further broken down into cryptographic protocols, symmetric algorithms, and asymmetric (or public-key) algorithms. You were introduced to cryptographic protocols that include the works of Needham-Schroeder and Otway-Rees. You saw examples of how the key lengths are important to how long a cryptographic solution may be viable. You were introduced to the common attack models. These included the Ciphertext only (COA), Known-Plaintext (KPA), Chosen-Plaintext (CPA), and Chosen-Ciphertext (CCA).

Perfect secrecy is the concept that states that nothing from the ciphertext reveals anything useful about the plaintext. In this chapter, you were able to explore the Python syntax that allows you to convert a message to hexadecimal and binary. You found that the use of XOR is critical to cryptography. The power of XOR is that it is self-decrypting. If you encrypt a value using XOR, you can easily reverse it with the same operation. You were also introduced to cryptographic hashing using Python.

References

B. Bryant. *Designing an Authentication System: A Dialogue in Four Scenes.* Project Athena, Massachusetts Institute of Technology, Cambridge, MA, 1988.

L. Gong, R. Needham, R. Yahalom. "Reasoning about Belief in Cryptographic Protocols." *Proceedings of the IEEE Symposium on Security and Privacy*, pp. 234–248, Oakland, CA, 1990.

J. Kohl, C. Neuman, T. T'so. "The Evolution of the Kerberos Authentication System." In *Distributed Open Systems*, pp. 78–94. IEEE Computer Society Press, 1994.

R. Needham, M. Schroeder. "Using Encryption for Authentication in Large Networks of Computers." *Communications of the ACM*, Vol. 21, No. 12, 1978.

R. Needham, M. Schroeder. "Authentication Revisited." *Operating Systems Review*, Vol. 21, No. 1, 1987.

D. Otway, R. Rees. "Efficient and Timely Mutual Authentication." *ACM SIGOPS Operating Systems Review*, Vol. 21, No. 1, 1987.

Classical Cryptography

Authentication protocols need to employ encryption to protect the session from exposure to intruders; over the past few years, we have heard time and time again of data breaches that have left user data vulnerable and passwords in the hands of bad actors. In a secure world, passwords are typically hashed, salted, and stretched, and electronic communications should be encrypted to ensure secrecy. Just hashing or encrypting data may not be enough, though. The best encryption schemes will not protect data from poorly constructed passwords. In this chapter, you'll be introduced to password practices, get an understanding of some common historical cryptography schemes, and learn the Python code that will bring all the topics together. Specifically, you will gain cryptographic knowledge as you do the following:

- Explore best practices for passwords
- Explore the basics of encryption schemes
- Explore the use of historical ciphers and their cryptanalysis
- Gain an understanding of why it is critical to use well-established encryption algorithms

Password Best Practices

Throughout this book, your purpose is to gain an understanding of how to use strong cryptographic schemes and how to identify and attack weak schemes. If you work as a security professional, you will also need to help people in your organization protect their data from themselves. You may be required to define policies, procedures, and controls regarding passwords. Even if our systems or cell phones are encrypted, once the password is entered, the system becomes vulnerable. In truth, the password is the only secret to the kingdom, and depending on the type of user account the person has, the more vulnerable the data. No system, encrypted or not, is safe with poor password management.

The following are some things to keep in mind regarding passwords:

- Users should sign an agreement with the system or data owners to keep their passwords confidential and safe. Passwords should not be written down.

- Temporary passwords should be used only once and immediately changed once a user logs in.

- Passwords should have length requirements and require the use of special characters to meet a defined complexity.

- Passwords should never be stored in clear text.

- A password for one system should not be used for another.

- Passwords should be changed regularly.

- Corporate policies must be in place to lock accounts that have excessive failed password attempts.

- Users should not be able to reuse passwords.

- Passwords should never be shared with support staff.

Most modern-day systems are getting better at forcing users to use stronger passwords, but for those systems that do not, it is critical that you understand password hashing, salting, stretching, and storage.

Password Storage

As just stated, as a security-minded professional, whether you are working as a security architect or a software designer, it is vital that you do not store user passwords in clear text. Doing so gives anyone who has access to the file, database, or server direct access to the users' passwords. One way to combat this is by hashing passwords that need to be stored.

Hashing Passwords

Python, like many other languages, provides you a way to call hashing functions that accept a message of any length and return a fixed-length result that is referred to as a *message digest* or *hash code*. Hashing functions use specific hashing algorithms but do not use secret keys. If the exact message is entered into a hashing function, the same hash code will be produced.

There are several reasons to use hash codes in communications. They can assist in ensuring the confidentiality and the integrity of the message. You can use a number of hashing algorithms, including MD5, SHA-3, SHA-512, HAVAL, and RIPEMD-160, just to name a few. The most important properties of hash algorithms are that the output is not predictable, different messages do not produce the same hash code, messages are not reversible, and given the same value, a hash algorithm should always produce the same result.

The following example shows the SHA-512 hash values for the words *password* and *Password*. Notice that even though only the first letter was capitalized, the entire message digest is different.

Here is the hash value for *password*:

```
b109f3bbbc244eb82441917ed06d618b9008dd09b3befd1b5e07394c706a8bb980b1d778
5e5976ec049b46df5f1326af5a2ea6d103fd07c95385ffab0cacbc86
```

Here is the hash value for *Password*:

```
e6c83b282aeb2e022844595721cc00bbda47cb24537c1779f9bb84f04039e1676e6ba857
3e588da1052510e3aa0a32a9e55879ae22b0c2d62136fc0a3e85f8bb
```

To examine the hashed password using SHA-512, type the following into Python:

```
import hashlib
plaintext_password = b'Password'
hashed_sha512 = hashlib.sha512(plaintext_password).hexdigest()
print(hashed_sha512)
```

There are two primary ways to attack hash functions: through cryptanalysis and through brute force. Storing passwords in the database in their hash code form still offers malicious users a way to figure out passwords. A rainbow table, which is a precomputed table for reversing cryptographic hash functions, can be used to crack password hashes. Rainbow tables are used in recovering a plaintext password up to a certain length consisting of a limited set of characters. This is where salting and stretching come in.

Salting Passwords

You have learned that you need to use cryptographic hashing to minimize readability when storing passwords, but just hashing alone isn't enough. *Salting* is the process of adding or concatenating a random chunk of bits to the end of the password before it goes through the hashing process. You would then save that random chunk of bits along with the hashed password. The reason salting is effective is that if bad actors attack your hashing scheme, they are unable to scale their attack to a large number of users or launch brute-force attacks across the enterprise.

Salting means that a rainbow attack must be recomputed for each individual user. That makes an attacker spend a lot more money per user, which is the way I tend to analyze security. As a fun exercise, you can type hashed values straight into the Google search engine. Try to get the plaintext for *161ebd7d-45089b3446ee4e0d86dbcf92*.

To examine salting in Python, type the following:

```
import hashlib
def saltPassword_sha512(password):
    salt = b'cHp3'
    hashed = hashlib.sha512(salt + password).hexdigest()
    print ("%s:%s" % (salt, hashed)) # Store these
    return hashed


plaintext_password = b'Password'
hashed_sha512 = saltPassword_sha512 (plaintext_password)
```

Stretching Passwords

Our next defense is the concept of key or password stretching. *Stretching* is a technique used to make a weak key, passphrase, or password more secure against brute-force attacks by increasing the time it takes to test each possible iteration. Key stretching works by accepting input that is fed into an algorithm, and the return result is an enhanced key. The enhanced key should be of a sufficient size to make it impractical to break using brute-force techniques. The key-stretching process may be repeated several times to consume a longer amount of processing time. The idea is that if the user knows the correct key, the additional second or two it takes to verify it doesn't impact the user; however, if the system is under attack, it should slow down the attacker significantly.

Password Tools

A number of Python libraries offer you ways to perform password functions without having to develop your own; you will probably be better served by using a library instead of rolling your own as it will keep your code simpler. One of the most popular libraries is bcrypt. You can install bcrypt by using the following statement:

```
pip3 install bcrypt
```

The bcrypt library may have dependencies on pycparser and cffi. A few alternatives are worth mentioning, but bcrypt is one of the more popular choices. Some alternatives include scrypt either using the hashlib or cryptography libraries. Simplecrypt also provides libraries for encryption, decryption, and salting.

To add a salt to your hashed password, examine the following Python code:

```
>>> import bcrypt
>>> passwd = b's$cret12'
>>> salt = bcrypt.gensalt()
>>> hashed = bcrypt.hashpw(passwd, salt)
>>>
>>> print(salt)
>>> print(hashed)

b'$2b$12$qfG2n514PG51LD5X0d/a8u'
b'$2b$12$qfG2n514PG51LD5X0d/a8unGLJxQJ8KbVppzf0yGbtk7aE6xjqPHO'
```

The generated output should look similar to what is shown here, but will not match completely because the salt is generated each time the code is executed. Even though the hashed password will be identical each time, the added salt ensures that the hashed password remains secure.

Obfuscating Data

Before jumping into cryptographic schemes to encrypt and decrypt data, we will examine various ways to obfuscate data. *Data obfuscation* (DO) is a technique used to mask data; it scrambles data to prevent unauthorized access to sensitive information.

There are two types of DO encryption: network security DO and cryptographic DO. Network security DO deals with payload attacks that are purposely used to avoid detection by network protection systems. Cryptographic DO is the input of data encoding prior to being transferred to another encryption scheme. Here, we will look at the latter. Using any of the schemes mentioned will remove the ability to use frequency analysis; we will explore frequency analysis in great depth in the next chapter.

You were first introduced to DO in the previous chapter when you learned about the XOR function. Here, we will continue examining techniques to mask data using ASCII encoding, Base64 encoding, binary data, and decoding. ASCII, abbreviated from American Standard Code for Information Interchange, is a character-encoding standard for electronic communication. ASCII codes represent text in computers, telecommunications equipment, and other devices. Most modern character-encoding schemes are based on ASCII, although they support many additional characters.

ASCII Encoding

In ASCII encoding, each letter is converted to one byte. Look at the following examples:

A = 65 or 0b01000001

B = 66 or 0b01000010

C = 67 or 0b01000011

ABC = 0b01000001 0b01000010 0b01000011

Base64 Encoding Text

Base64, also known as privacy enhanced electronic mail (PEM), is the encoding that converts binary data into a textual format; it can be passed through communication channels where text can be handled in a safe environment. PEM is primarily used in the email encryption process. To use the functions included in the Base64 module, you will need to import the library in your code. Base64 offers a decode and encode module that both accepts input and provides output.

To break ASCII encoding into Base64-encoded text, each sequence of six bits encodes to a single character. The characters used can be seen in the following examples:

```
A-Z: 0-25
a-z: 26-51
0, 1, 2, ..., 9: 52-61
+, /: 62 and 63
```

Examine the 24 bits from the previous section:

```
0b01000001 0b01000010 0b01000011
```

Break the line into 6-bit groups:

```
0b010000 010100 001001 000011
```

When you convert the four groups to decimal, you will see that they are equal to the following:

```
16 20 9 3
```

You now convert the numbers to Base64:

```
Q U J D
```

Therefore, when you encode "ABC" to Base64, you should end up with QUJD, as shown here:

```
>>> import base64
>>> value = 'ABC'.encode()
>>> print(base64.b64encode(value))
b'QUJD'
```

In the previous example, we used Python to encode three bytes at a time. When performing Base64 encoding, the text is broken down into groups of three. In the event that the text cannot be broken down into groups of three, you will see the padding character, which is shown using the equal sign (=). If the example had four bytes, then the output would look like the following:

```
>>> value = 'ABCD'.encode()
>>> print(base64.b64encode(value))
b'QUJDRA=='

>>> value = 'ABCDE'.encode()
>>> print(base64.b64encode(value))
b'QUJDREU='

>>> value = 'ABCDEF'.encode()
>>> print(base64.b64encode(value))
b'QUJDREVG'
```

The preceding padding uses null bytes, which equals A. The capital A is the first character you have in Base64; it stands for six bits of zero (000000). You can prove that with the following:

```
>>> value1 = 'ABCD'.encode()
>>> value2 = 'ABCD\x00".encode()
>>> value3 = 'ABCD\x00\x00".encode()
>>> print(base64.b64encode(value1))
b'QUJDRA=='
>>> print(base64.b64encode(value2))
b'QUJDRAA='
>>> print(base64.b64encode(value3))
b'QUJDRAAA'
```

Once you start evaluating Base64, it may become confusing to tell Base64 and ASCII apart. One of the major differences between the two is the encoding process. When you encode text in ASCII, you first start with a text string, and it is converted into a sequence of bytes. When you encode Base64, you are starting with a sequence of bytes and converting the bytes to text.

Binary Data

We will now examine binary data. The file types on your computer are composed of binary data. ASCII data always begins with a first bit of zero. When you open a file using Python, you can convert binary data to Base64:

```
With open('file.exe','rb') as f:
        data = f.read()
        data.encode()
```

Decoding

In this section, we will take what you have learned using the encode() methods and get the inverse using the decode() method. Examine the following syntax:

```
>>> # encode ABCD
>>> value1 = 'ABCD'.encode()
>>> value1
B'ABCD'

>>> #decode ABCD
>>> value1.decode()
'ABCD'
```

Once you have the binary values, you can use the base64 library to encode the values using b64encode. The inverse is the b64decode:

```
>>> myb64 = base64.b64encode(value1)
>>> myb64
B'QUJDRA=='

>>> my = base64.b64decode(myb64)
>> my
B'ABCD'

>>> print (my.decode())
ABCD
>>>
```

Historical Ciphers

Since the invention of writing, there has been the need for message secrecy. While most of the historical ciphers you will learn about in this chapter have been broken, it is important to understand their encryption scheme so that you have a better understanding of how to break them.

In fact, all historical codes used prior to 1980 have been broken except for the one the Native American code talkers used in World Wars I and II. During World War I, the Choctaw Indian language was used, and during World War II, the Navajo language was used. The US Marine Corps recruited Navajo men to serve as Marine Corps radio operators. Both languages served perfectly as they were unwritten and undecipherable due to their complexities.

Scytale of Sparta

One of the oldest cryptographic tools was the Spartan scytale, which was used to perform a transposition cipher. We will examine transposition ciphers in greater detail both later in this chapter and throughout the book. The scytale consisted of a cylinder with a strip of parchment; the parchment would wrap around the cylinder and then the message would be written lengthwise on the parchment. The key in this case would be the radius of the cylinder itself. If the parchment were wrapped around a cylinder of a different radius, the letters would not align in the same way, making the message unreadable.

Substitution Ciphers

The substitution cipher simply substitutes one letter in the alphabet for another based upon a cryptovariable. The substitution involves shifting positions in the alphabet. This includes the Caesar cipher and ROT-13, which will be covered shortly. Examine the following example:

Plaintext: WE HOLD THESE TRUTHS TO BE SELF-EVIDENT, THAT ALL MEN ARE CREATED EQUAL.

Ciphertext: ZH KROG WKHVH WUXWKV WR EH VHOI-HYLGHQW, WKDW DOO PHQ DUH FUHDWHG HTXDO.

The Python syntax to both encrypt and decrypt a substitution cipher is presented next. This example shows the use of ROT-13:

```
key = 'abcdefghijklmnopqrstuvwxyz'

def enc_substitution(n, plaintext):
    result = ''
    for l in plaintext.lower():
        try:
            i = (key.index(l) + n) % 26
            result += key[i]
        except ValueError:
            result += l
    return result.lower()
```

```
def dec_substitution(n, ciphertext):
    result = ''
    for l in ciphertext:
        try:
            i = (key.index(l) - n) % 26
            result += key[i]
        except ValueError:
            result += l

    return result

origtext = 'We hold these truths to be self-evident, that all men are
created equal.'
ciphertext = enc_substitution(13, origtext)
plaintext = dec_substitution(13, ciphertext)

print(origtext)
print(ciphertext)
print(plaintext)
```

Caesar Cipher

The Caesar cipher is one of the oldest recorded ciphers. De Vita Caesarum, Divus Iulis ("The Lives of the Caesars, the Deified Julius), commonly known as The Twelve Caesars, was written in approximately 121 CE. In The Twelve Caesars, it states that if someone has a message that they want to keep private, they can do so by changing the order of the letters so that the original word cannot be determined. When the recipient of the message receives it, the reader must substitute the letters so that they shift by four positions.

Simply put, the cipher shifted letters of the alphabet three places forward so that the letter A was replaced with the letter D, the letter B was replaced with E, and so on. Once the end of the alphabet was reached, the letters would start over:

A	B	C	D	E	F	G	H	I	J	K	L	M	N	O	P	Q	R	S	T	U	V	W	X	Y	Z
D	E	F	G	H	I	J	K	L	M	N	O	P	Q	R	S	T	U	V	W	X	Y	Z	A	B	C

The Caesar cipher is an example of a mono-alphabet substitution. This type of substitution substitutes one character of the ciphertext from a character in plaintext. Other examples that include this type of substitution are Atbash, Affine, and the ROT-13 cipher. There are many flaws with this type of cipher, the most obvious of which is that the encryption and decryption methods are fixed and require no shared key. This would allow anyone who knew this method to read Caesar's encrypted messages with ease. Over the years, there have been several variations that include ROT-13, which shifts the letters 13 places instead of 3. We will explore how to encrypt and decrypt Caesar cipher and ROT-13 codes using Python.

For example, given that x is the current letter of the alphabet, the Caesar cipher function adds three for encryption and subtracts three for decryption. While this could be a variable shift, let's start with the original shift of 3:

```
Enc(x) = (x + 3) % 26
Dec(x) = (x - 3) % 26
```

These functions are the first use of modular arithmetic; there are other ways to get the same result, but this is the cleanest and fastest method. The encryption formula adds 3 to the numeric value of the number. If the value exceeds 26, which is the final position of Z, then the modular arithmetic wraps the value back to the beginning of the alphabet. While it is possible to get the ordinal (ord) of a number and convert it back to ASCII, the use of the key simplifies the alphabet indexing. You will learn how to use the ord() function when we explore the Vigenère cipher in the next section. In the following Python recipe, the enc_caesar function will access a variable index to encrypt the plaintext that is passed in.

```
key = 'abcdefghijklmnopqrstuvwxyz'
def enc_caesar(n, plaintext):
    result = ''
    for l in plaintext.lower():
        try:
            i = (key.index(l) + n) % 26
            result += key[i]
        except ValueError:
            result += l
    return result.lower()

plaintext = 'We hold these truths to be self-evident, that all men are
created equal.'
ciphertext = enc_caesar(3, plaintext)
print (ciphertext)
```

The output of this should result in the following:

```
zh krog wkhvh wuxwkv wr eh vhoi-hylghqw, wkdw doo phq duh fuhdwhg htxdo.
```

The reverse in this case is straightforward. Instead of adding, we subtract. The decryption would look like the following:

```
key = 'abcdefghijklmnopqrstuvwxyz'
def dec_caesar(n, ciphertext):
    result = ''
    for l in ciphertext:
        try:
```

```
            i = (key.index(l) - n) % 26
            result += key[i]
        except ValueError:
            result += l
    return result

ciphertext = 'zh krog wkhvh wuxwkv wr eh vhoi-hylghqw, wkdw doo phq duh
fuhdwhg htxdo.'
plaintext = dec_caesar(3, ciphertext)
print (plaintext)
```

ROT-13

Now that you understand the Caesar cipher, take a look at the ROT-13 cipher. The unique construction of the ROT-13 cipher allows you to encrypt and decrypt using the same method. The reason for this is that since ROT-13 moves the letter of the alphabet exactly halfway, when you run the process again, the letter goes back to its original value.

To see the code behind the cipher, take a look at the following:

```
key = 'abcdefghijklmnopqrstuvwxyz'
def enc_dec_ROT13(n, plaintext):
    result = ''
    for l in plaintext.lower():
        try:
            i = (key.index(l) + n) % 26
            result += key[i]
        except ValueError:
            result += l
    return result.lower()

plaintext = 'We hold these truths to be self-evident, that all men are
created equal.'
ciphertext = enc_dec_ROT13(13, plaintext)
print (ciphertext)

plaintext = enc_dec_ROT13(13, ciphertext)
print (plaintext)

jr ubyq gurfr gehguf gb or frys-rivqrag, gung nyy zra ner perngrq rdhny.
we hold these truths to be self-evident, that all men are created equal.
```

Whether we use a Caesar cipher or the ROT-13 variation, brute-forcing an attack would take at most 25 tries, and we could easily decipher the plaintext results when we see a language we understand. This will get more complex as we explore the other historical ciphers; the cryptanalysis requires frequency analysis and language detectors. We will focus on these concepts in upcoming chapters.

Atbash Cipher

The Atbash cipher is one of many substitution ciphers you will explore. Similar to ROT-13, the Atbash cipher is also its own inverse, which means you can encode and decode using the same key; this also means we need to have only one function to perform both the encryption and decryption processes. The original cipher was used to encode the Hebrew alphabets but, in reality, it can be modified to encode or decode any alphabet. The Atbash cipher is often thought to be a special case of the Alphine cipher that we will be exploring next.

The following is the Atbash key as it maps to the English alphabet:

A	B	C	D	E	F	G	H	I	J	K	L	M	N	O	P	Q	R	S	T	U	V	W	X	Y	Z
Z	Y	X	W	V	U	T	S	R	Q	P	O	N	M	L	K	J	I	H	G	F	E	D	C	B	A

The Python code that implements the Atbash cipher is as follows:

```
def toAtBash(text):
    characters = list(text.upper())
    result = ""
    for character in characters:
        if character in code_dictionary:
            result += code_dictionary.get(character)
        else:
            result += character # preserve non-alpha chars found
    return result

alphabet = list("ABCDEFGHIJKLMNOPQRSTUVWXYZ")
reverse_alphabet = list(reversed(alphabet))
code_dictionary = dict(zip(alphabet, reverse_alphabet))
plainText= "we hold these truths to be self-evident"
print(plainText)
cipherText = toAtBash(plainText)
print(cipherText)
cipherText = toAtBash(cipherText)
print(cipherText)

we hold these truths to be self-evident
DV SLOW GSVHV GIFGSH GL YV HVOU-VERWVMG
WE HOLD THESE TRUTHS TO BE SELF-EVIDENT
```

Vigenère Cipher

The Vigenère cipher consists of using several Caesar ciphers in sequence with different shift values. To encipher, a table of alphabets can be used, termed a tabula recta, Vigenère square, or Vigenère table. It consists of the alphabet written out 26 times in different rows, each alphabet shifted cyclically to the left compared to the previous alphabet, corresponding to the 26 possible Caesar ciphers. At different points in the encryption process, the cipher uses a different alphabet from one of the rows. The alphabet used at each point depends on a repeating keyword.

Here's an example:

Keyword: **DECLARATION**

D	E	C	L	A	R	A	T	I	O	N
3	4	2	11	0	17	0	19	8	14	13

Plaintext: We hold these truths to be self-evident, that all men are created equal.

Ciphertext: zi jzlu tamgr wvwehj th js fhph-pvzdxvh, gkev llc mxv oeh gtpakew mehdp.

To create a numeric key such as the one shown, use the following syntax. You should see the output [3, 4, 2, 11, 0, 17, 0, 19, 8, 14, 13]:

```
def key_vigenere(key):
    keyArray = []
    for i in range(0,len(key)):
        keyElement = ord(key[i]) - 65
        keyArray.append(keyElement)
    return keyArray


secretKey = 'DECLARATION'
key = key_vigenere(secretKey)
print(key)
```

Once you have created the key, you can use it to create ciphertext. You should see the output dpnemvnmifrwgtpakewbsdxen:

```
def shiftEnc(c, n):
    return chr(((ord(c) - ord('A') + n) % 26) + ord('a'))


def enc_vigenere(plainttext, key):
    secret = "".join([shiftEnc(plainttext[i], key[i % len(key)]) for i
in range(len(plainttext))])
    return secret
secretKey = 'DECLARATION'
key = key_vigenere(secretKey)
plaintext = 'ALL MEN ARE CREATED EQUAL'
ciphertext = enc_vigenere(plaintext, key)
print(ciphertext)
```

When you know the key, such as in this case, you can decrypt the Vigenère cipher with the following:

```
def shiftDec(c, n):
    c = c.upper()
    return  chr(((ord(c) - ord('A') - n) % 26) + ord('a'))

def dec_vigenere(ciphertext, key):
    plain = "".join([shiftDec(ciphertext[i], key[i % len(key)]) for i in
range(len(ciphertext))])
    return plain

secretKey = 'DECLARATION'
key = key_vigenere(secretKey)
decoded = dec_vigenere(ciphertext, key)
```

We will examine how to brute-force the Vigenère cipher in a later chapter. We will do this by creating a random key that will use the same encryption function, and then we will use frequency analysis to help find the appropriate key. For now, it is more important to understand how the Python code works with this cryptography scheme.

Playfair

The Playfair cipher was used by the Allied forces in World War II; it is the most common digraphic system, and was named after Lord Playfair of England. With this scheme, the sender and the receiver use a shared keyword. The keyword is then used to construct a table that consists of five rows and five columns; the shared word is then populated into the table followed by the rest of the alphabet. As the table is being built out, letters that already appear in the key are skipped. In addition, the letters I and J use the same letter. For this example, we will use the word DECLARATION, as shown here:

D	E	C	L	A
R	T	I	O	N
B	F	G	H	K
M	P	Q	S	U
V	W	X	Y	Z

The Playfair table is read by looking at where the two letters of the blocks intersect. For example, if the first block, TH, were made into a rectangle, the letters at the other two corners of the rectangle would be OF. To see a graphical interpretation of this, examine the next table:

D	E	C	L	A
R	T	I	O	N
B	F	G	H	K
M	P	Q	S	U
V	W	X	Y	Z

When you have two letters that fall in the same column such as WE, you will need to incorporate the next lower letter, and wrap to the top of the column if necessary. This would form a block around the letters ET. The block WE would be encrypted as ET. The same rule applies if letters fall in the same row.

D	E	C	L	A
R	T	I	O	N
B	F	G	H	K
M	P	Q	S	U
V	W	X	Y	Z

Using the preceding table, examine the following plaintext and ciphertext:

Plaintext: He has obstructed the Administration of Justice by refusing his Assent to Laws for establishing Judiciary Powers

Ciphertext: flklyhhmitqafterfldeqrropondionrthazpogiawhvvntpmuorkxgouylu-plriwnnyadypwkntwapodkcoysorkxazcrigdnzystetom

To create a function in Python that encrypts plaintext using Playfair, type the following:

```
def Playfair_box_shift(i1, i2):
    r1 = i1/5
    r2 = i2/5
    c1 = i1 % 5
    c2 = i2 % 5
    out_r1 = r1
    out_c1 = c2
    out_r2 = r2
    out_c2 = c1
    if r1 == r2:
        out_c1 = (c1 + 1) % 5
        out_c2 = (c2 + 1) % 5
    elif c1 == c2:
        out_r1 = (r1 + 1) % 5
        out_r2 = (r2 + 1) % 5
    return out_r1*5 + out_c1, out_r2*5 + out_c2
```

```
def Playfair_enc(plain):
    random.shuffle(words)
    seed = "".join(words[:10]).replace('j','i')
    alpha = 'abcdefghiklmnopqrstuvwxyz'
    suffix = "".join( sorted( list( set(alpha) - set(seed) ) ) )
    seed_set = set()
    prefix = ""
    for letter in seed:
        if not letter in seed_set:
            seed_set.add(letter)
            prefix += letter
    key = prefix + suffix
    secret = ""
    for i in range(0,len(plain),2):
        chr1 = plain[i]
        chr2 = plain[i+1]
        if chr1 == chr2:
            chr2 = 'X'
        i1 = key.find(chr1.lower())
        i2 = key.find(chr2.lower())
        ci1, ci2 = Playfair_box_shift(i1, i2)
        secret += key[ci1] + key[ci2]
    return secret, key
```

As with the other historical ciphers presented in this chapter, the Playfair cipher can be cracked given enough text. Playfair has a weakness; it will decrypt to the same letter pattern in the plaintext for digraphs that are reciprocals of each other. Examine the next table. Notice how the letters DT and ER form a block. The letters ER (and their reverse RE) form a common digraph in the English language. Digraphs are often used for phonemes that cannot be represented using a single character, like the English *sh* in *ship* and *fish*. When using the English language, there are many words that contain these digraphs, such as *receiver*; notice how receiver contains both an RE and the reciprocal ER; these two letter combinations would encrypt to letter combinations that are easy to identify such as TD and DT. This weakness gives you additional foresight into the cryptographic scheme.

D	E	C	L	A
R	T	I	O	N
B	F	G	H	K
M	P	Q	S	U
V	W	X	Y	Z

Other digraphs in the English language include *sc, ng, ch, ck, gh, py, rh, sh, ti, th, wh, zh, ci, wr, qu*. Identifying nearby reversed digraphs in the ciphertext and matching the pattern to a list of known plaintext words containing the pattern is an easy way to generate possible plaintext strings with which to begin constructing the key.

Another way to break the Playfair cipher is with a method called *shotgun hill climbing*. This starts with a random square of letters. Then minor changes are introduced (i.e., switching letters, or rows, or reflecting the entire square) to see if the candidate plaintext is more like standard plaintext than before the change. The minor changes are examined through frequency analysis and language detectors. For now, here is the Python that decrypts the ciphertext using Playfair with a known shared key:

```python
def Playfair_box_shift_dec(i1, i2):
    r1 = i1/5
    r2 = i2/5
    c1 = i1 % 5
    c2 = i2 % 5
    out_r1 = r1
    out_c1 = c2
    out_r2 = r2
    out_c2 = c1
    if r1 == r2:
        out_c1 = (c1 - 1) % 5
        out_c2 = (c2 - 1) % 5
    elif c1 == c2:
        out_r1 = (r1 - 1) % 5
        out_r2 = (r2 - 1) % 5
    return out_r1*5 + out_c1, out_r2*5 + out_c2

def Playfair_dec(ciphertext, sharedkey):
    seed = "".join(sharedkey).replace('j','i')
    alpha = 'abcdefghiklmnopqrstuvwxyz'
    suffix = "".join( sorted( list( set(alpha) - set(seed) ) ) )
    seed_set = set()
    prefix = ""
    for letter in seed:
        if not letter in seed_set:
            seed_set.add(letter)
            prefix += letter
    key = prefix + suffix
    plaintext = ""
    for i in range(0,len(ciphertext),2):
        chr1 = ciphertext[i]
        chr2 = ciphertext[i+1]
        print chr1, chr2
        if chr1 == chr2:
            chr2 = 'X'
        i1 = key.find(chr1.lower())
        i2 = key.find(chr2.lower())
        ci1, ci2 = Playfair_box_shift_dec(i1, i2)
        plaintext += key[ci1] + key[ci2]
    return plaintext
```

Hill 2x2

The Hill 2x2 cipher is a polygraphic substitution cipher based on linear algebra. The inventor, Lester S. Hill, created the cipher in 1929. The cipher uses matrices and matrix multiplication to mix the plaintext to produce the ciphertext. To fully understand the Hill cipher, it helps to be familiar with a branch of mathematics known as number theory. The Hill cipher is often covered in depth in many textbooks on the number theory topic. The key used here is HILL, which corresponds to the numbers 7, 8, 11, and 11:

Key: 7, 8, 11, 11

Plaintext: SECRETMESSAG

Ciphertext: CIUBYTMUKGWO

To create a Python function that will create the Hill 2x2 encryption, type the following:

```python
import sys
import numpy as np


def cipher_encryption(plain, key):

    # if message length is an odd number, place a zero at the end.
    len_chk = 0
    if len(plain) % 2 != 0:
        plain += "0"
        len_chk = 1

    # msg to matrices
    row = 2
    col = int(len(plain)/2)
    msg2d = np.zeros((row, col), dtype=int)

    itr1 = 0
    itr2 = 0
    for i in range(len(plain)):
        if i%2 == 0:
            msg2d[0][itr1]= int(ord(plain[i]) - 65)
            itr1 += 1
        else:
            msg2d[1][itr2] = int(ord(plain[i]) - 65)
            itr2 += 1


    # key to 2x2
    key2d = np.zeros((2,2), dtype=int)
    itr3 = 0
    for i in range(2):
```

```
            for j in range(2):
                key2d[i][j] = ord(key[itr3]) - 65
                itr3 += 1

    print (key2d)

    # checking validity of the key
    # finding determinant
    deter = key2d[0][0] * key2d[1][1] - key2d[0][1] * key2d[1][0]
    deter = deter % 26

    # finding multiplicative inverse
    for i in range(26):
        temp_inv = deter * i
        if temp_inv % 26 == 1:
            mul_inv = i
            break
        else:
            continue

    if mul_inv == -1:
        print("Invalid key")
        sys.exit()

    encryp_text = ""
    itr_count = int(len(plain)/2)
    if len_chk == 0:
        for i in range(itr_count):
            temp1 = msg2d[0][i] * key2d[0][0] + msg2d[1][i] * key2d[0]
[1]
            encryp_text += chr((temp1 % 26) + 65)
            temp2 = msg2d[0][i] * key2d[1][0] + msg2d[1][i] * key2d[1]
[1]
            encryp_text += chr((temp2 % 26) + 65)
    else:
        for i in range(itr_count-1):
            temp1 = msg2d[0][i] * key2d[0][0] + msg2d[1][i] * key2d[0]
[1]
            encryp_text += chr((temp1 % 26) + 65)
            temp2 = msg2d[0][i] * key2d[1][0] + msg2d[1][i] * key2d[1]
[1]
            encryp_text += chr((temp2 % 26) + 65)

    print("Encrypted text: {}".format(encryp_text))
    return encryp_text




def cipher_decryption(cipher, key):
```

```
# if message length is an odd number, place a zero at the end.
len_chk = 0
if len(cipher) % 2 != 0:
    cipher += "0"
    len_chk = 1

# msg to matrices
row = 2
col = int(len(cipher)/2)
msg2d = np.zeros((row, col), dtype=int)

itr1 = 0
itr2 = 0
for i in range(len(cipher)):
    if i%2 == 0:
        msg2d[0][itr1]= int(ord(cipher[i]) - 65)
        itr1 += 1
    else:
        msg2d[1][itr2] = int(ord(cipher[i]) - 65)
        itr2 += 1


# key to 2x2
key2d = np.zeros((2,2), dtype=int)
itr3 = 0
for i in range(2):
    for j in range(2):
        key2d[i][j] = ord(key[itr3]) - 65
        itr3 += 1

# finding determinant
deter = key2d[0][0] * key2d[1][1] - key2d[0][1] * key2d[1][0]
deter = deter % 26

# finding multiplicative inverse
for i in range(26):
    temp_inv = deter * i
    if temp_inv % 26 == 1:
        mul_inv = i
        break
    else:
        continue

# adjugate matrix
# swapping
key2d[0][0], key2d[1][1] = key2d[1][1], key2d[0][0]

#changing signs
key2d[0][1] *= -1
key2d[1][0] *= -1
```

```
        for i in range(num_of_rows):
            for j in range(len(key)):
                arr[i][j] = plain_text[z]
                z += 1

        num_loc = get_number_location(key, keyword_num_list)

        cipher_text = ""
        k = 0
        for i in range(num_of_rows):
            if k == len(key):
                break
            else:
                d = int(num_loc[k])

                for j in range(num_of_rows):
                    cipher_text += arr[j][d]
                k += 1
        return cipher_text

def get_number_location(key, keyword_num_list):
    num_loc = ""
    for i in range(len(key) + 1):
        for j in range(len(key)):
            if keyword_num_list[j] == i:
                num_loc += str(j)
    return num_loc


def keyword_num_assign(key):
    alpha = "ABCDEFGHIJKLMNOPQRSTUVWXYZ"
    keyword_num_list = list(range(len(key)))
    init = 0
    for i in range(len(alpha)):
        for j in range(len(key)):
            if alpha[i] == key[j]:
                init += 1
                keyword_num_list[j] = init
    return keyword_num_list


def print_grid(plain_text, key):

    keyword_num_list = keyword_num_assign(key)

    for i in range(len(key)):
        print(key[i], end = " ", flush=True)

    print()
    for i in range(len(key)):
        print(str(keyword_num_list[i]), end=" ", flush=True)
    print()
```

```python
    print("------------------------")

    # in case characters don't fit the entire grid perfectly.
    extra_letters = len(plain_text) % len(key)

    dummy_characters = len(key) - extra_letters

    if extra_letters != 0:
        for i in range(dummy_characters):
            plain_text += "."

    num_of_rows = int(len(plain_text) / len(key))

    # Converting message into a grid
    arr = [[0] * len(key) for i in range(num_of_rows)]
    z = 0

    for i in range(num_of_rows):
        for j in range(len(key)):
            arr[i][j] = plain_text[z]
            z += 1

    for i in range(num_of_rows):
        for j in range(len(key)):
            print(arr[i][j], end=" ", flush=True)
        print()

def cipher_decryption(encrypted, key):

    keyword_num_list = keyword_num_assign(key)
    num_of_rows = int(len(encrypted) / len(key))

    num_loc = get_number_location(key, keyword_num_list)

    # Converting message into a grid
    arr = [[0] * len(key) for i in range(num_of_rows)]

    # decipher
    plain_text = ""
    k = 0
    itr = 0

    for i in range(len(encrypted)):
        d = 0
        if k == len(key):
            k = 0
        else:
            d: int = int(num_loc[k])
        for j in range(num_of_rows):
            arr[j][d] = encrypted[itr]
```

```
                itr += 1
            if itr == len(encrypted):
                break
            k += 1

    print()

    for i in range(num_of_rows):
        for j in range(len(key)):
            plain_text += str(arr[i][j])
    return plain_text

plain_text = "Attack by sea and land at dawn!"
key = "fleet"

msg = plain_text.replace(" ","").upper()
msgkey = key.upper()

encrypted = cipher_encryption(msg, msgkey)
decrypted = cipher_decryption(encrypted, msgkey)

print ("Plain Text: " + plain_text)
print ("Encrypted Text: " + encrypted)
print ("Decrypted Text: " + decrypted)
print ()
print_grid(msg, key)
```

Affine Cipher

Next on our list is the Affine cipher. The Affine cipher is a mono-alphabetic substitution cipher. The difference with the Affine cipher is that each letter is mapped to a numeric equivalent, encrypted using a mathematical function, and then converted back to a letter. While using the mathematical function may sound difficult, the process is fundamentally a standard substitution cipher with a set of rules that govern which letters map to other letters. The mathematical function makes use of the modulo m, where m is the length of the alphabet. Each letter is mapped to a number as shown in the following grid where A = 0, B = 1, . . . , Y = 24, Z = 25:

A	B	C	D	E	F	G	H	I	J	K	L	M	N	O	P	Q	R	S	T	U	V	W	X	Y	Z
00	01	02	03	04	05	06	07	08	09	10	11	12	13	14	15	16	17	18	19	20	21	22	23	24	25

The encryption process of the Affine cipher uses modular arithmetic to transform letters into their corresponding integers and then converts the integer into another number, which in turn is converted back into a letter. The encryption function for a single letter would look like the following:

```
Encrypt ( x ) = (a x + b) mod m
```

where x is the integer represented by the letter and m is the number of letters in the alphabet.

To decrypt the Affine cipher, you must find the inverse function. The first step is to convert the encrypted letter into an integer, use a mathematical function to convert the number to another number, and then convert the number back into a letter. The decryption process would look like the following:

```
Decrypt ( x ) = a^-1 (x - b) mod m
```

where x is the integer represented by the letter, m is the number of letters in the alphabet, and a^{-1} is the modular multiplicative inverse of a modulo m. We will explore the multiplicative inverse of a modulo in more detail in the next chapter. If you find yourself having a hard time understanding the code, feel free to review the next chapter and come back to this cipher.

For now, you will see a working example of the Affine cipher in practice. Let's re-examine the formula for the encryption process: $E(x) = (a x + b)$. You can use the previous table to find the letter in the top row and the corresponding integer in the second row. You are left needing to know what the value is for both a and b. This is the key for the cipher. In this case, we will set the value of $a = 17$ and $b = 20$:

Plaintext	C	O	D	E	B	O	O	K
Value of x	02	14	03	04	01	14	14	10
ax + b % 26	02	24	19	10	11	24	24	8
Encrypted	C	Y	T	K	L	Y	Y	I

Examine the letter E in the table. The letter maps to integer 04. You can use Python to validate the math using the following:

```
>>> print ((17 * 4 + 20) % 26)
10
```

The multiplicative inverse for the Affine cipher is $D(x) = 23 * (x - b) \% 26$. You will learn how it is derived in the next chapter. You should find that you are able to decode the cipher using the following table.

Encrypted	C	Y	T	K	L	Y	Y	I
Encrypted x	02	24	19	10	11	24	24	8
23 * (x-b) % 26	02	14	03	04	01	14	14	10
Plaintext	C	O	D	E	B	O	O	K

To prove the previous encryption and decryption scheme, examine the decryption of the letter K. The letter maps to integer 04. You can use Python to validate the math using the following:

```
>>> print ((23 * (10 - 20) % 26))
4
```

This explanation should give you a bit of insight as you examine the following Python script for implementing the Affine cipher:

```
# Extended Euclidean Algorithm for finding modular inverse
# eg: modinv(7, 26) = 15
def egcd(a, b):
    x,y, u,v = 0,1, 1,0
    while a != 0:
        q, r = b//a, b%a
        m, n = x-u*q, y-v*q
        b,a, x,y, u,v = a,r, u,v, m,n
    gcd = b
    return gcd, x, y


def modinv(a, m):
    gcd, x, y = egcd(a, m)
    if gcd != 1:
        return None  # modular inverse does not exist
    else:
        return x % m



# affine cipher encryption function
# returns the cipher text
def encrypt(text, key):
    '''
    E = (a * x + b) % 26
    '''
    return ''.join([ chr((( key[0]*(ord(t) - ord('A')) + key[1] ) % 26)
                + ord('A')) for t in text.upper().replace(' ', '') ])


# affine cipher decryption function
# returns original text
def decrypt(cipher, key):
    '''
    D = (a^-1 * (x - b)) % 26
    '''
```

```python
    return ''.join([ chr((( modinv(key[0], 26)*(ord(c) - ord('A') -
key[1]))
                    % 26) + ord('A')) for c in cipher ])


# Test the encrypt and decrypt functions
def main():
    # declaring text and key
    text = 'CODEBOOK'
    key = [17, 20]

    # calling encryption function
    encrypted_text = encrypt(text, key)

    print('Encrypted Text: {}'.format(encrypted_text ))

    # calling decryption function
    print('Decrypted Text: {}'.format
    (decrypt(encrypted_text, key) ))


if __name__ == '__main__':
    main()
```

Summary

Maintaining password best practices will help mitigate against brute-force attacks on your data. If you are responsible for creating your own authentication system, it is highly recommended that you hash, salt, and/or stretch passwords . As you have learned, just encrypting the data is not enough. In fact, in the next chapter, you will learn how to use Python to crack historical ciphers. We will be building on the mathematical concepts that will enable you to determine the language and encryption scheme of several historical ciphers and determine methods toward their cryptanalysis.

CHAPTER

4

Cryptographic Math and Frequency Analysis

By now, you have a basic understanding of historical ciphers and their cryptanalysis using Python. In this chapter, you'll turn your attention to the mathematics that is essential to understanding cryptography through the remainder of this book. This chapter introduces basic group theory and the Chinese remainder theorem, shows how to solve systems of linear equations, and gives a more in-depth look at modular arithmetic. You'll learn the proper importance of secure pseudorandom number generators and their use in cryptography. This chapter is the basis for the remainder of this book as you explore public-key cryptography. Finally, you'll start to construct a frequency analysis (FA) module that has a wide range of cryptanalysis functions. Through this chapter, you'll gain cryptographic knowledge as you do the following:

- Gain an understanding of modular arithmetic
- Understand the importance of the greatest common divisor (GCD)
- Gain an understanding of group theory
- Gain an understanding of pseudorandom numbers
- Create a Python script for frequency analysis

Modular Arithmetic and the Greatest Common Devisor

You witnessed briefly in the previous chapter how Python uses modular arithmetic in cryptography. In this chapter, you'll gain a greater understanding of it. The logic of modular arithmetic began with the quotient-remainder theorem. The quotient-remainder theorem states that for every integer A and positive B there exist different integers Q and R such that: $A = B * Q + R$, $0 = < r = < b$. When $a = 95$ and $b = 10$, what is the unique value of q (quotient) and r (remainder)? You find that the quotient equals 9 and the remainder equals 5.

Once you understand the quotient-remainder theorem, it is easier to understand our first bit of cryptographic math: modular arithmetic.

Here is an example: $23 \equiv 2(\text{mod}7)$, which reads as "23 is equivalent to 2 mod 7." You can also type it into a search engine as **23 mod 7** to see the answer. You can further examine the modulo by stating that $a \equiv b \ (\text{mod } q)$ when a minus b is a multiple of q. Another way to state it numerically would be: $123 \equiv 13$ $(\text{mod } 11)$ because $123 - 13 = 110 = 11 * 10$. An alternative way to think about it is to examine 53 $(\text{mod } 13)$, which would be to say that 53 is equivalent to $53 - 13 = 40$, which is equivalent to 27, which is equivalent to 14, which is equivalent to 1, which is equivalent to -12, which is equivalent to -25, and so on. In fact, $53 \equiv \{53 + k \cdot 13 \mid \forall k \in Z\}$ (you can read that as "is equivalent to the set of all numbers of form 53 plus an integer multiple of 13"). As shown in the previous chapter, we take the modulus by using the % sign.

To illustrate this example in Python, type the following:

```
>>> 53 % 13
1
>>> 40 % 13
1
>>> 27 % 13
1
>>> 14 % 13
1
>>> -12 % 13
1
```

Now that you understand modular arithmetic, we turn our attention to the greatest common divisor (GCD). The GCD is the largest number that perfectly divides two integers: a and b. For example, the GCD of 12 and 18 is 6. This is an excellent opportunity to introduce Euclid's algorithm, which is a technique for finding the GCD of two integers with negligible effort. To find the GCD of two integers A and B, use the following rules:

If $A = 0$ then $\text{GCD}(A, B) = B$

If $B = 0$ then $\text{GCD}(A, B) = A$

$A = B * Q + R$ and $B \neq 0$ then $GCD(A, B) = GCD(B,R)$

Therefore, write A using the quotient remainder form: $A = B * Q + R$

Find **GCD(B, R)**

Euclid's algorithm works by continuously dividing one number into another and calculating the quotient and remainder at each step. Each phase produces a decreasing sequence of remainders, which terminate at zero, and the last non-zero remainder in the sequence is the GCD. You will revisit Euclid's algorithm shortly when you examine the modular inverses; for now, you can use the algorithm to write a GCD function in Python:

```
def gcd(a,b):
  if b == 0:
    return a
  else:
    return gcd(b, a % b)

print(gcd(12,18))
```

Now that you know how to create your own GCD function, note that it is very inefficient due to its use of recursion. Prefer using Python's built-in GCD function, which is part of the standard Python math library. You will see an example of this when you explore Euler's totient function later in this chapter.

Prime Numbers

Prime numbers in cryptography are vital to the security of our encryption schemes. *Prime factorization*, also known as *integer factorization*, is a mathematical problem that is used to secure public-key encryption schemes. This is achieved by using extremely large semiprime numbers that are a result of the multiplication of two prime numbers. As you may remember, a prime number is any number that is only divisible by 1 and itself. The first prime number is 2. Additional prime numbers include 3, 5, 7, 11, 13, 17, 19, 23, and so on. An infinite number of prime numbers exist, and all numbers have one prime factorization. A semiprime number, also known as biprime, 2-almost prime, or a pq number, is a natural number that is the product of two prime numbers. The semiprimes less than 50 are 4, 6, 9, 10, 14, 15, 21, 22, 25, 26, 33, 34, 35, 38, 39, 46, and 49.

Prime numbers are significant in cryptography. Here is a simple Python script that tests if an integer value is prime:

```
def isprime(x):
    x = abs(int(x))
    if x < 2:
        return "Less 2", False
```

```
    elif x == 2:
        return True
    elif x % 2 == 0:
        return False
    else:
        for n in range(3, int(x**0.5)+2, 2):
            if x % n == 0:
                return n, False
        return True

print (isprime(100000007))
```

Computationally speaking, it is easy to generate large prime numbers that will require most humans to either perform math on paper or use a computer. You can calculate a fairly large number and then check if there are any available factors. Take, for example, 19 × 13 = 589. Both 19 and 13 are prime numbers as their only factors are themselves and 1; the product of the two numbers results in a semiprime. Multiplying 19 and 13 together is straightforward. However, finding the factors of 589 is a bit more challenging. To find all factors, you will need to examine all of the primes that are less than 589 until you find which prime numbers are used. You can achieve this reasonably quickly for smaller numbers, but once you start dealing with larger numbers, the amount of possible numbers that are required to check becomes so large that even modern computers are not able to calculate them within a reasonable time frame.

Prime Number Theorem

To estimate the generation of prime numbers, you can use the prime number theorem. The prime number theorem returns an approximate value for the number of primes less than or equal to a provided positive real number x. The usual notation for this number is $\pi(x)$, so that $\pi(2) = 1$, $\pi(3.5) = 2$, and $\pi(10) = 4$. To generate large prime numbers, you will need to take an approximation and then use a primality test to verify the number. You will see how this works at the end of this section when you review the code listing for generating large prime numbers.

You can write a number of primality tests in Python. Some of the examples provided in this chapter include the school primality test, Fermat's little theorem, and the Miller-Rabin primality test.

School Primality Test

The school primality test solves the problem of whether an integer is prime or not by iterating through all of the numbers starting from 2 to ($n/2$) using a loop for every number check to see if it divides n. If the program finds any number that divides *n*, the program will return false. In the reverse, if no numbers are found between 2 and (*n*/2) that divides *n*, the value is prime.

Here's a school primality test method:

```
# A school primality test method
def isPrime(n):
    # Corner case
    if n <= 1:
        return False

    # Check from 2 to n-1
    for i in range(2, n):
        if n % i == 0:
            return False;

    return True

print(isPrime(11))
print(isPrime(14))
```

For a little cleaner execution, you can optimize the preceding code by observing that all primes are of the form $6k \pm 1$, with the exception of 2 and 3. This is due to the fact that all integers can be expressed as $(6k \pm i)$ for some integer *k* and for *i* = −1, 0, 1, 2, 3, or 4; 2 divides $(6k + 0)$, $(6k + 2)$, $(6k + 4)$; 3 divides $(6k + 3)$. Therefore, a more efficient method is to test if *n* is divisible by 2 or 3, then to check through all the number of the form $6k \pm 1$.

```
# A optimized school method based
def isPrime(n):
    # Corner cases
    if (n <= 1):
        return False
    if (n <= 3):
        return True

    # This is checked so that we can skip
    # middle five numbers in below loop
    if (n % 2 == 0 or n % 3 == 0) :
        return False

    i = 5
    while(i * i <= n):
        if (n % i == 0 or n % (i + 2) == 0):
            return False
        i = i + 6

    return True

print(isPrime(11))
print(isPrime(15))
```

Fermat's Little Theorem

Fermat's little theorem is used in number theory to compute the powers of integers modulo prime numbers. The theorem is a special case of Euler's theorem. (We explore Euler's theorem later in this chapter.) Fermat's little theorem states let p be a prime number, and a be any integer.

If n is a prime number, then for every a, $1 < a < p - 1$,

$a^{p-1} \equiv 1 \pmod{p}$

or

$a^{p-1} \% p = 1$

To ensure this makes sense, let's look at an example:

p = prime integer number

a = integer which is not a multiple of p

According to Fermat's little theorem,

$2^{(17-1)} \equiv 1 \bmod (17)$

$65{,}536 \% 17 \equiv 1$

This means $(65{,}536 - 1)$ is a multiple of 17. This is proven by multiplying 17 * 3,855, which equals $(65{,}536 - 1)$ or 65,535. If you know the modulo m is prime, then you can also use Fermat's little theorem to find the inverse. We will cover this in more detail later in this chapter.

Here is a quick and easy function that will return whether an integer is prime or not:

```
>>> def CheckIfProbablyPrime(x):
...      return pow(2, x-1, x) == 1

>>> CheckIfProbablyPrime(19)
True
>>> CheckIfProbablyPrime(31)
True
>>> CheckIfProbablyPrime(589)
False
```

Miller-Rabin Primality Test

Similar to the other tests featured in this section, the Miller-Rabin primality test is a primality test; it was first discovered by M. M. Artjuhov in 1967. It was later rediscovered in 1976 by Gary L. Miller. Miller's version of the test is deterministic. Michael Rabin further modified the algorithm in 1980 to obtain an unconditional probabilistic algorithm.

In computer science, a *deterministic algorithm* is one that will always produce the same output when given a particular set of inputs. Deterministic algorithms are the most studied. To get a better understanding of how the Miller-Rabin primality test works, enter the following Python code:

```python
# Miller-Rabin primality test
import random

# Utility function to do modular exponentiation.
# Returns (x^y) % p
def power(x, y, p):

    # Initialize result
    res = 1;

    # Update x if it is more than or equal to p
    x = x % p;
    while (y > 0):

        # If y is odd, multiply x with result
        if (y & 1):
            res = (res * x) % p;

        # y must be even now
        y = y>>1; # y = y/2
        x = (x * x) % p;

    return res;

# This function is called for all k trials. It returns
# false if n is composite and returns false if n is
# probably prime. d is an odd
# number such that d*2^r = n-1 for some r >= 1

def millerTest(d, n):

    # Pick a random number in [2..n-2]
    # Corner cases make sure that n > 4
    a = 2 + random.randint(1, n - 4);

    # Compute a^d % n
    x = power(a, d, n);

    if (x == 1 or x == n - 1):
        return True;

    # Keep squaring x while one of the following doesn't happen
    # (i) d does not reach n-1
    # (ii) (x^2) % n is not 1
    # (iii) (x^2) % n is not n-1
```

```
    while not is_prime(p, 128):
        p = generate_prime_candidate(length)
    return p

print('Generate the value of n using two prime numbers p and q:')
print('\n')
print(generate_prime_number())
print('\n')
```

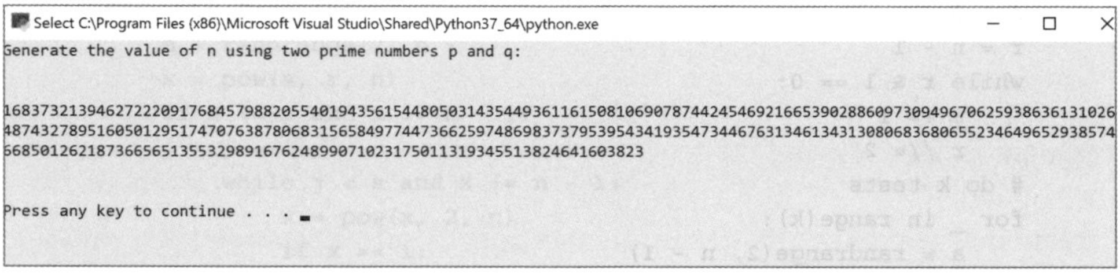

Figure 4.2: `Generate_large_primes.py`

Basic Group Theory

In abstract algebra and other fields of mathematics, group theory studies the algebraic structures known as *groups*. The concept of a group is central to abstract algebra: other familiar algebraic structures, such as vector spaces, rings, and fields, can all perform as groups endowed with additional operations and axioms. Group theory comes into play as you explore the Diffie-Hellman and RSA encryption systems in Chapter 8. For now, consider the idea that elements in groups (e.g., integers) have orders (i.e., cycle lengths), and this lets you use modular arithmetic to speed up significant computations. Group theory is exploited to build cryptographic schemes and the associated cryptanalysis.

To start your exploration into the basics of group theory, we define a group as a set, **G**, together with a binary operation * (called the *group law* of G) that combines any two elements to form another element. The operation may be multiplication, addition, rotation, composition, or any other action that consumes two elements and returns one.

To be eligible as a group, the set and operation (G, *) requires four properties, known as the *group axioms*.

- **Closure:** $a, b \in G$ implies $a * b \in G$
- **Identity:** There exists $e \in G$ such that $a * e = e * a = a$ for all $a \in G$
- **Inverse:** For each $a \in G$, there exists $a^{-1} \in G$ such that $a * a^{-1} = a^{-1} * a = e$
- **Associativity:** $a, b, c \in G$ implies $(a * b) * c = a* (b * c)$

Additionally, a group is said to be *abelian* if it satisfies the commutativity property, as shown here:

$A * b = b * a$ for all $a, b \in G$

This is simply stating that a group in which the result of applying the group **G** operation to two elements (a, b) has no dependency on the order in which they are written.

Furthermore, in an additive group, you write **0** instead of e; in a multiplicative group, you write **1** instead of e.

An example of this is shown in modular arithmetic. Suppose you have the group **G** = {0, 1, 2, 3, 4}; the group falls under the operation of addition modular 5. Review the following examples: 0 + 0 = 0, 0 + 4 = 4, 1 + 4 = 0, 2 + 4 = 1, 3 + 3 = 1. You will notice that adding any two elements in **G** together makes another element in **G**. This example has an identity 0: $x + 0 = 0 + x$ for each x. You should also notice that every element has an inverse that will return it to 0: 4 + 1 = 0, 3 + 2 = 0. The group example can be written as Z_5 (which reads "Z five" or "Z mod 5"). Modular arithmetic is also known as clock arithmetic; if you are struggling with the concept, think of a clock but instead of starting with 1, use 0. This will give you the group **G** = {0, 1, 2, 3, 4, 5, 6, 7, 8, 9, 10, 11}; when you add an hour to 11 (11 + 1), you return to 0. Therefore, 11 + 2 = 1, 11 + 3 = 2.

To continue, in a multiplicative group of numbers, the set {0, 1, 2, 3, 4} is not a group under multiplication modulo 5 since 1 is the identity element but 0 ∘ $x = 0$ and there can't be any element that would send 0 to 1; there is no inverse for 0 under multiplication modulo 5, but the group **G** = {1, 2} is a group multiplication modulo 3 (2·2 = 1, 2 is its inverse).

Orders of Elements

Suppose you have a group **G** with an identity element e. The order of $x \in G$ is the smallest positive integer n such that $x^n = e$. In abstract algebra, this is expressed as $|x| = n$. If there is no such n, then x has infinite order. Review the following example.

NOTE While this looks like the same notation as the absolute value, remember that in abstract algebra it is different.

The nonzero real numbers form a group under multiplication. You must omit zero since you cannot divide by zero; zero does not have a multiplicative inverse. In abstract algebra, you indicate that you are omitting zero with the symbol $\mathbf{R}^x$. As briefly mentioned earlier, the identity element in any group is 1. Incidentally, the order of $|1| = 1$; this is because $1^1 = 1$. Furthermore, the order of –1 is 2, notated as $|-1| = 2$; this is because $-1^2 = 1$. Other than 1 and –1, no other nonzero real number can be raised to a positive integer power to get 1. Therefore, all other real numbers have an infinite order in this group.

Now suppose you have a group **G**; it is possible to have a subset of **G** that is also a group. In abstract algebra, this is called a subgroup, and it is typically represented by the letter **H**. You specify that **H** is a subgroup of **G** by using the notation **H ≤ G**. Technically, you can use the notation **H < G** but **G** is also considered to be a subset of **G** and **H** could equal **G**.

When working with groups, you typically use additive notation (+) or multiplicative notation (×); this is true even when the elements of the group are not numbers, and the group operation is not numerical but is function compositions or geometrical transformations. A group **G** is considered a "cyclic" group if it can be generated by a single element: **G** = <x>. Review the following definition for cyclic groups:

Let **G** be a group with operation x

Pick $x \in$ **G**

Think about the smallest subgroup of **G** that contains x. First, you have x, but any group that contains x must also contain its inverse: x^{-1}. It also must contain the identity element, which you should remember is 1 for a multiplicative group. It must also contain all powers of x: x^2, x^3, x^4. Don't forget all powers of the inverse of x: $x^{-1}, x^{-2}, x^{-3}, x^{-4}$. Therefore, a set of all integral powers of x would be the smallest subgroup of G; it would look as follows: $\{\ldots x^{-4}, x^{-3}, x^{-2}, x^{-1}, 1, x, x^2, x^3, x^4, \ldots\}$. This is an example of a group generated by x.

<x> = $\{\ldots x^{-4}, x^{-3}, x^{-2}, x^{-1}, 1, x, x^2, x^3, x^4, \ldots\}$ = Group generated by x

If **G** = <x> for some x, then **G** is a cyclic group.

It is probably worth reviewing the same definition using additive notation:

Let **H** be a group with operation +

Pick $y \in$ **H**.

The group generated by y is the smallest subgroup of **H** containing y. It must contain y, its inverse (−y), and the identity element 0. It must also contain all multiples of y:

<y> = $\{\ldots, -3y, -2y, -y, 0, y, 2y, 3y, \ldots\}$ = Group generated by y.

If **H** = <y> for some y, then we call **H** a cyclic group.

There are two types of cyclic groups: infinite and finite. The infinite group contains all integers. The finite group contains the integers mod n. Cyclic groups are essential because of the fundamental theorem of finitely generated abelian groups. It states that any abelian group that is finitely generated can be broken apart into a finite number of cyclic groups and every cyclic group is the integers **Z** or the integers mod n. Cyclic groups are the building blocks for finite numbered abelian groups.

Ideally, you now have a general idea of groups and subgroups. Enter "cosets"; these are objects in abstract algebra that help you find subgroups using Lagrange's theorem. The theorem uses a simple rule that dramatically narrows down the possible list of subgroups.

Recall that the notation for group **H** is a subgroup of group **G**: **H** ≤ **G**. Every group has at least two subgroups. These include **G** itself and the trivial group = {e}. The trivial group consists of only the identity element. The idea of Lagrange's theorem is to find if a group has more than these two subgroups. The theorem states: if **H** ≤ **G**, then the order of **H** divides the order of **G**.

Recall that the order of a group **G** is the number of elements in the group and it is denoted using the absolute value symbol |**G**|. This notation allows you to write Lagrange's theorem by stating: **H** ≤ **G** → |**H**| divides |**G**|. What the theorem is stating is that the subgroup **H** cannot be just any size and that there are strong restrictions on the subsets of **G**. Here is a simplified example:

Let G be a group with |G| = 323 = 17 × 19

Divisors of 323: 1, 17, 19, 323

The results of the theorem present the possible orders of the subgroups include 1, 17, 19, and 323.

Every group has at least two subgroups: G (itself) and {e} (trivial group):

|G| = 323

|{e}| = 1

This means that if G has any other subgroups, their orders are 17 or 19. It is essential to understand that the theorem is not stating that there are indeed subgroups of order 17 and 19. In this case, it does, but there are many cases where it will not.

The proof of this is not that difficult. Mostly, a subgroup is closed under the operation in question, so if you have some element that is not in the subgroup, you can multiply or add it to the elements in the subgroup and get another set not equal to the subgroup that has the same size. Repeat the process, and you'll chunk all the elements in G into "cosets" of H.

Modular Inverses

You'll now turn your focus to modular inverses. For an integer a and a modulus m you want to find a number n; the notation looks like the following: a^{-1} such that $n \circ a \equiv 1 \pmod{m}$.

That is, it is the multiplicative inverse in the ring of integers modulo m. The multiplicative inverse of a modulo m exists if and only if a and m are coprime (i.e., if $gcd(a, m) = 1$).

For every number a and a prime p that $a^{p-1} \equiv 1 \pmod{p}$. If you need to compute the inverse of a modulo p since $a * a^{p-2} = a^{p-1} \equiv 1$, when the modulus is prime, you can compute $a^{p-2} \pmod{p}$.

If the modulus is prime, Python provides an internal function called pow that takes *a*, *p* − 2, and *p* to compute the inverse modulo. Consider the following example:

```
>>> a = 14
>>> p = 101
>>> a_inv = pow(a, p-2, p)
>>> a_check = a * a_inv % p
>>> print("The modular inverse is ", a_inv)
The modular inverse is  65
>>> print("The check value should equal 1. It equals ", a_check)
The check value should equal 1. It equals 1
```

Fermat's Little Theorem to Find the Inverse

As mentioned earlier in this chapter, we can use Fermat's little theorem to calculate the inverse if we know that *m* is prime:

$$a^{(m-1)} \equiv 1 \pmod{m}$$
$$a^{-1} \equiv a^{m-2} \pmod{m}$$

Here's the Python code to calculate the inverse if we know that *m* is prime:

```
# Fermat's little theorem.
# modular inverse of a under modulo m using
# Assumption: m is prime

def gcd(a,b):
    if (b == 0):
        return a
    else:
        return gcd(b, a % b)


# To compute x^y under modulo m
def power(x,y,m):

    if (y == 0):
        return 1
    p = power(x, y // 2, m) % m
    p = (p * p) % m

    return p if(y % 2 == 0) else  (x * p) % m

# Function to find modular inverse of a under modulo m

def modInverse(a,m):
    if (gcd(a, m) != 1):
        print("Inverse doesn't exist")

    else:
        # If a and m are relatively prime, then
```

```
        # modulo inverse is a^(m-2) mode m
        print("Modular multiplicative inverse is ",
            power(a, m - 2, m))

a = 3
m = 11
modInverse(a, m)
```

NOTE   In the preceding code listing, the code uses a `gcd()` function instead of using the built-in math library to help you understand how to code the GCD. You will find this helpful when you use the extended GCD.

Extending the GCD

To find the inverse when you have a nonprime modulus, you need to add a new trick: the extended Euclidean algorithm. The extended Euclidean algorithm is useful when two integers (*a*, *b*) are coprime; two numbers are said to be coprime if the only positive number that divides both numbers is 1.

The next example returns the inverse using the extended Euclidean algorithm:

```
def egcd(a, b):
    if a == 0:
        return (b, 0, 1)
    else:
        g, y, x = egcd(b % a, a)
        return (g, x - (b // a) * y, y)

def modinv(a, m):
    g, x, y = egcd(a, m)
    if g != 1:
        raise Exception('modular inverse does not exist')
    else:
        return x % m

a = 10272184008901526397898044
p = 676892447384205115543512

print modinv(a, p)

4751454584755824717584097
```

Euler's Theorem

Earlier in this chapter, you were introduced to Fermat's little theorem. We will now examine a generalization of Fermat's theorem known as Euler's theorem.

Both Fermat's and Euler's theorems play an important role in public-key cryptography, which will be explored in greater detail in Chapter 8.

In number theory, Euler's theorem, also known as Euler's totient theorem or the Fermat–Euler theorem, states that if n and a are coprime positive integers, then $a\varphi^{(n)} \equiv 1 \bmod n$ where $\varphi(n)$ is Euler's totient function. In 1736, Leonhard Euler published his proof of Fermat's little theorem, which Fermat had presented without proof. Subsequently, Euler presented other proofs of the theorem, culminating with "Euler's theorem" in his paper of 1763, in which he attempted to find the smallest exponent for which Fermat's little theorem was always true.

Euler investigated the properties of numbers; he specifically studied the distribution of prime numbers. One crucial function he defined is named the PHI function; the PHI function measures the breakability of a number. Assume you have the number n; the function calculates the number of integers that are less than or equal to n and do not share any common factor with n; you see it in the following notation: $\phi[n]$. For example, if you wanted to examine $\phi[8]$, you would examine all values from 1 to 8 and count all integers with which 8 does not share a factor greater than 1; the numbers are 1, 3, 5, 7. The function produces 4. As it turns out, calculating the PHI of a prime number P is simple. $\phi[P] = P - 1$. To calculate $\phi[7]$, you count all integers except 7 since none of the integers share a factor with 7; therefore, $\phi[7] = 6$. Assume a larger prime such as 21,377. $\phi[21{,}377] = 21{,}376$. The equation looks like the following:

$$ap - 1 \equiv 1 \bmod p$$

To take full advantage of this trick, which helps when you explore RSA, you need to see the general version. If you know the prime factorization of a modulus, then computing the Euler's totient works as follows:

$$\phi(p_1^{K1} \cdots p_n^{Kn}) = \phi(p_1^{K1}) \cdots \phi(p_n^{Ki-1}) \text{ where } \phi(p_i^{Ki}) - p_i^{Ki-1} = p^{Ki-1} \circ (p_i - 1)$$

We extend the ideas presented in this chapter into some classical number theory that also happens to be practical for cryptographers. Euler totient functions offer benefits to speed up modular inverse computations. You also learn why raising numbers to substantial powers is not expensive when you are working with modular arithmetic.

For instance:

$$\phi(3 \circ 5 \circ 23) = \phi(3) \circ \phi(5) \circ \phi(23) = 2 \circ 4 \circ 22 = 32$$

Euler's totient function $\Phi(n)$ for an input n is the count of numbers in the format of {1, 2, 3, 4, 5, n} that are relatively prime to n, i.e., the numbers whose GCD with n is 1. Examine the following six examples, which calculate the Euler's totient function $\Phi(n)$ in respect to the inputs 1 through 6. The output will be the number of positive integers that do not exceed n and also have no common divisors with n other than the common divisor 1:

$\Phi(1) = 1$

gcd (1, 1) is 1

$\Phi(2) = 1$

gcd (1, 2) is 1, but gcd (2, 2) is 2

$\Phi(3) = 2$

gcd (1, 3) is 1 and gcd (2, 3) is 1

$\Phi(4) = 2$

gcd (1, 4) is 1 and gcd (3, 4) is 1

$\Phi(5) = 4$

gcd (1, 5) is 1, gcd (2, 5) is 1,

gcd (3, 5) is 1, and gcd (4, 5) is 1

$\Phi(6) = 2$

gcd (1, 6) is 1 and gcd (5, 6) is 1

Use the following Python to test Euler's totient function on integers 1 through 20. The output should resemble Figure 4.3.

```python
import math

def phi(n):
    amount = 0
    for k in range(1, n + 1):
        if math.gcd(n, k) == 1:
            amount += 1
    return amount


for n in range(1,20) :
    print("Φ(",n,") = ",phi(n))
```

To add a little pizzazz to your Python program, you can use the `matplotlib` library and create a graph, as shown here:

```python
import math
import numpy as np
from matplotlib import pyplot as plt

def phi(n):
    amount = 0
    for k in range(1, n + 1):
        if math.gcd(n, k) == 1:
            amount += 1
    return amount
```

```
for i in range (500):
    phi_n = phi(i)
    #print (i ,phi_n)
    plt . plot (i ,phi_n , 'o ')

plt.xlabel("Value of x")
plt.ylabel("Value of y")
plt.title("Euler's Theorem")
plt.show()
```

Figure 4.4 shows the output of using Euler's theorem and the MatPlot library to create a graph.

```
Φ( 1 ) =  1
Φ( 2 ) =  1
Φ( 3 ) =  2
Φ( 4 ) =  2
Φ( 5 ) =  4
Φ( 6 ) =  2
Φ( 7 ) =  6
Φ( 8 ) =  4
Φ( 9 ) =  6
Φ( 10 ) =  4
Φ( 11 ) =  10
Φ( 12 ) =  4
Φ( 13 ) =  12
Φ( 14 ) =  6
Φ( 15 ) =  8
Φ( 16 ) =  8
Φ( 17 ) =  16
Φ( 18 ) =  6
Φ( 19 ) =  18
Φ( 20 ) =  8

Press any key to continue . . .
```

Figure 4.3: `Euler.py` test

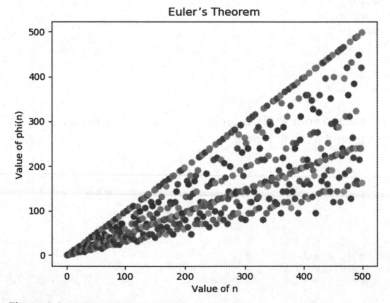

Figure 4.4: `EulerPlot.py` test

Pseudorandomness

You will now examine pseudorandom number generation (PRNG) and why it is insecure for use in cryptography. The goal of PRNG is to have a reproducible sequence of random-feeling numbers. PRNG offers benefits when running simulations that need to be consistent between each execution. Some examples of simulation that benefit from the consistency of a PRNG generator include testing stock market predictions, testing scientific experiments, rolling dice in games, and generating symmetric-key encryption.

In the early days of computing, when applications needed to simulate nuclear reactions but also needed to be reproducible in the case of an error in the program, John von Neumann generated one of the first pseudorandom generators using the middle-square method. The method generates a sequence of n-digit numbers based on the digits in the middle of the number and then squares them. For example, if you have a seed number of 682117, you square it to get 465283601689. The middle numbers are 283601. Square this number and repeat. So while the number appears random, you can reproduce the generated numbers as long as you start with the same seed.

Take a look at how this can be done using Python:

```
n = int(input("Please enter a six-digit number: "))
for i in range(1,10):
    n = int(str(n * n).zfill(12)[3:9])
    print(n)

Please enter a six-digit number: 682117
283601
429527
493443
485994
190168
163868
852721
133103
716408
```

PRNG in encryption needs to have two properties that ensure its security. When the properties exist, the PRNG is known as a *cryptographically secure pseudorandom number generator* (CSPRNG). A CSPRNG must have the following properties:

- **Next-bit test:** You should not be able to guess the next bit with no better than 50% probability. This means given $S_{i+1}, S_{i+2}, S_{i+3}, \ldots, S_{i+n}$ you should not be able to guess S_{i+n+1}.

- **State compromised extension:** You should not be able to calculate $S_i, S_{i-1}, \ldots,$ given $S_{i+1}, \ldots, S_{i+n}$.

```
# find the inverse of A
A_inverse = np.linalg.inv(A)
print (A_inverse)

# solve for X
X = A_inverse * B
print (X)
```

You can alternatively use the NumPy array method to accomplish the same task, as shown here:

```
import numpy as np

# solve the following linear equation
print ('1a + 1b = 35')
print ('2a + 4b = 94')

# create equations
a = np.array([[1, 1],[2,4]])
b = np.array([35, 94])

# print answers
print (np.linalg.solve(a, b))
```

Now we will examine a practical example to show how matrices can be used for encryption.

In this example, we will encrypt the message "prepare to negotiate."

Message = "prepare to negotiate"

The encoding matrix for this example is as follows:

$$\begin{bmatrix} -3 & -3 & -4 \\ 0 & 1 & 1 \\ 4 & 3 & 4 \end{bmatrix}$$

Assign a number to each letter in the alphabet much like you did for a Caesar cipher. The letters do not have to map to the same numbers as long as both the sender and receiver know the assignments. Python uses the ord() function to assign a letter to a numerical value. You can convert the number back to a letter using the chr() function.

A	B	C	D	E	F	G	H	I	J	K	L	M	N	O	P	Q	R	S	T	U	V	W	X	Y	Z
01	02	03	04	05	06	07	08	09	10	11	12	13	14	15	16	17	18	19	20	21	22	23	24	25	26

This message that we want to encrypt will look like the following:

P	R	E	P	A	R	E		T	O		N	E	G	O	T	I	A	T	E
16	18	05	16	01	18	05	27	20	15	27	14	05	07	15	20	09	01	20	05

Because we started with a 3×3 encoding matrix, we will break the enumerated message into a sequence of 3×1 vectors:

$$\begin{bmatrix} 16 \\ 18 \\ 05 \end{bmatrix} \begin{bmatrix} 16 \\ 01 \\ 18 \end{bmatrix} \begin{bmatrix} 05 \\ 27 \\ 20 \end{bmatrix} \begin{bmatrix} 15 \\ 27 \\ 14 \end{bmatrix} \begin{bmatrix} 05 \\ 07 \\ 15 \end{bmatrix} \begin{bmatrix} 20 \\ 09 \\ 01 \end{bmatrix} \begin{bmatrix} 20 \\ 05 \\ 27 \end{bmatrix}$$

There are only 20 characters in the message; since we have a matrix with 21 positions, we need to populate the last position with a space (27) to complete the last vector. We may now encode the message by multiplying each of the preceding vectors by the original encoding matrix:

$$\begin{bmatrix} -3 & -3 & -4 \\ 0 & 1 & 1 \\ 4 & 3 & 4 \end{bmatrix} \begin{bmatrix} 16 & 16 & 05 & 15 & 05 & 20 & 20 \\ 18 & 01 & 27 & 27 & 07 & 09 & 05 \\ 05 & 18 & 20 & 14 & 15 & 01 & 27 \end{bmatrix}$$

This will produce the following encoded message that can be transmitted in a linear form:

−122, 23, 138, −123, 19, 139, −176, 47, 181, −182, 41, 197, −96, 22, 101, −91, 10, 111, −183, 32, 203

To decrypt the message, the recipient writes the message as a sequence of a 3×3 matrices and uses the inverse of the encoding matrix:

$$\begin{bmatrix} 1 & 0 & 1 \\ 4 & 4 & 3 \\ -4 & -3 & -3 \end{bmatrix}$$

With the inverse, you can perform matrix multiplication on the received message:

$$\begin{bmatrix} 1 & 0 & 1 \\ 4 & 4 & 3 \\ -4 & -3 & -3 \end{bmatrix} \begin{bmatrix} -122 & -123 & -176 & -182 & -96 & -91 & -183 \\ 23 & 19 & 47 & 41 & 22 & 10 & 32 \\ 138 & 139 & 181 & 197 & 101 & 111 & 203 \end{bmatrix}$$

The matrix multiplication should produce the following:

$$\begin{bmatrix} 16 & 16 & 05 & 15 & 05 & 20 & 20 \\ 18 & 01 & 27 & 27 & 07 & 09 & 05 \\ 05 & 18 & 20 & 14 & 15 & 01 & 27 \end{bmatrix}$$

Once you have the matrix calculated, you should be able to expand the message and map the numbers back to their original letters:

P	R	E	P	A	R	E		T	O		N	E	G	O	T	I	A	T	E
16	18	05	16	01	18	05	27	20	15	27	14	05	07	15	20	09	01	20	05

Frequency Analysis

The primary focus of this section is to teach the computer to recognize when a set of letters matches the frequency distribution of plaintext English. You can apply the information in this section in a number of different ways. The ultimate goal is to give you the tools you need to be able to crack a number of classical ciphers.

Frequency analysis is the study of the frequency of letters or the combination of letters. It is based on the fact that, within any written language, certain letters and combinations of letters will occur with varying frequencies. When you examine the frequency of letters used in the English language, you find that the letters *E*, *T*, *A*, and *O* are the most common, while *Z*, *Q*, and *X* are found with much less frequency. Examine Figure 4.5 to see the occurrence of each letter.

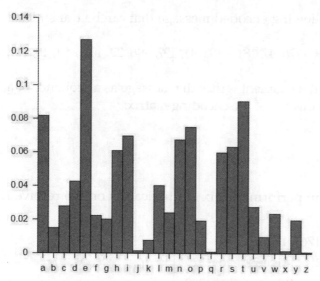

Figure 4.5: `FA.py`

We will also find higher frequency of letter combinations such as *TH*, *ER*, *ON*, and *AN*. These combinations are known as bigrams or digraphs. There are also common pairs of repeating letters such as *SS*, *EE*, *TT*, and *FF*. When you encrypt English plaintext into ciphertext using many historical ciphers, these same properties will be preserved and can be exploited in a ciphertext-only attack.

As you will recall, historical substitution ciphers replace each letter in the plaintext with an alternate letter. If you use the Caesar cipher to encrypt the letter *E* with a key of 3, then each occurrence of *E* will now be *H*. If you have enough text to determine that *H* is the letter with the most frequency, then you may determine that the key is the difference between the letters *H* and *E*. This would give you enough details to attempt to break the cipher. With the Caesar cipher, you will be able to brute-force a solution within 25 rounds. More advanced substitution ciphers, like the Vigenère cipher, offer a little more of a challenge.

We will first take a look at understanding how frequency analysis works; we will then apply the analysis to both the Caesar and the Vigenère cipher so that you can truly understand the power of frequency analysis. Frequency analysis isn't always helpful. Take the case of the novel *Gadsby*. *Gadsby* is a 1939 novel by Ernest Vincent Wright written as a lipogram, which does not include words that contain the letter *E*. Our first example will take a small set of text and count the occurrence of each letter, as shown here:

```
# initializing string
test_str = "We hold these truths to be self-evident, that all men are
created equal, "
test_str += "that they are endowed by their Creator with certain
unalienable Rights, "
test_str += "that among these are Life, "
test_str += "Liberty and the pursuit of Happiness."

# get count of each element in string
all_freq = {}

for i in test_str:
    if i in all_freq:
        all_freq[i] += 1
    else:
        all_freq[i] = 1

# printing result
print()
print ("Count of all characters in the provided text is :\n " + str(all_freq))

# frequency using collections.Counter()
from collections import Counter

# initializing string
test_str = "We hold these truths to be self-evident, that all men are created equal, "
test_str += "that they are endowed by their Creator with certain unalienable Rights, "
test_str += "that among these are Life, "
test_str += "Liberty and the pursuit of Happiness."

# using collections.Counter() to get
# count of each element in string
res = Counter(test_str)
```

```
# printing result
print()
print ("Count of all characters in the provided text is :\n " + str(res))
```

Figure 4.6 shows the occurrence of letters that are present in the test_str value. The first part of the execution shows the letters as they appear in the message, while the second part of the execution sorts the letters by their occurrence.

```
Count of all characters in the provided text is :
{'W': 1, 'e': 28, ' ': 34, 'h': 12, 'o': 6, 'l': 7, 'd': 6, 't': 22, 's': 8, 'r': 11, 'u': 5, 'b': 4, 'f': 3, '-': 1,
'v': 1, 'i': 10, 'n': 9, ',': 4, 'a': 16, 'm': 2, 'c': 2, 'q': 1, 'y': 3, 'w': 2, 'C': 1, 'R': 1, 'g': 2, 'L': 2, 'p': 3,
'H': 1, '.': 1}

Count of all characters in the provided text is :
Counter({' ': 34, 'e': 28, 't': 22, 'a': 16, 'h': 12, 'r': 11, 'i': 10, 'n': 9, 's': 8, 'l': 7, 'o': 6, 'd': 6, 'u': 5,
'b': 4, ',': 4, 'f': 3, 'y': 3, 'p': 3, 'm': 2, 'c': 2, 'w': 2, 'g': 2, 'L': 2, 'W': 1, '-': 1, 'v': 1, 'q': 1, 'C': 1,
'R': 1, 'H': 1, '.': 1})

Press any key to continue . . .
```

Figure 4.6: `Frequency.py`

Frequency analysis works best in situations where you have a great deal of text. In our next example, you will open a copy of the Declaration of Independence and then process the frequency analysis for it. A number of books are available at the Gutenberg project (`gutenberg.org`) that you can use to try a variety of texts in a number of languages. One of the techniques you are going to want to implement is the removal of unwanted characters, numbers, and spaces; we also typically make the letter case uniform, such as making each letter lowercase. The reason we do this is so that we can use modular arithmetic on a group of letters from *a* to *z* and when we reach *z*, we start back over with a like a typical Caesar cipher.

Review the following code to examine the frequencies of the letters:

```
import urllib.request, ssl

# get the text of the Declaration of Independence
response = urllib.request.urlopen("https://raw.githubusercontent.com/
noidentity29/AppliedCryptoPython/master/declaration.txt", context=ssl._
create_unverified_context())
originalText = response.read()

# Strip out all non-alphabet characters
# There are a number of ways to do this but this is the simplest to understand
modifiedText = str(originalText.strip())
modifiedText = modifiedText.replace(" ", "")
modifiedText = " ".join(modifiedText.split())
```

```
modifiedText = modifiedText.lower()

plaintext = ""
for c in modifiedText:
    if (c.isalpha()):
        plaintext = plaintext + c


# Determine the frequency analysis of the plaintext
frequency = {}
for ascii in range(ord('a'), ord('a')+26):
    frequency[chr(ascii)] = float(plaintext.count(chr(ascii)))/
len(plaintext)

sum_freqs_squared = 0.0
for ltr in frequency:
    sum_freqs_squared += frequency[ltr]*frequency[ltr]

# Results
print()
print ("The frequency should be near .065 if plaintext in English: " +
str(sum_freqs_squared))
```

Figure 4.7 shows the frequency analysis of the text of the Declaration of Independence. Since the document is in English, the frequency analysis should be near the value .065. When you are checking to see if your cryptanalysis is complete, your result should be similar.

```
The frequency should be near .065 if plaintext in English: 0.06843095088936661
Press any key to continue . . .
```

Figure 4.7: `declaration_freq.py`

Cryptanalysis with Python

Now that you understand the importance of frequency analysis (FA), you can start to explore how to use FA to start cracking classical ciphers. The techniques you learn here can be applied to a number of substitution-type ciphers such as the Caesar, ROT-13, and Vigenère ciphers. As your understanding grows, you will also be able to apply these techniques to the other classical ciphers that are outlined in Chapter 3.

The next cryptanalysis code listing we will examine will take the Declaration of Independence and encrypt it using a randomly generated key. It will then use FA to examine all key possibilities; remember that when using a letter-shifting cipher such as the Caesar cipher, there are only 26 possible keys. The code listing will brute-force the decryption by examining the frequency analysis of each attempt. You will know you have the correct key once you have a frequency analysis of .065:

```
import urllib.request, ssl, random

# get the text of the Declaration of Independence
response = urllib.request.urlopen("https://raw.githubusercontent.com/
noidentity29/AppliedCryptoPython/master/declaration.txt", context=ssl._
create_unverified_context())
originalText = response.read()

# Strip out all non-alphabet characters
# There are a number of ways to do this but this is the simplest to
understand
modifiedText = str(originalText.strip())
modifiedText = modifiedText.replace(" ", "")
modifiedText = " ".join(modifiedText.split())
modifiedText = modifiedText.lower()

plaintext = ""
for c in modifiedText:
    if (c.isalpha()):
        plaintext = plaintext + c

# Encrypt the plaintext using a random Caesar shift
def shiftBy(c, n):
    return chr(((ord(c) - ord('a') + n) % 26) + ord('a'))

caesar_key = random.randint(1,25)
print ("shhh the secret caesar key is: ", caesar_key)
encrypted = list(map(lambda x: shiftBy(x, caesar_key), plaintext))

# Use FA to determine Caesar key for encrypted text
normal_freqs = {'a': 0.080642499002080981, 'c': 0.026892340312538593,
'b': 0.015373768624831691,
'e': 0.12886234260657689, 'd': 0.043286671390026357, 'g': 0.019625534749730816, 'f':
0.024484713711692099, 'i': 0.06905550211598431, 'h': 0.060987267963718068, 'k':
0.0062521823678781188, 'j': 0.0011176940633901926, 'm': 0.025009719347800208, 'l':
0.041016761327711163, 'o': 0.073783151266212627, 'n': 0.069849754102356679, 'q':
0.0010648594165322703, 'p': 0.017031440203182008, 's': 0.063817324270355996, 'r':
0.06156572691936394, 'u': 0.027856851020401599, 't': 0.090246649949305979, 'w':
0.021192261444145363, 'v': 0.010257964235274787, 'y': 0.01806326249861108, 'x':
0.0016941732664605912, 'z': 0.0009695838238376564}
```

```
frequency = {}
for ascii in range(ord('a'), ord('a')+26):
    frequency[chr(ascii)] = float(encrypted.count(chr(ascii)))/len(plaintext)

sum_freqs_squared = 0.0
for ltr in frequency:
    sum_freqs_squared += frequency[ltr]*frequency[ltr]

print ("Will be near .065 despite Caesar: " + str(sum_freqs_squared))

for possible_key in range(1, 26):
    sum_f_sqr = 0.0
    for ltr in normal_freqs:
        caesar_guess = shiftBy(ltr, possible_key)
        sum_f_sqr += normal_freqs[ltr]*frequency[caesar_guess]
    if abs(sum_f_sqr - .065) < .005:
        print ("Key is probably: ", possible_key, " f_sqr is ",sum_f_sqr)
```

Figure 4.8 shows the key that was randomly generated to encrypt the text. The code will then return the FA of the encrypted code, which will be relatively close to .065 since it is a substitution cipher. The code looks for which key gets the closest to .065 and will then recommend that result as a key. Each time you execute your solution, you will generate a new key.

```
shhh the secret caesar key is:  7
Will be near .065 despite Caesar: 0.0684309508893666
Key is probably:  7  f_sqr is  0.06694645595370748
Press any key to continue . . .
```

Figure 4.8: `Cearsar_FA.py`

Using an Online Word List

One useful technique to help identify when you have successfully decrypted a historical cipher is to use known word lists. In the following example, we simply load a text file containing 10,000 common English words. In the technique shown we will read in the words using the `.split()` method to break them into a list of words. Additionally, you will see that we are interested only in the words that are at least three letters long. The quickest way to filter these words is to use a filter with the lambda function. *Lambda functions* are functions that do not require a name like the defined functions do. The lambda function returns a function object that can be assigned to a variable. In Python, the most common use for lambda functions is for a simple one-line function. You will typically see the lambda functions used in conjunction with a map or filter function.

Here's the example code to read in the words using the `.split()` method to break them into a list of words. Using the following Python code, you will download a file from the Internet called `common_en_words.txt`, which contains 10,000 common words in the English language. The output will show each of these words on their own line:

```
import urllib.request, ssl

# URL to Common English Words
commonWordsPath = "https://raw.githubusercontent.com/noidentity29/
AppliedCryptoPython/master/common_en_words.txt"

# create URL request
response = urllib.request.urlopen(commonWordsPath, context=ssl._create_
unverified_context())
readText = response.read()

# the file is in a binary format, decode
fileOfWords = readText.decode('utf-8')

# create an array for each word
words = fileOfWords.split()

# print word list
for word in words:
    print (word)

# filter out the shorter words
longerwords = list(filter(lambda x: len(x)> 2, words))

# print out longer words
for word in longerwords:
    print (word)
```

Determining the Frequency

The trick to decrypting historical ciphers using cryptanalysis relies on being able to determine the frequency of letters regardless of their encryption state. In the next example, you will see how to examine the frequency of letters used in text. The online provided file, `ch4_encrypted.txt`, is encrypted with a computer-generated key that represents the letters of the alphabet. From our previous lessons, you learned that the most common letters include E, T, A, O, I, N. Armed with this, you can start examining the frequency of letters in text and if the words are not readable in English, you can start swapping the most common letters with the frequency key of letters produced by the following code:

```python
import urllib.request, random, ssl
import operator


def getLetterFreqs(text):
    frequency = {}
    for ascii in range(ord('a'), ord('a')+26):
        frequency[chr(ascii)] = float(text.count(chr(ascii)))/len(text)

    sum_freqs_squared = 0.0
    for ltr in frequency:
        sum_freqs_squared += frequency[ltr]*frequency[ltr]
    return sum_freqs_squared

def getFitnessScore(message):
    lower = message.lower()
    score = 0.0
    for word in longerwords:
        wordWeight = lower.count(word)
        if wordWeight>0:
            score += wordWeight * 50 * len(word)
    return score

def getFreqKey(text):
    frequency = {}
    message = text.lower()
    normal_freqs = {'a': 0.080642499002080981, 'c': 0.026892340312538593, 'b':
0.015373768624831691, 'e': 0.12886234260657689, 'd': 0.043286671390026357, 'g':
0.019625534749730816, 'f': 0.024484713711692099, 'i': 0.069055502115984431, 'h':
0.060987267963718068, 'k': 0.0062521823678781188, 'j': 0.0011176940633901926, 'm':
0.025009719347800208, 'l': 0.041016761327711163, 'o': 0.073783151266212627, 'n':
0.069849754102356679, 'q': 0.0010648594165322703, 'p': 0.017031440203182008, 's':
0.063817324270355996, 'r': 0.06156572691936394, 'u': 0.027856851020401599, 't':
0.090246649949305979, 'w': 0.021192261444145363, 'v': 0.010257964235274787, 'y':
0.01806326249861108, 'x': 0.0016941732664605912, 'z': 0.0009695838238376564}

    tolerance = .013
    for ascii in range(ord('a'), ord('a')+26):
        frequency[chr(ascii)] =  message.count(chr(ascii))
    sorted_x = sorted(frequency.items(), key=operator.itemgetter(1),
reverse=True)
    print (sorted_x)
    sortedkey = ""
```

```
    commonWordsPath = "https://raw.githubusercontent.com/noidentity29/
AppliedCryptoPython/master/common_en_words.txt"
    ALPHA = 'ABCDEFGHIJKLMNOPQRSTUVWXYZ'


    # create URL request
    response = urllib.request.urlopen(commonWordsPath, context=ssl._
create_unverified_context())
    readText = response.read()

    # the file is in a binary format, decode
    fileOfWords = readText.decode('utf-8')

    # create an array for each word
    words = fileOfWords.split()

    # filter out the shorter words
    longerwords = list(filter(lambda x: len(x) > 2, words))

    return longerwords

def getKeyLength(encryptedText):
    highest = 0;
    highCtr = 0;
    encryptedText = encryptedText.lower()
    for KeyLength in range(1,26):
        sampling = encryptedText[::KeyLength]
        freqCheck =  getFreqs(sampling)
        if highest < freqCheck:
            highest = freqCheck
            highCtr = KeyLength

    return highCtr

def getFreqs(text):
    frequency = {}
    for ascii in range(ord('a'), ord('a')+26):
        frequency[chr(ascii)] = float(text.count(chr(ascii)))/len(text)

    sum_freqs_squared = 0.0
    for ltr in frequency:
        sum_freqs_squared += frequency[ltr]*frequency[ltr]
    return sum_freqs_squared

myDictionary = getDictionary()
cipherText = getEncryptedData()
freqScore = getLetterFreqs(cipherText)
fitScore = getFitnessScore(cipherText, myDictionary)
keyLength = getKeyLength(cipherText)
```

```
print ()
print ("The frequency score for this file is: ", freqScore)
print ()
print ("The fitness score for this file is: ", fitScore)
print()
print ("The key length for this file is: ", keyLength)
print ()
```

Figure 4.10 shows the initial frequency and fitness score of the file; based on this the output specifies the determined key length that should be used to crack the encryption.

```
The frequency score for this file is:  0.039258265526867064

The fitness score for this file is:  1196000.0

The key length for this file is:  16

Press any key to continue . . .
```

Figure 4.10: `Vigenere_break.py`

Now that we can determine the length of the key, we can use the knowledge we gained on cracking Caesar ciphers and apply it to cracking the Vigenère cipher. When we examine every letter that is in a specific position, we can use frequency analysis to find the best letter for each position.

The following program may take up to 20 minutes but should reveal the secret key used to encrypt the file:

```
import urllib.request, random, ssl
import operator
from itertools import cycle
from functools import reduce


def shiftBy(c, n):
    shift = chr(((ord(c) - ord('a') + n) % 26) + ord('a'))
    return shift

def getLetterFreqs(text):
    frequency = {}
    for ascii in range(ord('a'), ord('a')+26):
        frequency[chr(ascii)] = float(text.count(chr(ascii)))/len(text)

    sum_freqs_squared = 0.0
    for ltr in frequency:
        sum_freqs_squared += frequency[ltr]*frequency[ltr]
    return sum_freqs_squared
```

```python
def getTextOnly(text):
    # Strip out all non-alphabet characters
    # There are a number of ways to do this but this is the simplest to
understand
    modifiedText = str(text.strip())
    modifiedText = modifiedText.replace(" ", "")
    modifiedText = " ".join(modifiedText.split())
    modifiedText = modifiedText.lower()
    return modifiedText

def getEncryptedData():
    encryptedFilePath = "https://raw.githubusercontent.com/noidentity29/
AppliedCryptoPython/master/encryptedmoby.txt"

    response = urllib.request.urlopen(encryptedFilePath, context=ssl._
create_unverified_context())
    readText = response.read()
    readText = readText.decode('utf-8')
    textOnly = getTextOnly(readText)
    return textOnly

def getFitnessScore(message, longerwords):

    score = 0.0
    for word in longerwords:
        wordWeight = message.count(word)
        if wordWeight>0:
            score += wordWeight * 50 * len(word)
    return score

def getDictionary():

    commonWordsPath = "https://raw.githubusercontent.com/noidentity29/
AppliedCryptoPython/master/common_en_words.txt"
    ALPHA = 'ABCDEFGHIJKLMNOPQRSTUVWXYZ'


    # create URL request
    response = urllib.request.urlopen(commonWordsPath, context=ssl._
create_unverified_context())
    readText = response.read()

    # the file is in a binary format, decode
    fileOfWords = readText.decode('utf-8')

    # create an array for each word
    words = fileOfWords.split()

    # filter out the shorter words
    longerwords = list(filter(lambda x: len(x)> 2, words))
```

```
        return longerwords

def getKeyLength(encryptedText):
    highest = 0;
    highCtr = 0;
    encryptedText = encryptedText.lower()
    for KeyLength in range(1,26):
        sampling = encryptedText[::KeyLength]
        freqCheck =  getFreqs(sampling)
        if highest < freqCheck:
            highest = freqCheck
            highCtr = KeyLength

    return highCtr

def getFreqs(text):
    frequency = {}
    for ascii in range(ord('a'), ord('a')+26):
        frequency[chr(ascii)] = float(text.count(chr(ascii)))/len(text)

    sum_freqs_squared = 0.0
    for ltr in frequency:
        sum_freqs_squared += frequency[ltr]*frequency[ltr]
    return sum_freqs_squared

def decryptIndex(keys, ciphertext):
    """Decrypt the string and return the plaintext"""
    key = ""
    ALPHA = 'abcdefghijklmnopqrstuvwxyz'
    ciphertext = ciphertext.upper()
    ALPHA = 'ABCDEFGHIJKLMNOPQRSTUVWXYZ'
    for i in range(len(keys)):
        key = key + chr(keys[i] + 65)

    pairs = list(zip(ciphertext, cycle(key)))
    result = ''


    for pair in pairs:
        total = reduce(lambda x, y: ALPHA.index(x) - ALPHA.index(y),
pair)
        result += ALPHA[total % 26]

    return result

def findKeyPos(message, keyLength, keyPos):
    frequency = {}
    allKeys = []
    return_key = 0
    tolerance = .01
```

```
    normal_freqs = {'a': 0.080642499002080981, 'c': 0.026892340312538593, 'b':
    0.015373768624831691, 'e': 0.12886234260657689, 'd': 0.043286671390026357, 'g':
    0.019625534749730816, 'f': 0.024484713711692099, 'i': 0.06905550211598431, 'h':
    0.060987267963718068, 'k': 0.0062521823678781188, 'j': 0.0011176940633901926, 'm':
    0.025009719347800208, 'l': 0.041016761327711163, 'o': 0.073783151266212627, 'n':
    0.069849754102356679, 'q': 0.0010648594165322703, 'p': 0.017031440203182008, 's':
    0.063817324270355996, 'r': 0.06156572691936394, 'u': 0.027856851020401599, 't':
    0.090246649949305979, 'w': 0.021192261444145363, 'v': 0.010257964235274787, 'y':
    0.01806326249861108, 'x': 0.0016941732664605912, 'z': 0.0009695838238376564}


    lowerMessage = message.lower()
    sampling = lowerMessage[keyPos::keyLength]

    for ascii in range(ord('a'), ord('a')+26):
        frequency[chr(ascii)] = float(sampling.count(chr(ascii)))/
len(sampling)

    sum_freqs_squared = 0.0
    for ltr in frequency:
        sum_freqs_squared += frequency[ltr]*frequency[ltr]

    for possible_key in range(1, 26):
        sum_f_sqr = 0.0
        for ltr in normal_freqs:
            caesar_guess = shiftBy(ltr, possible_key)
            freqCalc = normal_freqs[ltr]*frequency[caesar_guess]
            sum_f_sqr += freqCalc

            engValue = abs(sum_f_sqr - .065)
            if engValue < tolerance:
                allKeys.append(possible_key)

    return allKeys

def getKey(encrypted, kl, dictionary):

    keys = []
    testKey = []
    defaultKey = []

    for i in range (0,kl):
        keyPos = findKeyPos(encrypted,16,i)
        answerLen =  len(keyPos)
        answerIndex = 0
        if answerLen > 1:
            defaultKey = keys[:]
            testKey = keys[:]
            defaultKey.append(keyPos[0])
            decrypted = decryptIndex(defaultKey,encrypted)
```

```
                    defaultScore = getFitnessScore(decrypted, dictionary)
                    for a in range(1,answerLen):
                        testKey.append(keyPos[a])
                        decrypted = decryptIndex(testKey,encrypted)
                        testScore = getFitnessScore(decrypted, dictionary)
                        if testScore > defaultScore:
                            answerIndex = a
                            defaultKey = testKey

                keys.append(keyPos[answerIndex])
                fullKey = ""
                for i in range(len(keys)):
                    fullKey = fullKey + chr(keys[i] + 65)

            fullKey = ""
            for i in range(len(keys)):
                fullKey = fullKey + chr(keys[i] + 65)

            return (fullKey)


myDictionary = getDictionary()
cipherText = getEncryptedData()
freqScore = getLetterFreqs(cipherText)
fitScore = getFitnessScore(cipherText, myDictionary)
keyLength = getKeyLength(cipherText)
decryptKey = getKey(cipherText, keyLength, myDictionary)


print ()
print ("The frequency score for this file is: ", freqScore)
print ()
print ("The fitness score for this file is: ", fitScore)
print()
print ("The key length for this file is: ", keyLength)
print ()
print ("The decryption key for this file is: ", decryptKey)
print ()
```

Figure 4.11 shows the output of an encrypted Moby Dick file and uses frequency analysis to find the frequency, fitness score, and key length to decrypt the file.

```
The frequency score for this file is:  0.039258416716995266

The fitness score for this file is: 1196000.0

The key length for this file is:  16

The decryption key for this file is:  YKVWVPLXDDRSNHCT

Press any key to continue . . . ■
```

Figure 4.11: Vigenere_crypto.py

Summary

This chapter was fairly heavy on the important mathematical concepts you need to break classical ciphers. You may find yourself referring to this chapter several times as you progress through the remaining chapters. Before moving on to the next chapter, make sure you have a pretty good understanding of modular arithmetic and how to find the inverse. In addition, you should have an understanding of basic group theory, the Chinese remainder theorem, and solving linear equations. A number of Python libraries are available that will simplify a great deal of the concepts offered in this chapter. It is vital that you remember the importance of using cryptographically secure pseudorandom generators and also understand how to determine the random number generation that is offered using C's `rand()` function. Frequency analysis will be your greatest ally. As you generate decryption keys, knowing how frequency analysis works will help you decrypt many of these ciphers without knowing the keys or key lengths.

We will be continuing our exploration of cryptanalysis as you progress through the remaining chapters, but you should have a good understanding of how to decrypt a wide variety of cryptographic schemes.

## CHAPTER 5

Stream Ciphers and Block Ciphers

In this chapter, you'll learn the means of support of the entire cryptographic world. You will learn how to encrypt and decrypt messages with a shared secret, which is how the vast majority of today's encryption on the Internet functions. In fact, encryption is used every day using techniques you'll learn in this chapter. This chapter introduces you to the development of stream ciphers, block ciphers, and cryptographically secure pseudorandom number generators. You'll gain an understanding of some of the analyses of the underlying algorithms and the best attacks that exist in the real world. You'll also learn the amount of security you must build in, based on the client you are serving, and how long it needs to stay secure. You'll walk away with being able to randomize every message you send, which will help you build a solid career in cryptography. Through this chapter, you'll gain cryptographic knowledge as you do the following:

- Learn how to convert between hexdigest and plaintext
- Gain an understanding of stream ciphers and CSPRNGs
- Learn about block ciphers
- Explore various modes of encryption and their weaknesses
- Gain an understanding of blocks as streams

Convert between Hexdigest and Plaintext

Before we dive into stream and block ciphers, I will show you some of the harder bits that involve the conversion between hexdigest and plaintext. To perform the conversions in Python, you'll use the `binascii` library. The `binascii` module provides several methods to convert between ASCII-ended binary expressions and binary. It comprises low-level functions written in C for superior performance.

In this section, you will learn about `hexlify` and `unhexlify`, modules in the `binascii` library. `Hexlify` returns the hexadecimal representation; each byte of data converts into a two-digit hex representation. The output results in the returned hexadecimal being twice the length of the data passed into the `hexlify` function. The following code converts the string "`apples are red`" to its hexadecimal representation. You will find that the length of the value referenced by `passhex` is twice the size of the value referenced by the `password` variable.

```
import binascii
password = b"apples are red"
print(password)

apples are red

>>> passhex =  binascii.hexlify(password)
>>> print(passhex)
b'6170706c65732061726520726564'

>>> print(len(password))
14
>>> print(len(passhex))
28
```

You probably noticed that the first two digits of the `passhex` variable equal 61; you can look up the code, hex, and characters in an ASCII table. To demonstrate how to convert from characters, code, and hex, examine the following Python code:

```
>>> passhex
b'6170706c65732061726520726564'
>>> print(ord('a'))
97
>>> print(hex(97))
0x61
>>> print(format(ord('a'), 'x'))
61
```

The `binascii` function `unhexlify`, which takes a hexadecimal string as a parameter, is the inverse. As you might imagine, the hexadecimal string must contain an even number of hexadecimal digits. Since the output of the `hexlify` function returns twice the length, `unhexlify` returns half the length. Here's an example of using `unhexlify` to convert back to binary from hexadecimal:

```
>>> unpasshex = binascii.unhexlify(passhex)
>>> unpasshex
b'apples are red'
```

Furthermore, Python allows you to use an `x` escape character to convert from hexadecimal back to plaintext, as shown here:

```
>>> hx = '\x61'
>>> hx
'a'
```

Use Stream Ciphers

Let's now start exploring private-key cryptography by looking at what stream ciphers are and then examine them as a combination of the one-time pad (OTP) and cryptographically secure pseudorandom number generators (CSPRNGs). The concepts of the OTP that make it perfectly secure are what you capitalize on to make a more robust cipher. As you may recall from Chapter 2, the one-time pad takes a message of n bits and a uniformly random secret key of the same length and generates a ciphertext by bitwise XOR. The encryption and decryption methods are identical operations.

When you examine the elegance of the OTP, you will undoubtedly see its weaknesses as well:

- You must arrange a key exchange between the sender and receiver of the message; this is true in all symmetric schemes.

- You can use the key only once.

- The key length is equal to the message length; if you have a way to send the key securely, then perhaps you could have just sent the message.

You could resolve one of the most significant OTP problems if both parties could generate keys on the fly with the other party. Ideally, both parties would use an unpredictable pseudorandom number generator that would start from the same seed and generate a uniformly random stream of noise that acts like the one-time pad key. As you witnessed in the previous chapter, PRNGs can be predictable and therefore can be cracked. Thus, we need to find improved cryptographically secure pseudorandom number generators.

The goal of this section is to guide you through the creation of your first "do it yourself" stream cipher. We will utilize an insecure stream cipher as an experiment to gain an understanding of the underlying mechanics. Once you complete it, you should feel comfortable with the use of XOR, seeds, and the general structure of a stream cipher. This section builds the base in which we add improvements with true security in mind.

In building your first stream cipher, you take the idea of the one-time pad mixed with the convenience of PRGNs to create an encryption scheme. Since we haven't explored any nonbreakable PRNGs yet, we will work with an insecure one, but the mechanics are identical when you have a more secure source of pseudorandom bits. It is important to know that since you want to use the stream cipher to work on real-world data, it is going to have to encrypt ASCII characters, which means you need to think about the use of random bytes more than the use of random bits. It is not much of a change, but it is worth mentioning.

To start, we select the C rand() function as our PRNG since we have code for it from Chapter 4. It generates 31 bits at a time (the numbers are mod 2^{31}), and you want 8 bits at a time. For the sake of this example, use the lowest 24 bits of each number that comes out and generate three bytes of randomness for our stream. Using these guidelines, this should allow you to generate a convention that matches the partner with which you are communicating. A rand()-generated number might look like temp = 2158094741372. If you want three bytes of randomness from that, you could follow these steps:

```
>>> temp = 2158094741372
>>> temp % 2**8
124
>>> (temp >> 8) % 2**8
111
>>> (temp >> 16) % 2**8
120
```

The code should produce three numbers uniformly chosen between 0 and 255. Now let's write our own simple PRNG function. It should produce four output numbers, [1471611625, 1204518815, 463882823, 963005816]:

```
def crand(seed):
    r=[]
    r.append(seed)
    for i in range(30):
        r.append((16807*r[-1]) % 2147483647)
        if r[-1] < 0:
            r[-1] += 2147483647
    for i in range(31, 34):
        r.append(r[len(r)-31])
    for i in range(34, 344):
        r.append((r[len(r)-31] + r[len(r)-3]) % 2**32)
    while True:
        next = r[len(r)-31]+r[len(r)-3] % 2**32
```

```
        r.append(next)
        yield (next >> 1 if next < 2**32 else (next % 2**32) >> 1)

mygen = crand(2018)
firstfour = [next(mygen) for i in range(4)]
print firstfour
[1471611625, 1204518815, 463882823, 963005816]
```

Now that you have your PRNG producing a predictable output, let's take the message "Hello world!" using the secret seed of 2018. We'll take the bytes in largest to smallest order for convenience, as shown here:

```
import binascii
def crand(seed):
    r=[]
    r.append(seed)
    for i in range(30):
        r.append((16807*r[-1]) % 2147483647)
        if r[-1] < 0:
            r[-1] += 2147483647
    for i in range(31, 34):
        r.append(r[len(r)-31])
    for i in range(34, 344):
        r.append((r[len(r)-31] + r[len(r)-3]) % 2**32)
    while True:
        next = r[len(r)-31]+r[len(r)-3] % 2**32
        r.append(next)
        yield (next >> 1 if next < 2**32 else (next % 2**32) >> 1)

mygen = crand(2018)
rands = [next(mygen) for i in range(4)]
plaintext = b"Hello world!"

hexplain = binascii.hexlify(plaintext)
hexkey = "".join(map(lambda x: format(x, 'x')[-6:], rands))

cipher_as_int = int(hexplain, 16) ^ int(hexkey, 16)
cipher_as_hex = format(cipher_as_int, 'x')
```

Armed with what you have learned thus far, can you find the original message to the following?

```
Hex: e5d8443c6ac32d3ee5c7398ecf7f9e03f619
Seed: 54321
```

If you get stuck, you can find the solution in the ch5_decrypt file on this book's website.

One crucial concept you'll now explore is the use of the nonce, also called the initialization vector (IV). These concepts, which would have been monumental during World War II, are the encryption version of a salt and save us from the inherent risks of a user sending the same message several times. You have explored how to fix one flaw of the one-time pad by generating a key that is the same length as the message; you still cannot use the same key multiple times. Two possible fixes could include the following:

- **Do not restart the PRNG:** Not restarting the PRNG requires both sides to carefully coordinate with each other so that they stay at the same part of the communication stream on the encryption and decryption side; this could offer challenges if some messages are lost in transit or if there are parallel message-sending channels.

- **Use some public randomness to change the secret key effectively:** This idea is that you generate, from a true entropy source, a nonce. A nonce is a one-time set of random bytes that mingles with the private key to change the output of the encryption scheme.

The ultimate goal of this is to allow you to send the same message 100 times in a row, with the same private key, and each time it would look entirely random and uncorrelated. From here on out, your goal is to use a nonce/IV so that the same message is never encrypted the same way twice. Most computers have a source of randomized bytes from entropy that we can pull data from to build random bytes. They pool sources of entropy like temperature, user actions, timings, and other unique factors. This information is then used by CSPRNGs to turn that entropy into uniform random bytes. A poorly generated key or initial seed will cripple even the most secure CSPRNG.

In the previous encryption scheme, you created a PRNG function along with a secret seed. Now we begin by generating a nonce so that when you are encrypting a message, you first generate some entropy bytes that pass along with the ciphertext. The nonce should be sent in the clear, so it should look random. To generate six bytes of noise, use the following Python code:

```
import os
nonce = os.urandom(6)
print(nonce)
```

Ideally, you need a convention to translate the nonce and your secret key (54321) into a new seed or key. Other schemes may have their ways of letting the nonce interact with the scheme; in this case, changing the seed is excellent for learning the concepts. The method presented here will be to concatenate the nonce and the secret key (as hex), then to apply the SHA256 hash function to those bytes (not hex), and take the lowest 32 bits as the new seed.

Here is what the Python looks like:

```
import os, hashlib, binascii
nonce = os.urandom(6)
```

```
hexnonce = binascii.hexlify(nonce)
oursecret = 54321
concatenated_hex = hexnonce + format(oursecret, 'x')
even_length = concatenated_hex.rjust(len(concatenated_hex) +
len(concatenated_hex) % 2, '0')
hexhash = hashlib.sha256(binascii.unhexlify(even_length)).hexdigest()
newseed = (int(hexhash, 16)) % 2**32

print(newseed)
```

To get a consistent key on both the sending and receiving side, we directly pass the nonce. To test this, replace the previous nonce with "cc4304c09aee" and keep the original seed of 54321. The new seed that generates should equate to "3336748862." Now you need a system for sending the nonce in your ciphertext. If you have the first six bytes as nonce bytes and the remaining bytes as the ciphertext, you can pass everything in the same message. Since the underlying generator is C's `rand` function, the encryption is still not strong enough to protect any secrets, but it is much stronger than it was.

Knowing the first six bytes are nonce bytes, here is a new challenge for you:

```
Secret Key: 61983
Message: 3e08816f1377f89f1c596fc197dd52946c92577bfd7c25c3
```

If you get stuck, you can find the solution in the ch5_decrypt2 file on this book's website.

Answer: Seed is `42847799`; the message is `'this is a message.'`

Ideally, by now, you are gaining an understanding of how stream ciphers work. Stream ciphers are generally not as secure or well-understood as block ciphers (which we study next). In software, you will most likely deal with block ciphers, though there are tools such as Wireguard which will use stream ciphers. Wireguard is a software VPN protocol that uses the ChaCha20 stream cipher; you will learn more about ChaCha20 later in this chapter. So, while some tools may use stream ciphers, stream ciphers play a more significant role in the hardware ecosystem. With space-constrained devices that need encrypted data streams, we need fast hardware implementations that encrypt bit-by-bit. So, as you code these, imagine the hardware version. As outlined in the previous section, the encryption schemes are still not strong enough to protect any classified data. In this part, you examine a full-strength encryption scheme called Trivium. Bart Preneel and Christophe De Cannière created it and submitted it to the eSTREAM competition. eSTREAM is a project that was organized by the EU Ecrypt network to help identify new stream ciphers that may be suitable for widespread adoption. The project began in November 2004 and completed in April 2008. It is designed to provide a reasonably efficient software encryption implementation and is specified as an International Standard under ISO/IEC 29192-3.

In Chapter 4, you first learned about pseudorandomness. A linear-feedback shift register (LFSR) is an algorithm for generating pseudorandom numbers. The sequence of pseudorandom numbers generated by an LFSR can be used as the one-time pad for an encryption algorithm. However, it has a major weakness: the numbers generated are periodic, and an attacker can figure out the key using a known plaintext attack. In the previous section, you used a PRNG to make a stream cipher. The next level of complexity that you can utilize would be something similar to the Trivium stream cipher, which uses a CSPRNG that generates one bit at a time. It tries to make the LFSR idea more secure by having multiple registers that interfere with each other. The intuitive notion is that LFSRs yield to linear algebra, so let's add just enough complexity to be nonlinear. Figure 5.1 represents a schematic of a three-register Trivium implementation.

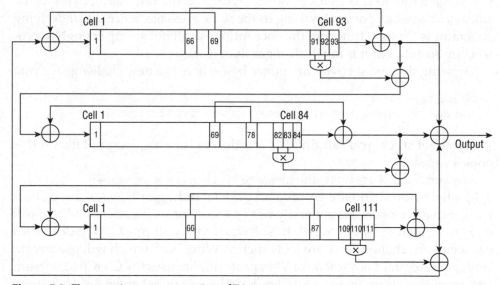

Figure 5.1: Three-register representation of Trivium

When looking at Figure 5.1, you see it as three separate registers that each produce their own output. The final output bit is the XOR of all three output bits. The output of each register is also used to help form the input of another register.

For the initialization, to kick-start Trivium, it accepts two inputs: an 80-bit key and an 80-bit IV. The 80-bit key is loaded into the leftmost 80 bits of the first register. The 80-bit IV is loaded into the leftmost 80 bits of the second register. Finally, the final 3 bits of the third register are set to 1 (the rightmost bits).

The stream is then run 4 × 288 times with the output discarded; this is now the opening state.

Let's do the first (tossed-out) run using an all 1 key and an all 1 IV, to show the idea. Bits 1–80 are all 1, bits 94–173 are all 80, and bits 286–288 are all 1; everything else is 0. The first output bit is an XOR of three different bits, so let's look at the first register. The output of register 1 is the XOR of bit 66 (1) and bit 93 (0), which is 1. Register 2's output is bit 162 XOR bit 177, which is also 1. Finally, register 3 is the XOR of bit 288 (1) and bit 243 (0), so also a 1. Thus, the first output is 1. Now everything must slide, so let's look at the feedback. The input to register 2 is the XOR of bit 171 (1) and the XOR of that first register's output bit (1) and the product of bits 91 and 92 (0), so 1 + 1 + 0 = 0 is the new input bit to register 2. All the other bits in register 2 slide one to the right. (Register 2 is now 0 in bit 94, 1 in bits 95–174, and 0 everywhere else.) Likewise, you can trace that the new input bit of register 3 is a 1. The new input bit for register 1 is a 0.

Now that we have introduced stream ciphers, you can examine some additional stream ciphers, namely, ARC4, Vernam, Salsa20, and the ChaCha20 ciphers. Both the Salsa20 and the ChaCha20 are similar in nature as they were created by the same author.

ARC4

The RC4 stream cipher was created by Ron Rivest in 1987. RC4 was classified as a trade secret by RSA Security but was eventually leaked to a message board in 1994. RC4 was originally trademarked by RSA Security so it is often referred to as ARCFOUR or ARC4 to avoid trademark issues. ARC4 would later become commonly used in a number of encryption protocols and standards such as SSL, TLS, WEP, and WPA. In 2015, it was prohibited for all versions of TLS by RFC 7465. ARC4 has been used in many hardware and software implementations. One of the main advantages of ARC4 is its speed and simplicity, which you will notice in the following code:

```
"""
Implement the ARC4 stream cipher. - Chapter 5
"""

def arc4crypt(data, key):
    x = 0
    box = range(256)
    for i in range(256):
        x = (x + box[i] + ord(key[i % len(key)])) % 256

        # swap range objects
        box = list(box)
        box[i], box[x] = box[x], box[i]
    x = 0
    y = 0
    out = []
    for char in data:
        x = (x + 1) % 256
        y = (y + box[x]) % 256
```

```
        box[x], box[y] = box[y], box[x]
        out.append(chr(ord(char) ^ box[(box[x] + box[y]) % 256]))

    return ''.join(out)

key = 'SuperSecretKey!!'
origtext = 'Dive Dive Dive'
ciphertext = arc4crypt (origtext, key)
plaintext = arc4crypt (ciphertext, key)

print('The original text is: {}'.format(origtext))
print()
print('The ciphertext is: {}'.format(ciphertext))
print()
print('The plaintext is {}'.format(plaintext))
print()
```

The ARC4 example should produce the same output that you see in Figure 5.2.

```
The original text is: Dive Dive Dive

The ciphertext is: °WU' »▯~▯▯à¬!W

The plaintext is Dive Dive Dive

Press any key to continue . . .
```

Figure 5.2: ARC4 stream cipher

Vernam Cipher

The Vernam cipher was developed by Gilbert Vernam in 1917. It is a type of one-time pad for data streams and is considered to be unbreakable. The algorithm is symmetrical, and the plaintext is combined with a random stream of data of the same length using the Boolean XOR function; the Boolean XOR function is also known as the Boolean exclusive OR function. Claude Shannon would later mathematically prove that it is unbreakable. The characteristics of the Vernam cipher include:

- The plaintext is written as a binary sequence of 0s and 1s.
- The secret key is a completely random binary sequence and is the same length as the plaintext.
- The ciphertext is produced by adding the secret key bitwise modulo 2 to the plaintext.

One of the disadvantages of using an OTP is that the keys must be as long as the message it is trying to conceal; therefore, for long messages, you will need a long key:

```
def VernamEncDec (text, key):
      result = "";
      ptr = 0;
      for char in text:
            result = result + chr(ord(char) ^ ord(key[ptr]));
            ptr = ptr + 1;
            if ptr == len(key):
                  ptr = 0;
      return result

key = "thisismykey12345";

while True:
      input_text = input("\nEnter Text To Encrypt:\t");
      ciphertext = VernamEncDec(input_text, key);
      print("\nEncrypted Vernam Cipher Text:\t" + ciphertext);
      plainttext = VernamEncDec(ciphertext, key);
      print("\nDecrypted Vernam Cipher Text:\t" + plainttext);
```

Salsa20 Cipher

The Salsa20 cipher was developed in 2005 by Daniel Bernstein, and submitted to eSTREAM. The Salsa20/20 (Salsa20 with 20 rounds) is built on a pseudorandom function that is based on add-rotate-xor (ARX) operations. ARX algorithms are designed to have their round function support modular addition, fixed rotation, and XOR. These ARX operations are popular because they are relatively fast and cheap in hardware and software, and because they run in constant time, and are therefore immune to timing attacks. The rotational cryptanalysis technique attempts to attack such round functions.

The core function of Salsa20 maps a 128-bit or 256-bit key, a 64-bit nonce/IV, and a 64-bit counter to a 512-bit block of the keystream. Salsa20 provides speeds of around 4–14 cycles per byte on modern x86 processors and is considered acceptable hardware performance. The numeric indicator in the Salsa name specifies the number of encryption rounds. Salsa20 has 8, 12, and 20 variants. One of the biggest benefits of Salsa20 is that Bernstein has written several implementations that have been released to the public domain, and the cipher is not patented.

same operation on multiple data points simultaneously. Most modern-day CPU designs include SIMD instruction to improve the performance of multimedia.

The second difference is that ChaCha builds the initial matrix with all attacker-controlled input words at the bottom:

Constant	Constant	Constant	Constant
Key	Key	Key	Key
Key	Key	Key	Key
Input	Input	Input	Input

These constants are the same as in Salsa20. The first round of ChaCha adds keys into the constants. The key words are copied in order; the input words are the block counter followed by the nonce.

The third difference is that ChaCha processes through rows in the same order in every round. The first round modifies first, fourth, third, second, first, fourth, third, second along columns, and the second round modifies first, fourth, third, second, first, fourth, third, second along southeast diagonals:

```
quarter_round (x0,x4,x8,x12)
quarter_round (x1,x5,x9,x13)
quarter_round (x2,x6,x10,x14)
quarter_round (x3,x7,x11,x15)
quarter_round (x0,x5,x10,x15)
quarter_round (x1,x6,x11,x12)
quarter_round (x2,x7,x8,x13)
quarter_round (x3,x4,x9,x14)
```

The four quarter-round words are always in top-to-bottom order in the matrix. A couple libraries are available that will offer ChaCha as an encryption scheme. You may also elect to use a pure Python implementation. To implement ChaCha using Python, use the following recipe:

```
"""
Implement the ChaCha20 stream cipher.
"""


import struct
import sys, os, binascii
from base64 import b64encode

def yield_chacha20_xor_stream(key, iv, position=0):
  # Generate the xor stream with the ChaCha20 cipher."""
  if not isinstance(position, int):
    raise TypeError
  if position & ~0xffffffff:
    raise ValueError('Position is not uint32.')
  if not isinstance(key, bytes):
```

```
        raise TypeError
    if not isinstance(iv, bytes):
        raise TypeError
    if len(key) != 32:
        raise ValueError
    if len(iv) != 8:
        raise ValueError

    def rotate(v, c):
        return ((v << c) & 0xffffffff) | v >> (32 - c)

    def quarter_round(x, a, b, c, d):
        x[a] = (x[a] + x[b]) & 0xffffffff
        x[d] = rotate(x[d] ^ x[a], 16)
        x[c] = (x[c] + x[d]) & 0xffffffff
        x[b] = rotate(x[b] ^ x[c], 12)
        x[a] = (x[a] + x[b]) & 0xffffffff
        x[d] = rotate(x[d] ^ x[a], 8)
        x[c] = (x[c] + x[d]) & 0xffffffff
        x[b] = rotate(x[b] ^ x[c], 7)

    ctx = [0] * 16
    ctx[:4] = (1634760805, 857760878, 2036477234, 1797285236)
    ctx[4 : 12] = struct.unpack('<8L', key)
    ctx[12] = ctx[13] = position
    ctx[14 : 16] = struct.unpack('<LL', iv)
    while 1:
        x = list(ctx)
        for i in range(10):
            quarter_round(x, 0, 4,  8, 12)
            quarter_round(x, 1, 5,  9, 13)
            quarter_round(x, 2, 6, 10, 14)
            quarter_round(x, 3, 7, 11, 15)
            quarter_round(x, 0, 5, 10, 15)
            quarter_round(x, 1, 6, 11, 12)
            quarter_round(x, 2, 7,  8, 13)
            quarter_round(x, 3, 4,  9, 14)
        for c in struct.pack('<16L', *(
                (x[i] + ctx[i]) & 0xffffffff for i in range(16))):
            yield c
        ctx[12] = (ctx[12] + 1) & 0xffffffff
        if ctx[12] == 0:
            ctx[13] = (ctx[13] + 1) & 0xffffffff

def chacha20_encrypt(data, key, iv=None, position=0):
    # Encrypt (or decrypt) with the ChaCha20 cipher.
    if not isinstance(data, bytes):
        raise TypeError
    if iv is None:
        iv = b'\0' * 8
```

```python
        if isinstance(key, bytes):
            if not key:
                raise ValueError('Key is empty.')
            if len(key) < 32:
                key = (key * (32 // len(key) + 1))[:32]
            if len(key) > 32:
                raise ValueError('Key too long.')

    return bytes(a ^ b for a, b in
            zip(data, yield_chacha20_xor_stream(key, iv, position)))

def main():
    #key = os.urandom(32)
    key = b'superSecretKey!!'
    print('The key that will be used is {}'.format(key))
    print()
    plaintext = b'We all live in a yellow submarine.'
    print('The plaintext is {}'.format(plaintext))

    iv = b'SecretIV'
    print()
    enc = chacha20_encrypt(plaintext, key, iv)
    decode_enc = b64encode(enc).decode('utf-8')
    print('The encrypted string is {}. '.format(decode_enc))
    print()
    dec = chacha20_encrypt(enc,key, iv)
    print('The decrypted string is {}. '.format(dec))
    print()

if __name__ == "__main__":
    sys.exit(int(main() or 0))
```

The preceding code should produce output that looks similar to Figure 5.3.

```
The key that will be used is b'superSecretKey!!'

The plaintext is b'We all live in a yellow submarine.'

The encrypted string is CMV6nLRZsVBBeR69BKOb9OsC45T0zE7uaBa4/ns4vzBlGg==.

The decrypted string is b'We all live in a yellow submarine.'.

Press any key to continue . . .
```

Figure 5.3: Python implementation of ChaCha20

If you would like to use a prepackaged implementation, you can install the `chacha20ploy1305` library; you will need to perform a `pip install chacha20poly1350`. Once you do, you can implement ChaCha20 using the following code:

```python
import os
from chacha20poly1305 import ChaCha20Poly1305
```

```
# generate a random key that has 32 bits
key = os.urandom(32)

print('The key that will be used is {}'.format(key))
print()
plaintext = b'Attack the yellow submarine.'
print('The plaintext is {}'.format(plaintext))
print()

# generate a random IV that has 12 bits
iv = os.urandom(12)
cip = ChaCha20Poly1305(key)

ciphertext = cip.encrypt(iv, plaintext)
print(ciphertext)
print()

plaintext = cip.decrypt(iv, ciphertext)
print(plaintext)
print()
```

The preceding use of the ChaCha20Poly1305 library should produce output similar to Figure 5.4.

The key that will be used is b'\x87\xbb\x16\x850:\xc1\xbfA\x8b\x9a\xd0\xe8D9\xc0\x820Dn\x1f]~\x16F\xe7\xc7&\xa9Z\x90\xdc'

The plaintext is b'Attack the yellow submarine.'

bytearray(b'\xb0[\x1d\xcd\x0fm~F\xe2\xc3\xc1GH\xf8\xde7\x0e\xf2vik\xbd;T[\xc0\xfa\xf4xH\xac\xf7Q\x1f_#\xf9h\xbfj/\xcf\x0eR')

bytearray(b'Attack the yellow submarine.')

Press any key to continue . . .

Figure 5.4: ChaCha20Poly1305

An alternative library that you may find helpful as well is the Crypto library. You can import ChaCha20 from the Crypt.Cipher library:

```
import json
from base64 import b64encode
from Crypto.Cipher import ChaCha20
from Crypto.Random import get_random_bytes
plaintext = b'Attack at dawn'
key = get_random_bytes(32)
cipher = ChaCha20.new(key=key)
ciphertext = cipher.encrypt(plaintext)
nonce = b64encode(cipher.nonce).decode('utf-8')
ct = b64encode(ciphertext).decode('utf-8')
```

```
result = json.dumps({'nonce':nonce, 'ciphertext':ct})
print(result)

{"nonce": "IZScZh28fDo=", "ciphertext": "ZatgU1f30WDHriaN8ts="}
```

Use Block Ciphers

Stream ciphers work by generating pseudorandom bits and XORing them with your message. Block ciphers take in a fixed-length message, a private key, and they produce a ciphertext that is the same length as the fixed-length plaintext message. Now we will examine the construction of block ciphers.

AES and Triple DES are the most common block ciphers in use today. From the student's point of view, DES is still interesting to study, but due to its small 56-bit key size, it is considered insecure. In 1999, two partners, Electronic Frontier Foundation and `distributed.net` collaborated to publicly break a DES key in 22 hours and 15 minutes. Here, we will use the `PyCrypto` library to demonstrate how to use DES to encrypt a message. The following recipe is using the ECB block mode; you will learn about the various modes later in this chapter. To execute the following recipe, perform a `pip install PyCrypto`:

```
from Crypto.Cipher import DES

key = b'shhhhhh!'
origText = b'The US Navy has submarines in Kingsbay!!'
des = DES.new(key, DES.MODE_ECB)
ciphertext = des.encrypt(origText)

plaintext = des.decrypt(ciphertext)

print('The original text is {}'.format(origText))
print('The ciphertext is {}'.format(ciphertext))
print('The plaintext is {}'.format(plaintext))
print()
```

This should produce the following output:

```
The original text is b'The US Navy has submarines in Kingsbay!!'
The ciphertext is b'\xf6\x0bb\xf9L\x15I\xf9\x0f\xe2\xee_^\xdaQX\xe1y\
xe5\xea\xd3Z\xc8y\xee\xd3\x86H\xf0Nn\x83\x93\nOd@6H\xd4'
The plaintext is b'The US Navy has submarines in Kingsbay!!'

Press any key to continue . . .
```

The key was 'shhhhhh!' and the message was 'The US Navy has submarines in Kingsbay!!'. The ciphertext was 40 bytes long; 40 mod 8 = 0, so there is no need to pad this example. If you were to implement a block cipher in reality, you should use a padding function that ensures the block length.

> **NOTE**   If you are following along in the code, you will note that `DES.key_size` and `DES.block_size` are both 8. This outdated scheme takes 64-bit keys (really 56 bits for the key and 8 bits for parity error checking) and 64-bit message blocks and encrypts them into 64-bit ciphertexts.

There are a few things you need to be aware of when using block ciphers. First, block ciphers only encrypt a fixed number of bytes at a time. If you played around with the preceding example, you noticed that the message had to have a length in multiples of 8; therefore, the message would need to be 8, 16, 24, 32, and so on. If your message is more than one block length, you would have to handle it; padding the message, or adding extra bytes to the end, is the most common option.

Second, block ciphers are considered a cryptographic primitive, or a basic building block to a more useful cryptographic message system. If you needed to handle larger blocks of arbitrary length, you would use a block cipher mode of operation, which describes how to apply a single-block operation to securely transform data chunks that are larger than blocks. You may have also noted that the example did not provide a nonce. That is another task of the mode you select. The block cipher itself has one job only: straight encryption with a single key and a fixed-length message. It is the cryptographic version of software engineering.

Third, block ciphers are pseudorandom shuffles that can be encrypted and decrypted; every input has one and only one output. In mathematics, this is called a function. An invertible function is one that also has a unique input for every output. Imagine a block cipher with a block length of 512. It takes in a 512-bit binary string and maps it to another 512-bit binary string. Since you can decrypt a 512-bit binary ciphertext, the decryption process is considered invertible to the encryption process. This relationship allows us to conclude that a block cipher is a permutation. The strength of the cipher is the extent to which its shuffling is indistinguishable from random shuffling. If a block cipher does its job well, then specifying a key should be like grabbing a random permutation from the set of all possible permutations. If we can determine that a particular scheme has some pattern in it that we can use to distinguish the cipher from genuinely random permutations, then the block cipher is considered weak. You explore various modes such as the CTR (counter) and OFB (output feedback) in the next chapter as they relate to various modes and which ones are recommended for image encryption. For now, all you need to know is the following:

- **CTR style:** If the nonce is 6, then get the random stream out of our permutation done in CTR style.
- **OFB style:** If the IV is 6, then get the random stream out of our permutation in OFB mode.

Note that the length of the permutation cycles has something to do with the strength of OFB as a CSPRNG. CTR is more resistant to this issue as a CSPRNG.

Block Modes of Operations

In the cryptography world, a *block cipher mode* of operation is an algorithm that uses a block cipher to provide encryption. A block cipher, when used alone, is only appropriate for the encryption or decryption of one fixed-length group of bits called a block. A mode of operation describes how to repeatedly apply a cipher's single-block operation to securely encrypt or decrypt amounts of data that are larger than a block.

A block cipher mode of operation uses an IV to ensure distinct ciphertexts even when the same key and plaintext are used for the encryption. Block ciphers can operate on more than one block size, though the block size is required to be fixed. Therefore, any blocks that may be smaller than the required size will require padding to ensure that the block size is full. (There are, however, modes that do not require padding because they effectively use a block cipher as a stream cipher.)

The earliest modes of operation include the ECB, CBC, OFB, and CFB, which were all specified in FIPS 81 (1981), DES Modes of Operation. The US National Institute of Standards and Technology (NIST) revised the list of approved modes of operation by including AES as a block cipher and adding the CR mode in 2001 as specified in NIST SP800-38A. In January 2010, NIST added XTS. While there are other modes of operations, they have not been approved by NIST.

The block cipher modes ECB, CBC, OFB, CFB, CTR, and XTS provide confidentiality, but they fail to protect against malicious tampering or accidental modification. Tampering or modification can be detected with a digital certificate or using a separate message authentication code such as CBC-MAC. We will cover CBC-MAC in Chapter 7.

ECB Mode

The ECB mode, formally named Electronic Codebook, divides the message into blocks and each block is encrypted separately. In Chapter 6, you will see visual examples of the weakness of encryption using ECB. Hint: you may still be able to determine what the original image is when using ECB mode even with strong encryption. ECB mode is typically used as an example of how to use block ciphers incorrectly. In Figure 5.5, you will see that plaintext enters the ECB block mode cipher encryption mode, which accepts a key and produces the encryption. Each block is encrypted the same, thus decreasing the scheme's effectiveness.

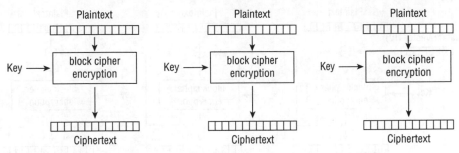

Figure 5.5: ECB mode encryption

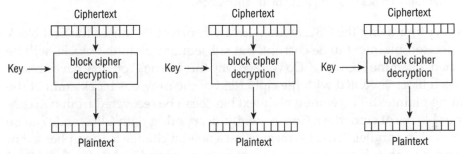

Figure 5.6: ECB mode decryption

In Figure 5.6, you will see that ciphertext enters the block cipher decryption mode, which accepts a key and produces the decryption.

CBC Mode

The CBC mode, formally named Cipher Block Chaining, was created in 1976 by Ehrsam, Meyer, Smith, and Tuchman. When using CBC mode, each block of plaintext is XOR'd with the previous ciphertext block. This ensures that each ciphertext block depends on all plaintext blocks processed up to that point. As shown in Figure 5.4, the IV is used on the initial block and then the produced ciphertext is used to encrypt the plaintext of the next block. Figure 5.7 shows the inverse operation.

CBC is the dominant mode of operation. Its major drawback is that encryption must be performed sequentially as opposed to encrypting in parallel. A second drawback is that the message must be padded to a multiple of the cipher block size.

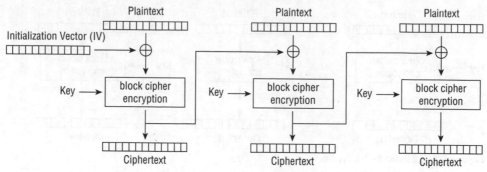

Figure 5.7: Cipher Block Chaining (CBC) mode encryption

Decrypting using the CBC mode with an incorrect IV causes the first block of generated plaintext to be corrupt, but subsequent plaintext blocks will be corrected. Examine Figure 5.8. Do you see why this is true? You may have noticed that each block is XOR'd with the ciphertext of the previous block and not the resulting plaintext. Therefore, a plaintext block can be recovered from two contiguous blocks of ciphertext. Consequently, decrypting with CBC mode can be performed in parallel. This also means that a one-bit change to the ciphertext in that particular block causes corruption of the corresponding blocks of plaintext and inverts the corresponding bit in the subsequent block of plaintext, but the remaining blocks should remain intact. This may make the CBC mode vulnerable to different padding oracle attacks such as POODLE.

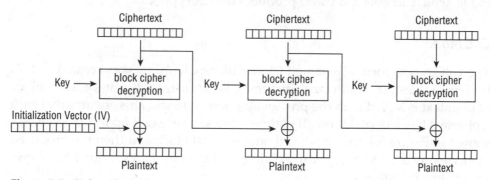

Figure 5.8: Cipher Block Chaining (CBC) mode decryption

NOTE   In cryptography, an oracle is a black box that responds to queries.

CFB Mode

We now explore a close relative to the CBC. The CFB, more formally known as the Cipher Feedback mode, makes a block cipher into a self-synchronizing stream cipher. While the CFB encryption and decryption modes are very similar, some small differences exist. As you examine Figure 5.9, you will notice that an initialization vector (IV) is only used to encrypt the first block. After the first block, the encrypted blocks are used in place of the IV; this continues until the end of the process.

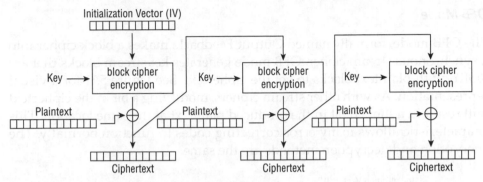

Figure 5.9: Cipher Feedback (CFB) mode encryption

Self-synchronizing protects the cipher if part of the ciphertext is lost; this helps recover data due to transmission errors. If an error occurs, the receiver will only lose part of the original message and should still be able to continue decrypting correctly. CFB also allows for operations that do not include a self-synchronizing process, in which synchronizing will only occur if an entire block of ciphertext is lost. If only a single bit or byte is lost, the decryption will be corrupt. If you need to make a self-synchronizing stream cipher that will work for any multiple of x bits, you will need to initialize a shift register of the size of the block with the IV; this process will provide an encrypted block cipher with the x bits of the results XOR'd with x bits of the plaintext to produce x bits of the ciphertext.

Similar to the CBC mode, any changes that propagate from the plaintext will affect the ciphertext, and encryption cannot be performed in parallel. You can, however, parallelize the decryption procedure, which is shown in Figure 5.10.

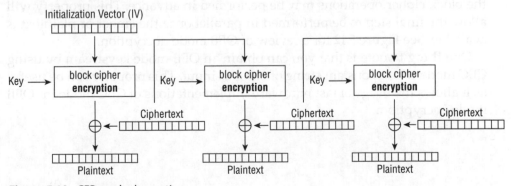

Figure 5.10: CFB mode decryption

CFB offers two advantages over CBC mode with the stream cipher modes OFB and CTR: first, the block cipher is only used in the encryption process, and second, the message does not need to be padded to a multiple of the cipher block size.

OFB Mode

The OFB mode, formally named Output Feedback, makes a block cipher into a synchronous stream cipher. OFB mode generates keystream blocks that are XOR'd with plaintext blocks to get the ciphertext. See Figure 5.11 for a visual representation. As with other stream ciphers, modifying a bit in the ciphertext will result in a flipped bit in the produced plaintext at the same location. This characteristic allows many error-correcting codes to function normally. The encryption and decryption methods are the same.

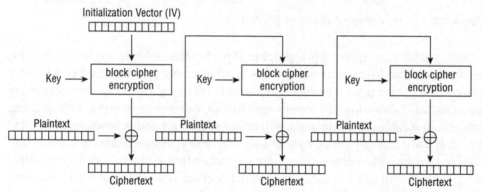

Figure 5.11: Output Feedback (OFB) mode encryption

As with the CBC mode, the OFB cipher operation depends on the previous blocks and therefore cannot be performed in parallel. One notable difference is that because the ciphertext and plaintext are only used for the final XOR, the block cipher operations may be performed in advance. This property will allow the final step to be performed in parallel once the cipher or plaintext is available. See Figure 5.12 for a review of OFB mode decryption.

One thing to note is that you can obtain an OFB mode keystream by using CBC mode with a constant string of zeros as input. This property can be useful as it allows the usage of fast hardware implementations of CBC mode for OFB mode encryption.

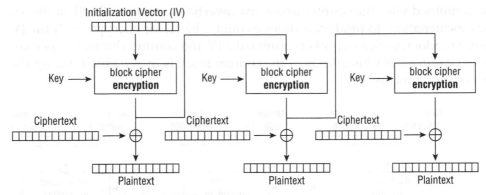

Figure 5.12: Output Feedback (OFB) mode decryption

CTR Mode

CTR mode, also known as Integer Counter mode or Segmented Integer Counter mode, turns a block cipher into a stream cipher. CTR mode was introduced in 1979 by Whitfield Diffie and Martin Hellman. These are two names we will explore in the following chapters. You will see in Figure 5.13 that the CTR generates the keystream block by encrypting successive values of a counter that can be any function that generates a sequence that is guaranteed not to repeat; typically, the simplest counter is to increment by one, although some critics believe using the counter is considered a risk. However, CTR mode is widely accepted and is recommended along with CBC by Niels Ferguson and Bruce Schneier.

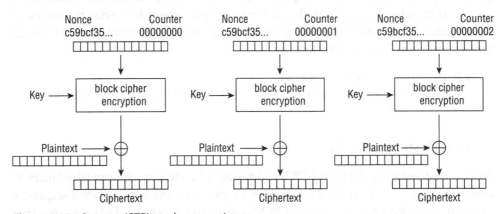

Figure 5.13: Counter (CTR) mode encryption

CTR mode allows a random-access property during the decryption process. CTR mode is considered well-suited to operate on a multiprocessor computer where blocks can be encrypted in parallel. If you generate a random IV, it can

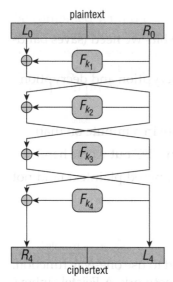

Figure 5.15: Feistel Network encryption

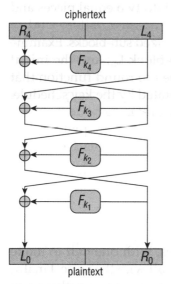

Figure 5.16: Feistel Network decryption

To build the encryption scheme, write a function that consumes a length 64 string and a salt that now acts like a key. Have your scheme do four rounds of a Feistel network and return a hex string of the 512-bit output. For now, you can use 5,000 iterations per super-hash.

Advanced Encryption Standard (AES)

AES stands for Advanced Encryption Standard, and it is the only public encryption scheme that the NSA approves for confidential information. We focus on its use as our main block cipher from now on. AES is the current de facto block cipher, and it works on 16 bytes at a time. It has three possible key lengths: 16-byte, 24-byte, or 32-byte. We know that a block cipher is effectively a deterministic permutation on binary strings, like a fixed-length reversible hash. Given a proper-length key and a 16-byte input we should always get the same 16-byte output. Note that there are typically three ways to work with bytes: plain ASCII, hex digest, and base64 (we haven't played with this yet but we will). A good chunk of your bugs come from transferring between hex and raw. You explore AES in the next chapter as you manipulate images.

Using AES with Python

Earlier in this chapter, you were introduced to PyCrypto as a Python module that enables block ciphers using DES; it also has methods for encrypting AES. The PyCrypto module is similar to the Java Cryptography Extension (JCE) that is used in Java.

The first step we will take in our AES encryption is to generate a strong key. As you know, the stronger the key, the stronger the encryption. The key we use for our encryption is oftentimes the weakest link in our encryption chain. The key we select should not be guessable and should provide sufficient entropy, which simply means that the key should lack order or predictability. The following Python code will create a random key that is 16 bytes:

```
import os
import binascii

key = binascii.hexlify(os.urandom(16))
print ('key', [x for x in key] )
```

```
key [97, 53, 99, 97, 102, 99, 102, 102, 50, 101, 98, 57, 97, 51, 50, 50,
51, 52, 102, 49, 101, 51, 102, 52, 100, 49, 48, 51, 51, 49, 56, 51]
```

Now that you have generated a key, you will need an initialization vector. The IV should be generated for each message to ensure a different encrypted text each time the message is encrypted. The IV adds significant protection in case the message is intercepted; it should mitigate the use of cryptanalysis to infer message or key data. The IV is required to be transmitted to the message receiver to ensure proper decryption, but unlike the message key, the IV does not need to be kept secret. You can add the IV to process the encrypted text. The message receiver will need to know where the IV is located inside the message. You can create a random IV by using the following snippet; note the use of `random.randint`. This method of generating random numbers is less effective and it has a lower entropy, but in this case we are using it to create the IV that will be used in the encryption process so there is less concern with the use of `randint` here:

```
iv = ''.join([chr(random.randint(0, 0xFF)) for i in range(16)]) )])
```

The next step in the process is to create the ciphertext. In this example, we will use the CBC mode; this links the current block to the previous block in the stream. See the previous section to review the various AES block modes.

Remember that for this implementation of AES using PyCrypto, you will need to ensure that you pad the block to guarantee you have enough data in the block:

```
aes = AES.new(key, AES.MODE_CBC, iv)
data = 'Playing with AES' # <- 16 bytes
encd = aes.encrypt(data)
```

To decrypt the ciphertext, you will need the key that was used for the encryption. Transporting the key, inside itself, can be a challenge. You will learn about key exchange in a later chapter. In addition to the key, you will also need the IV. The IV can be transmitted over any line of communication as there are no requirements to encrypt it. You can safely send the IV along with the encrypted file and embed it in plaintext, as shown here:

```
from base64 import b64encode
from Crypto.Cipher import AES
from Crypto.Util.Padding import pad
import binascii, os
import random

data = b"secret"
key = binascii.hexlify(os.urandom(16))
iv = ''.join(chr(random.randint(0, 0xFF)) for i in range(16))
#print ('key: ', [x for x in key] )
#print()

cipher = AES.new(key, AES.MODE_CBC)
ct_bytes = cipher.encrypt(pad(data, AES.block_size))
ct = b64encode(ct_bytes).decode('utf-8')
print('iv: {}'.format(iv))
print()
print('ciphertext: {}'.format(ct))
print()
```

```
iv: öhLÒô™Ï2q]>°mâ

ciphertext: BDE+z8ME6r0QgkraNXLuuQ==
```

File Encryption Using AES

Next, you can encrypt a file using AES by implementing the following Python recipe. The primary difference is opening the file and passing the packs into blocks:

```
aes = AES.new(key, AES.MODE_CBC, iv)
filesize = os.path.getsize(infile)
with open (encrypted, 'w') as fout:
     fout.write(struct.pack('<Q', filesize))
fout.write(iv)
```

File Decryption Using AES

To decrypt the previous example, use the following code to reverse the process:

```
with open(verfile, 'w') as fout:
    while True:
        data = fin.read(sz)
        n = len(data)
        if n == 0:
            break
        decd = aes.decrypt(data)
        n = len(decd)
        if fsz > n:
            fout.write(decd)
        else:
            fout.write(decd[:fsz]) # <- remove padding on last block
        fsz -= n
```

Summary

After completing this chapter, you should feel comfortable converting between hexdigest and plaintext using the `binascii` library. The `binascii` module provides several methods to convert between ASCII-ended binary expressions and binary. We then took a survey of how both stream ciphers and block ciphers work. You should understand that a stream cipher is a symmetric key cipher where plaintext digits are combined with a pseudorandom cipher digit stream. In a stream cipher, each plaintext digit is encrypted one at a time with the corresponding digit of the keystream, to give a digit of the ciphertext stream.

While most stream ciphers are used at the hardware layer, you now understand how to both create and use the Salsa20, ChaCha20, and Vernam ciphers. We then turned our focus on block ciphers and the various modes of operations. We concluded the block cipher exploration by examining which modes allow block ciphers to operate like stream ciphers. We also explored how to create a DIY cipher using a Feistel Network. We finished with an introduction to the Advanced Encryption Standard (AES) cryptosystem. You will explore more about block mode operations and AES in the next chapter as you learn to encrypt images.

CHAPTER

6

Using Cryptography with Images

At this point, you should be feeling confident in your ability to encrypt and decrypt messages. In this chapter, you will expand on what you know to include the cryptography of images. Through exercises in this chapter, you will be able to identify problems with different modes of encryption and learn alternative ways to get results. To complete our study of image cryptography, we will close the chapter with steganography. Through this chapter, you will do the following:

- Gain an understanding of image and cryptography libraries
- Learn about AES modes of operations
- Explore various cryptography methods for images
- Hide and read media within an image using Python

Simple Image Cryptography

Before we get into various libraries that can be used for image cryptography, I wanted to share a simple method that will allow you to encrypt and decrypt a file. The entire process relies on looping through the bits of an image and then bitwise exclusive (XOR) them with the bit and the key. To decrypt the image, we simply reverse the XOR operation.

In the following example and the subsequent ones in this chapter, we will be encrypting the original image and then saving it with an *e* in front of the name. When we decrypt the image, we save it with a *d* in front of the name. The reason we're doing this is to be able to compare the original image with the decrypted image to see if there is any apparent data loss.

Figure 6.1 shows the original image we will use. Feel free to create your own for this exercise. It is a fairly small file, which is fine until we get to the end of the chapter. For hiding BLOB data, you may need a much larger file. Time for a little code.

Figure 6.1: Original `ch6_secret_image.jpg` file

```
print('The program is looking for a file named: ch6_secret_image.jpg')
fo = open("Chapter6\ch6_secret_image.jpg", "rb")
image = fo.read()
fo.close()

print()
print("The secret key is 42.")
image = bytearray(image)
key = 42

for index, value in enumerate(image):
    image[index] = value^key

print()
print('The image has been encrypted. Review e_ch6_secret_image.jpg')
fo = open("Chapter6\e_ch6_secret_image.jpg", "wb")
fo.write(image)
fo.close()

image = bytearray(image)

for index, value in enumerate(image):
    image[index] = key^value
```

```
print()
print('The image has now been decrypted. Review d_ch6_secret_image.jpg')
fo = open("Chapter6\d_ch6_secret_image.jpg", "wb")
fo.write(image)
fo.close()
```

While the image is now unreadable, it may also throw an error depending on the software you are using (see Figure 6.2). This isn't a showstopper, though, as you can still email the file anywhere and you will not have to worry about someone decrypting it without the key, which in this case is 42.

Figure 6.2: Error message for `e_ch6_secret_image.jpg`

Decrypting will reproduce the image without data loss, as shown in Figure 6.3. This is important to examine as some modes will have some loss. The image on the left is the original, while the image on the right has been encrypted and then decrypted. Later, we will examine various encryption modes that work well on regular files but fail on images. One such example is the use of the ECB mode discussed shortly.

In the next section, we will start exploring more complex solutions using cryptographic libraries.

Figure 6.3: Side by side of `ch6_secret_image.jpg` and `d_ch6_secret_image.jpg`

Images and Cryptography Libraries

Let's change our focus to implementing libraries that will make our cryptography lives a little easier. We will revisit the Cryptography library that we introduced in Chapter 1, and we will introduce the Cryptosteganography library that will give us the ability to explore steganography using Python later in this chapter.

Understanding the Cryptography Library

`Cryptography` is the name of a Python package that provides cryptographic primitives and recipes. The library boasts to be your "cryptographic standard library," and it currently supports various versions in Python. To install the library, perform a `pip install cryptography`.

The Cryptography library includes both high-level recipes and low-level interfaces to common cryptographic algorithms such as symmetric ciphers, message digests, and key derivation functions. The Fernet example shown next highlights an example of a high-level interface. Check out the following quick sample code to ensure that you have the Cryptography library installed:

```
from cryptography.fernet import Fernet
key = Fernet.generate_key()
f = Fernet(key)
print ("The key is %s", f)
print ()
ciphertext = f.encrypt(b"This is a secret message.")
print (ciphertext)
print ()
```

```
plaintext = f.decrypt(ciphertext)
print (plaintext)
```

If you have the Cryptography library installed correctly, you should be able to generate a new key and encrypt and decrypt `This is a secret message.` Your output should look like Figure 6.4, except it will have a unique key.

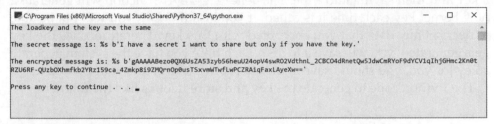

Figure 6.4: Cryptography library test

Understanding the Cryptosteganography Library

Steganography is the art of concealing information within different types of media objects such as images or audio files, in such a way that no one, apart from the sender and intended recipient, suspects the existence of the message. By itself, steganography is a type of security through obscurity. In this section, we will not only explore how to hide unencrypted messages inside an image but also store encrypted media inside an image. If you choose to hide unencrypted data, you can find a number of freeware tools that can extract your message, so feel free to encrypt the data prior to adding it to the image.

The second library that we are going to examine is the Cryptosteganography library. The module allows you to store messages or files that are protected using AES-256 inside an image. To take advantage of the library, perform a `pip3 install cryptosteganography` inside your project or your working environment. The Cryptosteganography library is designed to work in Python 3 and higher.

Image Cryptography

We will explore image cryptography using a variety of formats and tools. We will first review file cryptography using the Fernet library. This will give you the basis of using the Fernet library to encrypt and decrypt image files. You will then explore how the AES block modes of operation affect how your images are encrypted.

File Cryptography Using Fernet

In this section, we will explore image cryptography using Fernet, which is an implementation of symmetric authenticated cryptography. Symmetric encryption, which you may remember is synonymous for "same key," means that we use the same key to both encrypt and decrypt. You will begin by generating a key and then saving it to a file. The `generate_key()` function will generate a new Fernet key each time it is called; if you lose this key, you will not be able to decrypt any data that you encrypted with this key. Therefore, once the key gets generated, you will save it to disk. Each time you have the system generate a key for you, you should save it; the alternative is to create your own key.

The Python code to generate the key and store it looks like the following:

```
key = Fernet.generate_key()
with open("ch6.key", "wb") as key_file:
    key_file.write(key)
```

To load the key file once it is stored, you can use the following Python code:

```
return open("ch6.key", "rb").read()
```

Once you have an encryption system and a key, you should be ready to encrypt your message. Do not forget to encode your message; this will convert the string to bytes suitable for encrypting. Your message assignment should look like the following:

```
plaintext = "I have a secret I want to share but only if you have the key.".encode()
```

From here, we are ready to start our encryption process:

```
f = Fernet(key)
ciphertext = f.encrypt(plaintext)
print (ciphertext)
```

Assuming you are playing along, you should have something similar to Figure 6.5.

Figure 6.5: Python output for Fernet

Next, we will load a file with plaintext data and then encrypt the data using the `encrypt()` method. The file is then saved to storage:

```
filename = "sometextfile.txt"
f = Fernet(key)
with open(filename, "rb") as file:
    # read all file data
    file_data = file.read()
# encrypt data
encrypted_data = f.encrypt(file_data)
# write the encrypted file
with open(filename, "wb") as file:
    file.write(encrypted_data)
```

The decryption process is almost identical, but we use the `decrypt()` function of the Fernet object:

```
$filename = "sometextfile.txt"
f = Fernet(key)
with open(filename, "rb") as file:
    # read the encrypted data
    encrypted_data = file.read()
# decrypt data
decrypted_data = f.decrypt(encrypted_data)
# write the original file
with open(filename, "wb") as file:
    file.write(decrypted_data)
```

Now that you have the concepts, you can wrap all these snippets up into something a little more flexible. The following Python code accepts a key, a file, and either a decryption or encryption flag:

```
from cryptography.fernet import Fernet
import os

def write_key():
    # Generates a key and save it into a file
    key = Fernet.generate_key()
    with open("ch6.key", "wb") as key_file:
        key_file.write(key)

def load_key():
    #Loads the key from the current directory named 'ch6.key'
    return open("ch6.key", "rb").read()

def encrypt(filename, key):
    # encrypts the file and writes it using filename and key
    f = Fernet(key)
    with open(filename, "rb") as file:
        # read all file data
```

```
            file_data = file.read()
        # encrypt data
        encrypted_data = f.encrypt(file_data)
        # write the encrypted file
        with open(filename, "wb") as file:
            file.write(encrypted_data)


def decrypt(filename, key):
    # decrypts the file and writes it using the filename and key
    f = Fernet(key)
    with open(filename, "rb") as file:
        # read the encrypted data
        encrypted_data = file.read()
    # decrypt data
    decrypted_data = f.decrypt(encrypted_data)
    # write the original file
    with open(filename, "wb") as file:
        file.write(decrypted_data)


if __name__ == "__main__":
    import argparse
    parser = argparse.ArgumentParser(description="Simple File Encryptor
Script")
    parser.add_argument("file", help="File to encrypt/decrypt")
    parser.add_argument("-g", "--generate-key", dest="generate_key",
action="store_true",
                        help="Whether to generate a new key or use
existing")
    parser.add_argument("-e", "--encrypt", action="store_true",
                        help="Whether to encrypt the file, only -e or -d
can be specified.")
    parser.add_argument("-d", "--decrypt", action="store_true",
                        help="Whether to decrypt the file, only -e or -d
can be specified.")

    args = parser.parse_args()
    file = args.file
    generate_key = args.generate_key

    if generate_key:
        write_key()
    # load the key
    key = load_key()

    encrypt_ = args.encrypt
    decrypt_ = args.decrypt
```

```
    if encrypt_ and decrypt_:
        raise TypeError("Please specify whether you want to encrypt the
file or decrypt it.")
    elif encrypt_:
        encrypt(file, key)
    elif decrypt_:
        decrypt(file, key)
    else:
        raise TypeError("Please specify whether you want to encrypt the
file or decrypt it.")
```

Image Cryptography Using Fernet

Using our previous example, you can now write a solution that will allow you to specify the original image and change the encrypted file to a specific name; in this case, the `ch6_secret_image.jpg` file will be encrypted as `e_ch6_secret_image.jpg` and then immediately decrypted to `d_ch6_secret_image.jpg`. The image resolution between the original file and the decrypted file is identical as the Fernet algorithm operates on the file itself and does not alter the pixels of the image.

In the following example, I removed the reading and writing key since the encryption and decryption are happening in the same process. The encryption process here is not specific to just images and can be used on a variety of data types. The takeaway from this program should be the full encryption at the file level and not the pixel level:

```
def encrypt(filename, newfile, key):
    """
    Given a plain image (str), the new file name,  and key (bytes), it
encrypts the file and write it
    """
    f = Fernet(key)
    with open(filename, "rb") as file:
        # read all file data
        file_data = file.read()
    # encrypt data
    encrypted_data = f.encrypt(file_data)
    # write the encrypted file
    with open(newfile, "wb") as file:
        file.write(encrypted_data)

def decrypt(filename, newfile, key):
    """
    Given a encrypted file (str), the new file name, and key (bytes), it
decrypts the file and write it
    """
    f = Fernet(key)
```

```
        with open(filename, "rb") as file:
            # read the encrypted data
            encrypted_data = file.read()
        # decrypt data
        decrypted_data = f.decrypt(encrypted_data)
        # write the original file
        with open(newfile, "wb") as file:
            file.write(decrypted_data)

    key = Fernet.generate_key()

    enc = encrypt("ch6_secret_image.jpg", "e_ch6_secret_image.jpg", key)
    dec = decrypt("e_ch6_secret_image.jpg", "d_ch6_secret_image.jpg", key)
```

AES and Block Modes of Operations

AES stands for Advanced Encryption Standard, and it is the only public encryption scheme that the NSA approves for confidential information. We focus on its use as our main block cipher from now on. AES is the current de facto block cipher, and it works on 16 bytes at a time. It has three possible key lengths: 16 bytes, 24 bytes, or 32 bytes. A number of AES block cipher modes are part of the AES specification; in this section, we will examine ECB and CBC.

The following code examples will utilize the PyCrypto library that was discussed in the Advanced Encryption Standard (AES) section of Chapter 5. To install the library, you will need to perform a `pip install PyCrypto`; the library provides us with the following modes we can use:

- `MODE_ECB`: Electronic Code Book (ECB)
- `MODE_CBC`: Cipher-Block Chaining (CBC)
- `MODE_CFB`: Cipher Feedback (CFB)
- `MODE_PGP`: Pretty Good Privacy (PGP)
- `MODE_OFB`: Output Feedback (OFB)
- `MODE_CTR`: CounTer Mode (CTR)
- `MODE_OPENPGP`: Open Pretty Good Privacy (OPENPGP)

Each of the block sizes will need to equal 16 bytes, while the key sizes for each of the supported modes support 16, 24, and 32 bytes. The encryption for the majority of these modes will be identical to using the CBC mode. If you do not specify a mode, the Electronic Code Book (ECB) mode will be used. More recent libraries may require you to specify an encryption mode. Either way, you should specify a mode so that it is obvious which mode you are using.

The simplest block mode is ECB; the cipher mode processes each 128-bit block of data. Each block is then then independently encrypted using AES with the same encryption key. The decryption process is the reverse. When using the ECB mode process, identical blocks of plaintext will be encrypted the same and will yield identical blocks of ciphertext or an encrypted image. While the weaknesses of the cipher mode may not be initially apparent, when we examine the mode in image cryptography, a major security vulnerability appears. In Figure 6.6, you will see the difference between the ECB mode versus the other modes that are available.

Figure 6.6: Image encryption modes

Exploring a Simple ECB Mode Example

For our first example, we will examine how to produce the ECB mode encrypted image. First, we start out with a bitmap file that has a distinct pattern, as shown in Figure 6.7.

Figure 6.7: Plane image in BMP format

The first step is to import the library and set a key. For this example, we will use a 16-byte key, although 24-byte and 32-byte keys are supported:

```
>>> from Crypto.Cipher import AES
>>> key = b"aaaabbbbccccdddd"
>>> cipher = AES.new(key, AES.MODE_ECB)
```

The next step is to file read the `plane.bmp` image; we will store the binary file into a variable named `byteblock`:

```
>>> with open("plane.bmp", "rb") as f:
>>>    byteblock = f.read()
```

The `byteblock` will need to be in multiples of 16 bytes. If not, it will result in an error that states: *Input strings must be a multiple of 16 in length.* The `byteblock` value will depend on the size of the image. To examine the `byteblock`, you can examine the length of the variable:

```
>>> print (len(byteblock))
261654
```

Since the input string must be a multiple of 16, we will need to examine how many bytes are left over when we take the modulo. In this case, it is 6:

```
>>> print (len(byteblock)%16)
6
```

Our goal is now to move the bytes that are multiples of 16 into a variable that we can use to isolate the block while subtracting the overflow. Here, we will store the value in `byteblock_trimmed`:

```
byteblock_trimmed = byteblock[64:-6]

>>> print (len(byteblock_trimmed))
261584
>>> print (len(byteblock_trimmed)%16)
0
```

To ensure that the image can be encrypted and decrypted without a data loss, you will need to combine the two sets of byte blocks:

```
# byteblock_trimmed must not have extra bytes or an error will occur
ciphertext = cipher.encrypt(byteblock_trimmed)
ciphertext = byteblock[0:64] + ciphertext + byteblock[-6:]
```

Now, all that is needed for the image is to save it using the ciphertext:

```
with open("plane_ecb.jpg", "w") as f:
    f.write(ciphertext)
```

The resulting image will look like Figure 6.8.

Figure 6.8: ECB encrypted plane

Now we will reverse the process. The decryption process will look like the following:

```
with open("plane_ecb.bmp", "rb") as f:
    byteblock = f.read()

byteblock_trimmed = byteblock[64:-6]

plaintext = cipher.decrypt(byteblock_trimmed)
plaintext = byteblock[0:64] + plaintext + byteblock[-6:]

with open("dplane_ecb.bmp", "wb") as f:
    byteblock = f.write(plaintext)
```

The result, shown in Figure 6.9, will produce a decrypted version that matches the original version.

Figure 6.9: ECB decrypted plane

Depending on the image you choose, you will have a variable of bytes that will need to be captured. The following code stores the value in a pad variable. To simplify the code, I multiplied it by –1 to produce a negative number. The following code will combine everything you have learned and encrypt our secret `.bmp` image:

```
from Crypto.Cipher import AES
key = b"aaaabbbbccccdddd"

cipher = AES.new(key, AES.MODE_ECB)

# encrypt using ECB mode

with open("chapter6/ch6_secret_image.bmp", "rb") as f:
    byteblock = f.read()

pad = len(byteblock)%16 * -1

byteblock_trimmed = byteblock[64:pad]

ciphertext = cipher.encrypt(byteblock_trimmed)
ciphertext = byteblock[0:64] + ciphertext + byteblock[pad:]

with open("e_ch6_secret_image.bmp", "wb") as f:
    f.write(ciphertext)

# decrypt using the reverse process

with open("e_ch6_secret_image.bmp", "rb") as f:
    byteblock = f.read()

pad = len(byteblock)%16 * -1
byteblock_trimmed = byteblock[64:pad]
plaintext = cipher.decrypt(byteblock_trimmed)
plaintext = byteblock[0:64] + plaintext + byteblock[pad:]
with open("d_ch6_secret_image.bmp", "wb") as f:
    byteblock = f.write(plaintext)

print ("done")
```

One of the critical takeaways I want you to walk away with is to understand that bitmap files that have large uniform areas will not encrypt the way you want them to and can potentially expose information you want to hide. You saw in Figure 6.8 that the outline of the airplane was still visible. This next example does a little better at obfuscating the image but still provides too much information. Examine the output for the preceding code recipe in Figure 6.10. This vulnerability is unique to the ECB mode encryption and, in this case, is only an issue if the image is a `.bmp` file. Some image types, such as `.jpg` files, are not vulnerable to the same issue.

Figure 6.10: ECB security issue

Exploring a Simple CBC Mode Example

Now that you understand how to encrypt and decrypt using ECB block mode, we will examine the CBC mode. One important difference between the two modes is the use of an initialization vector (IV) and the specification of the block mode, which in this case is `AES.MODE _ CBC`:

```
from Crypto.Cipher import AES

iv = "1111222233334444"
key = "aaaabbbbccccdddd"
cipher = AES.new(key, AES.MODE_CBC, iv)

# encrypt using CBC mode

with open("plane.bmp", "rb") as f:
   byteblock = f.read()

pad = len(byteblock)%16 * -1

byteblock_trimmed = byteblock[64:pad]

ciphertext = cipher.encrypt(byteblock_trimmed)
ciphertext = byteblock[0:64] + ciphertext + byteblock[pad:]

with open("plane_cbc.bmp", "w") as f:
   f.write(ciphertext)

# decrypt using the reverse process
```

```
with open("plane_cbc.bmp", "rb") as f:
   byteblock = f.read()

pad = len(byteblock)%16 * -1
byteblock_trimmed = byteblock[64:pad]
plaintext = cipher.decrypt(byteblock_trimmed)
plaintext = byteblock[0:64] + plaintext + byteblock[pad:]
with open("dplane_cbc.bmp", "w") as f:
   byteblock = f.write(plaintext)


print ("done")
```

The result, shown in Figure 6.11, will produce an encrypted version that does not show the same vulnerability as the ECB mode.

Figure 6.11: CBC encrypted plane

Applying the Examples

You have all the tools you need to create a solution that offers a number of AES block modes. The following code will allow you to specify a filename, key, and IV; it can be used to test a variety of block modes:

```
from Crypto.Cipher import AES


def Open_File(filename):
    with open(filename, "rb") as f:
        byteblock = f.read()
    return byteblock

def Save_File(filename, block):
    with open(filename,"wb") as f:
        f.write(block)

def Get_Padding(block):
    l = len(block) %16
    return (l * -1)
```

```
def Encrypt(cipher,read_filename, save_filename):
    block = Open_File(read_filename)
    pad = Get_Padding(block)
    block_trimmed = block[64:pad]
    ciphertext = cipher.encrypt(block_trimmed)
    ciphertext = block[0:64] + ciphertext + block[pad:]
    Save_File(save_filename, ciphertext)

def Decrypt(cipher,read_filename, save_filename):
    block = Open_File(read_filename)
    pad = Get_Padding(block)
    block_trimmed = block[64:pad]
    ciphertext = cipher.decrypt(block_trimmed)
    ciphertext = block[0:64] + ciphertext + block[pad:]
    Save_File(save_filename, ciphertext)

def Init_Cipher(key, mode, iv):
    cipher = AES.new(key, mode, iv)
    return cipher

# set the key and iv values
key = "aaaabbbbccccdddd"
iv = "1111222233334444"

# Available AES Block Modes
# AES.MODE_ECB = 1
# AES.MODE_CBC = 2
# AES.MODE_CFB = 3
# AES.MODE_OFB = 5
# AES.MODE_CTR = 6
# AES.MODE_OPENPGP = 7

mode = AES.MODE_CBC

c = Init_Cipher(key,mode, iv)

Encrypt(c, "plane.bmp", "eplane.bmp")
Decrypt(c, "eplane.bmp", "dplane.bmp")
```

Steganography

Steganography, which means "concealed writing" in Greek, is the art of concealing data within another file, image, video, or message. The first recorded use of the term was by Johannes Trithemius in his book titled *Steganographia* in 1499. While his book was on the topics of cryptography and steganography, it was masqueraded as a book on magic; the book contains hidden cipher messages. After almost 500 years these cryptograms have been detected and solved. As a result, *Steganographia* can no longer be regarded as one of the main early modern demonological treatises, but instead stands unambiguously revealed as the first book-length treatment of cryptography in Europe.

Typically with steganography, the hidden messages appear as images, articles, lists, or other textual items. Hidden messages may be written between the lines of letters using invisible ink. The goal of steganography is to not attract attention to the article itself and for those messages without keys, apply the concept of security through obscurity. The primary difference between steganography and cryptography is that the latter focuses on protecting the contents of a message, whereas steganography is concerned with concealing both the message and its contents.

Steganography, today, includes the concealment of information or data within computer files or electronic communications. In this section, we will explore how to hide data within other electronic media using Python. Earlier in this chapter, you learned about the `Cryptosteganography` module. We will first start using this module to conceal data and then explore other methods. Some of the caveats of using this module is that the output is limited to PNG formatted files and it does not work if the file is greater than the original input file. You may need larger images to store big blocks of data.

Storing a Message Inside an Image

Let us turn our attention to storing data inside a digital image. Each image, no matter the format, is constructed of small digital values called pixels. Pixels are the equivalent to cells in the human body and are the smallest element that makes up an image. Each pixel value represents the brightness of a given color at any specific point. When you examine an image at the pixel level, you will find that the image is made up of a series of pixels that form rows and columns. Images that provide the most accurate representation of the original image require more pixels. In digital images, the color is represented by three or four component intensities such as cyan, magenta, yellow, and black (CMYK), or red, green, and blue (RGB). The RGB model is the combination of adding red, green, and blue in various ways to produce a wide variety of colors. The RGB value is composed of 3 values (red, green, blue) which are each 8-bit values that range from 0 to 255. When breaking down an RGB color digitally, you will see the colors represented with three numbers; an example would be [124, 196, 143], which is a variance of green. You can examine any number of arrangements by finding color pickers on the web. Each value in the RGB scale is represented by a binary code. The binary code is broken down into 8-bit binary digits. The leftmost bit is the most significant bit. The number 128 is represented by 10000000, whereas the number 177 is represented by 10110001. On the rightmost side of the digits, we have the least significant bit. If we change the rightmost value, it will have less impact on the final value. Small changes to the least significant bit will not be noticeable to the naked eye. This will come into play when hiding data using the Least Significant Bit or LSB method of steganography. In an RGB image, an 8-bit image means three 8-bit channels for the RGB data; each color has its own 8-bit channel, which provides one byte for each red, green, and blue color; this mode is also known as 24-bit color depth. This gives an image a color palette of 16.7 million colors. The LSB method replaces bits in the image, but not all these bits are needed to show the image. You can also use this same method to hide data in audio files. Another method of hiding data inside images is to append extra bytes to the end of the image, while still leaving the image file technically valid, or encoding the extra bytes in the image metadata fields. This method will increase the size of the image in most cases. When adding bits to a file, the secret message could appear in the file header portion, which contains the information such as file type, color depth, and resolution of the image. Each type of file also has an explicit end of file so data can be hidden after the end of the file without modifying the image data and corrupting the image.

Our goal here is to use the CryptoSteganography module to take a secret message and hide it in an image. Let's jump into some code and we will explore some tools afterward to help discover hidden data inside our images.

The first thing that you need to do is import the CryptoSteganography library:

```
>>> from cryptosteganography import CryptoSteganography
```

The next step is to create a key and pass it into the CryptoSteganography object. The key is critical in order to extract the messages you conceal; the key you select can be a passphrase or any selected password:

```
>>> key = "1111222233334444!"
>>> crypto_steganography = CryptoSteganography(key)
```

Now, create three variables to specify the original image file, the altered or modified file, and the message you want to hide in the image. Use the crypto_steganography object to hide the details in the image using the hide() method:

```
>>> origfile = "ch6_secret_image.jpg"
>>> modfile = "steg_ch6_secret_image.png"
>>> message = "This is the secret message."
>>> crypto_steganography.hide(origfile, modfile, message)
```

Now that we have an image that contains a secret message, use the retrieve() method to extract the message. Once you have that, you can print it to the screen to verify that it is correct:

```
>>> secret = crypto_steganography.retrieve(modfile)
>>> print(secret)
This is the secret message.
```

We now examine how the module works when you do not supply the correct key. Change the key to anything else and then pass the new key into the `CryptoSteganography` class:

```
>>> key = "AnotherKey"
>>> crypto_steganography = CryptoSteganography(key)
```

You can now use the `retrieve()` method to attempt to extract the message. This time, when you print the retrieved value, you will get the value None, indicating that the key is incorrect:

```
>>> secret = crypto_steganography.retrieve(modfile)
>>> print(secret)
None
```

Now that you have seen the components, let's put them all together and show how hiding information using steganography changes the original file:

```
from cryptosteganography import CryptoSteganography

key = "1111222233334444!"
crypto_steganography = CryptoSteganography(key)

print()
print('The program is looking for an image named ch6_secret_image.png\n')
origfile = "chapter6\steg\ch6_secret_image.png"
print('The image with the hidden message will be called steg_ch6_secret_
image.png\n')
modfile = "chapter6\steg\steg_ch6_secret_image.png"

secretMsg = ""
message1 = "Sympathy for the favorite nation, facilitating the illusion
of an imaginary common "
message2 = "interest in cases where no real common interest exists, and
infusing into one the "
message3 = "enmities of the other, betrays the former into a
participation in the quarrels and "
message4 = "wars of the latter without adequate inducement or
justification."
secretMsg = secretMsg.join([message1, message2, message3, message4])


crypto_steganography.hide(origfile, modfile, secretMsg)
secret = crypto_steganography.retrieve(modfile)
print("The secret that is hidden in the file is:\n")
print(secret)
print()
```

```
print('Now we will try the wronge secret.\n')
key = "AnotherKey"
crypto_steganography = CryptoSteganography(key)
secret = crypto_steganography.retrieve(modfile)
print('The secret message is: {} \n'.format(secret))
```

The preceding code will hide a quote from George Washington in an image named `ch6_secret_image.png`. I converted the original file for this chapter to a PNG file so that we could examine the change in file size. The original file in this case does not need to be in a PNG format, but it makes it easier to compare the original with the modified version. Many times, when I have hidden data in pictures, the picture size has increased, but as you will see in Figure 6.12, the original image was 87 KB and the image with the hidden message is only 75 KB. You are not able to guess which image has the secret hidden inside just by examining the file sizes.

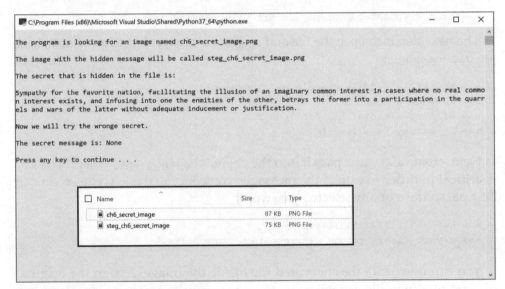

Figure 6.12: Steganography example

Additionally, you will notice that without the proper key, the secret message is not revealed. So, the next question is, how can you determine if there is hidden data inside an image? A number of free tools are available online that you can use to embed and extract data from images. One tool that I have used several times is Invisible Secrets. Now, we will explore a more complex setup with binary data.

Storing a Binary File Inside an Image

For our next example, we will take a media file and hide it in an image. The file I am using for this example was retrieved from `file-examples.com`. The file is 747 KB in size. If you would like to use the same file, you can find it here: `https://file-examples.com/index.php/sample-audio-files/sample-mp3-download/`.

Our goal here is to use the `CryptoSteganography` module to take a secret message and hide it in an image. The first thing that you need to do is reference the `CryptoSteganography` library. The larger the media file, the longer it will take to encrypt and decrypt. In this next example, I will also be using a much larger image file because the media file I've selected is too large for the secret image I used in the previous example. As you work through this example, you may be attempting to store more data than the image will support. In those cases, you will see an exception that states: *The message you want to hide is too long*. Here we will start breaking down the code you need:

```
>>> from cryptosteganography import CryptoSteganography
```

The next step is to open the file and assign the binary data to a variable; here we use `'message'`:

```
>>> mediafile = "file_example_MP3_700KB.mp3"
>>> message = None
>>> with open(mediafile, "rb") as f:
>>>     message = f.read()
```

Next, create a key and pass it into the `CryptoSteganography` object. The key is critical in order to extract the messages you conceal; the key you select can be a passphrase or any selected password:

```
>>> key = "1111222233334444!"
>>> crypto_steganography = CryptoSteganography(key)
```

You can now store the encrypted file inside the image. Assign the original file and modified file variables:

```
>>> origfile = "dogs.png"
>>> modfile = "steg_audio_dogs.png "
>>> crypto_steganography.hide(origfile, modfile, message)
```

Now that we have our media hidden, it is time to extract it. You can use the previous `crypto_steganography` object, but the code here will instantiate a new object. This will allow you to change or modify the key if you like. Here, we will use the same key. In addition, specify the steganography image and the name of the file you wish to store the MP3 as:

```
>>> key = "1111222233334444!"
>>> crypto_steganography = CryptoSteganography(key)
```

```
>>> modfile = 'stegaudio_dogs.png'
>>> decrypted = 'decrypted_sample.mp3'
```

Use the `retrieve()` method to pull out the media file and write it to a new file that was specified in the decrypted variable:

```
>>> secret_bin = crypto_steganography.retrieve(modfile)
>>> with open(decrypted, 'wb') as f:
>>>    f.write(secret_bin)
```

Now we will put it together with a working example that will hide a media file inside an image of dogs named `dogs.jpg`. There is nothing special about this image shown in Figure 6.13. It is simply just a photo of my two dogs taken with my cell phone camera; it is, however, a large enough file in which to hide a 700 KB MP3 file.

Figure 6.13: High-definition photo of dogs

The following code will take an MP3 file and hide it inside a large JPG file.

```
from cryptosteganography import CryptoSteganography

# open sound file
mediafile = 'chapter6/steg/file_example_MP3_700KB.mp3'
message = None

with open(mediafile, "rb") as f:
    message = f.read()
```

```
print()
print('The program is looking for an image named dogs.jpg\n')
origfile = "chapter6\steg\dogs.jpg"
print('The image with the hidden audio file will be called steg_audio_
dogs.png\n')
modfile = "chapter6\steg\steg_audio_dogs.png"

key = "1111222233334444!"
crypto_steganography = CryptoSteganography(key)
crypto_steganography.hide(origfile, modfile, message)

print('The extracted data will be called decrypted_sample2.mp3 \n')
decrypted = 'decrypted_sample2.mp3'
secret_bin = crypto_steganography.retrieve(modfile)

# Save the data to a new file
with open(decrypted, 'wb') as f:
    f.write(secret_bin)
```

In Figure 6.14, you will see the output from the preceding Python recipe. The code takes a media file and encrypts it inside the dogs.jpg image. You will see that the original size of the dogs image is 598 KB. Once you embed the media file, the outputted file is 4,983 KB. The previous example also extracts the media file from the image and stores it as decrypted_sample.mp3. You can compare the two MP3 files; you will find that they are identical.

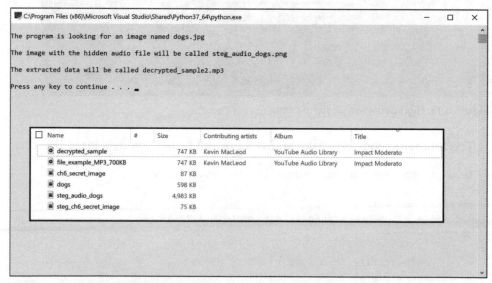

Figure 6.14: Steganography with media

Working with large images

While we are on the topic of images and the ability to hide data inside them, I want to introduce you to the FITS image type. FITS stand for Flexible Image Transport System; it is an open standard that defines a digital file format that is used for the transmission, processing, and storage of data within a single file. FITS is typically used for digital files produced in astronomical research or satellite data. The amount of data inside the file can be astronomical, pun intended. The data inside the file can be represented in several dimensional formats. The important aspect to understand about how this format works is that there is human-readable text stored in the header portion of the file format. The header details may list any parameters that could tell where the image was taken, which satellite or telescope produced it, and any number of pieces of metadata that the author wants to include; the only limit to the header metadata is that the label must be eight characters or less. A FITS file consists of one or more Header + Data Units; these are known as HDUs. The first HDU that is created is called the primary HDU or primary array. The primary HDU can be empty or contain an N-dimensional array of pixels such as a 1-D spectrum, a 2-D image, or a 3-D data cube. The best way to get an understanding of the FITS standard is to dive in with some Python code; in order to follow along with the following code, you will need to include the `astropy` library. Another library that you can use is `PyFITS`. The `.io` FITS module is identical to PyFITS except by name. `PyFITS` was ported into `astropy`. You can do this by typing `pip install astropy`. Let's create a FITS file that stores some random `numpy` array in a file named `random_array.fits`. The output of the file will give you the default header information along with the contents of the data.

```
import numpy as np
from astropy.io import fits

file_name = "chapter6/fits/random_array.fits"
hdu = fits.PrimaryHDU()
hdu.data = np.random.random((128,128))
# Note that setting the data automatically populates the header with
basic information:
hdu.writeto(file_name, overwrite=True)

data = fits.getdata(file_name)
header = fits.getheader(file_name)

print(header)
print()
print(data)
```

Now that you understand the components that make up a FITS file, we can explore FITS for images where you might want to keep some of the header information confidential. You already know how to encrypt strings, so here, I'll just assume you've encrypted the data using your favorite algorithm. Since the labels are restricted to eight characters, the labels do not make great candidates for encryption but the actual data does. If there was data that you wanted to keep secret, the following Python code would do the trick.

```python
import matplotlib.pyplot as plt
import numpy as np

from PIL import Image
from astropy.io import fits
from astropy.visualization import astropy_mpl_style

location_lat = "Encrypted latitude"
location_long = "Encrypted longitude"
author = "Encrypted name here"
satellite = "Encrypted satellite name"

# load image as pixel array
img_file = Image.open('chapter6/fits/ch6_secret_image.jpg')
xsize, ysize = img_file.size
print("Image size: {} x {}".format(xsize, ysize))
plt.style.use(astropy_mpl_style)
plt.imshow(img_file)

# split the image into color channels
r, g, b = img_file.split()
r_data = np.array(r.getdata())
g_data = np.array(g.getdata())
b_data = np.array(b.getdata())
print(r_data.shape)

r_data = r_data.reshape(ysize, xsize)
g_data = g_data.reshape(ysize, xsize)
b_data = b_data.reshape(ysize, xsize)

red = fits.PrimaryHDU(data=r_data)
red.header["AUTHOR"] = author
red.header["LATOBS"] = location_lat
red.header["LONGOBS"] = location_long
red.header["SATNAME"] = satellite
red.writeto('chapter6/fits/red.fits', overwrite=True)

green = fits.PrimaryHDU(data=g_data)
green.header["AUTHOR"] = author
green.header["LATOBS"] = location_lat
green.header["LONGOBS"] = location_long
green.header["SATNAME"] = satellite
green.writeto('chapter6/fits/green.fits', overwrite=True)
```

```
blue = fits.PrimaryHDU(data=b_data)
blue.header["AUTHOR"] = author
blue.header["LATOBS"] = location_lat
blue.header["LONGOBS"] = location_long
blue.header["SATNAME"] = satellite
blue.writeto('chapter6/fits/blue.fits', overwrite=True)
```

The output of the previous code takes our secret image from the beginning of the chapter and creates three unique FITS files using red, green, and blue channels. You will see in Figure 6.15 that the header for green.fits contains our secret information. As you might expect, we could easily encrypt the image too.

Figure 6.15: FITS Files

Summary

In this chapter, you were introduced to a couple of libraries that perform cryptographic and steganography tasks on images. It is important for you to understand how various AES block modes work and how they apply to image files. We concluded the chapter by using the CryptoSteganography library to hide various types of files. Hiding messages inside an image could affect the properties of the image. This was obvious when we hid a 30-second MP3 file inside an image. The decryption process for each of these examples is dependent on the use of a secret key; if the recipient of the file does not have the secret key, your message will remain a secret even if the recipient can see that the visual properties of the file have changed. Finally, we explored the FITS file format. While the FITS format may not provide much value on the surface, the amount of data that can be stored and encrypted is incredible.

Summary

Message Integrity

You should be comfortable at this stage with symmetric key cryptography. In this chapter, you learn to generate message authentication codes to let message recipients validate that the message they are receiving has not been tampered with while it was in transit. In the context of message integrity, a hash function is used to produce a fixed-length message digest from a variable-size message. The most common message digests range in length from 160 to 512 bits. Any alteration to the input message produces a dramatically different message digest. The message digests help detect unauthorized alterations and message forgeries. The principles you learn and develop here continue in the next chapter as you explore public-key cryptography; throughout this chapter, you gain cryptographic knowledge as you:

- Learn about Message Authentication Codes (MACs)
- Ensure that your signature is not compromised and does not get forged
- Explore how to make forgeries when someone else failed to protect their signatures
- Explore sending encrypted data over nonsecure channels

Message Authentication Codes

You were first introduced to hash functions and message authentication codes in Chapter 2. You now dive into those same concepts at a deeper level. Message Authentication Codes, also called tags, or MACs as they are more commonly known, play an essential role in ensuring messages are not tampered with while they are en route to their destination. MACs ensure message integrity in addition to validating the message authenticity by allowing the parties involved to verify the message using a shared secret. A MAC involves three separate functions:

- A key-generation function that returns a key k from an input
- A signing function that returns a MAC or tag t when given the key k
- A verifying function that verifies the authenticity of the message (m) given the value of k and t

The formal definition of the MAC is as follows:

A MAC relies on a secret key that both the sender and receiver know; therefore, it uses a symmetric key value. The MAC is built by taking the message (m) and the key (k) and using a defined algorithm where the tag (t) that gets returned. The recipient gets both the original message (m) and the tag (t). If the message and key produce the same tag, then the receiver has verified the message; if the tag cannot be verified, the message may have been altered by a reprehensible party.

The goal of your adversary is to generate a different message and tag that the receiver would verify as correct. No authentication at the receiving end could be achieved if both the message and its hash value are accessible to an adversary wanting to tamper with the message. There are several ways in which one could incorporate message hashing.

- **Concatenate message and MAC:** In this scheme, the sender would use symmetric-key encryption and concatenate the message and its MAC to form a composite message that is then encrypted and sent to the recipient. The receiver then decrypts the message using the symmetric key and separates the message and the MAC. The MAC would then provide the authentication, and the encryption provides the confidentiality.

- **MAC encryption:** This scheme is a modification of the previous one outlined. In this scheme, only the MAC is encrypted. This scheme is efficient to use when confidentiality is not the main concern, but message authentication is critical. Only the receiver with access to the secret key knows the real MAC; this ensures that the receiver can verify whether the message is authentic and remains tamper-free.

- **Public-key MAC encryption:** This scheme is similar to MAC encryption and uses public-key encryption to encrypt the MAC with the sender's private key. This means that anyone who has the sender's public key can decrypt the MAC; this method is to ensure authentication. This scheme is the basic concept behind a digital signature.

- **Symmetric public-key confidentiality:** This scheme builds on the public-key MAC encryption where the message is concatenated with the encrypted public-key MAC, but then the concatenated message is encrypted again with a symmetric key. The scheme is frequently used when both authentication and confidentiality are needed.

- **Hidden secret:** In the next scheme, nothing is encrypted. The sender appends a secret string S, also known to the receiver, to the message before computing its MAC; the sender then removes the secret string. Before checking the MAC of the received message for its authentication, the receiver appends the same secret string S to the message and computes the MAC to confirm both matches.

- **Symmetric key confidentiality:** This scheme is similar to symmetric public-key confidentiality with the exception that instead of using a public key to encrypt the MAC, the sender uses a symmetric key. He then concatenates the MAC to the message and encrypts the message again.

You might wonder why we do not do something simple like H(K|m) for some secure hash function H. We do not explore the details of how hash functions compress large amounts of data down to something fixed length, but they use something analogous to a block cipher mode for compression, called the Merkle-Damgård construction. The heart of most hash functions is a "compressor" that takes in two fixed-length inputs and spits out one output of that length. Then it concatenates the block compressions into the final hash. Knowing that, we can forge signatures with an unknown secret key. Next, you will learn how to generate your first cryptographically secure MAC, which is a clever application of hashing to generate a difficult-to-forge tag. The system is called the Hash-based Message Authentication Code, or HMAC.

Hash-based Message Authentication Code

A cryptographically secure MAC is known as a Hash-based Message Authentication Code (HMAC). For a hash function to be considered cryptographically secure, it must satisfy two properties:

- **One-way property:** The one-way property refers to a hash function that makes it computationally infeasible to find a message that corresponds to a given MAC.

- **Strong collision resistance property:** The strong collision resistance property refers to a hash function that makes it computationally infeasible to find two different messages that hash to the same MAC.

It is important to note that hash functions that are not collision resistant can be vulnerable to the birthday attack; you learn more about this attack shortly. First, you will explore the HMAC function and learn how to incorporate the same logic into a standard hash library. Open the Python interpreter and enter the first two lines of code to verify that you are getting the same tag:

```
import hmac, hashlib
print(hmac.new(b"secretkey", b"our secret message", hashlib.sha256).
hexdigest())

78c736db86abd16023a23355f4ad3005e77dec6d8c960d06ea3c4a9aba9c449f
```

SHA256 has a 64-byte block length; to build an HMAC by hand, you need to build K^+, ipad, and opad:

```
import binascii, hashlib
k = b"secretkey"
msg = b"our secret message"

kplus = k + b"\x00"*(64-len(k))
ipad = b"\x36"*64
opad = b"\x5C"*64

def XOR(raw1, raw2):
    return binascii.unhexlify(format(int(binascii.hexlify(raw1), 16) ^
int(binascii.hexlify(raw2), 16), 'x'))

tag = hashlib.sha256(XOR(kplus, opad) + hashlib.sha256(XOR(kplus, ipad)
+ msg).digest()).digest()

print(binascii.hexlify(tag))
```

Confirm that this manual computation matches the library implementation. In our next script, we will apply an HMAC digest to a signed message.

Using HMAC to Sign Message

The file that we are creating the message digest for is a simple text file that contains only Hello. When run, the code reads a data file and computes an HMAC signature for it:

```
import hmac

myKey = b'this_is_my_secret'
digest_maker = hmac.new(myKey)

with open('test.txt', 'rb') as f:
    while True:
```

```
            block = f.read(1024)
            if not block:
                break
digest_maker.update(block)
digest = digest_maker.hexdigest()
print (digest)
```

The output should produce the following results:

```
c2b5ac0978608c196f6237ab3983ebd2
```

Message Digest with SHA

MD5 is one of the most common algorithms used for hashing, but over the years MD5 hashes have proven to have a number of weaknesses such as collisions and are vulnerable to length extension attacks. The SHA family of algorithms offer stronger options and should be used instead, but many of these algorithms are also susceptible to the length extension attack; we will review this later in the chapter.

The new() function on the hmac object takes three arguments. The first is the secret passphrase or key; this will be needed by both the sender and receiver. The second value is an initial message. If the message content that needs to be authenticated is small, such as a timestamp or HTTP POST, the entire body of the message can be passed to the function; if not, you will need to use the update() method. The last argument is the digest module to be used. The default is hashlib.md5. The following example will create a test.txt file that contains Hello and then checks if the hash is using SHA256:

```
import hmac
import hashlib

myKey = b'this_is_my_secret'
digest_maker = hmac.new(myKey, b'', hashlib.sha256,)

with open("chapter7/test.txt", "wb") as hello_file:
    hello_file.write(b'Hello')
    hello_file.close()


# the test.txt file contains the bytes 'Hello'
with open('chapter7/test.txt', 'rb') as f:
    while True:
        block = f.read(5)
        if not block:
            break
```

```
          digest_maker.update(block)
          digest = digest_maker.hexdigest()
print(digest)
```

```
6833cebacb9495c1cccba617d4b5f3aefda3dc03fcb3f8d070d61a09a4084a02
```

Binary Digests

The previous examples used the `hexdigest()` method to produce a printable digest. The `hexdigest()` is a different representation of the value calculated by the `digest()` method, which is a binary value that may include unprintable characters, including NUL. Some web services such as Amazon S3 and Google checkout use the Base64-encoded version of the binary digest instead of the `hexdigest()`. To see the difference, I am using the same Hello text file from the previous example:

```python
import base64
import hmac
import hashlib

myKey = b'this_is_my_secret'
with open('test.txt', 'rb') as f:
    body = f.read(5)

hash = hmac.new(myKey, body, hashlib.sha256,)
digest = hash.digest()
print(base64.encodebytes(digest))
```

The output generated should resemble the following:

```
b'aDPOusuUlcHMy6YX1LXzrv2j3AP8s/jQcNYaCaQISgI=\n'
```

HMAC authentication should be used for any public network service, and any time data is stored where security is important. For example, when sending data through a pipe or socket, that data should be signed, and then the signature should be tested before the data is used. We will explore how to do this later in this chapter when we explore secure channels.

The first step is to establish a function to calculate a digest for a string, and a simple class to be instantiated and passed through a communication channel:

```python
import hashlib
import hmac

def make_digest(message):
    "Return a digest for the message."
    myKey = b'this_is_my_secret'
    hash = hmac.new(myKey, message, hashlib.sha3_256)
    return hash.hexdigest().encode('utf-8')
```

```
# You must encode your message before it is hashed.
message = b'This is a test of the emergency broadcast system; it is only
a test.'
rd = make_digest(message)
print (rd)
```

The preceding code listing should produce a digest for our intended message. Your output should look identical to the output shown in Figure 7.1.

```
import hashlib
import hmac

def make_digest(message):
    "Return a digest for the message."
    myKey = b'this_is_my_secret'
    hash = hmac.new(myKey, message, hashlib.sha3_256)
    return hash.hexdigest().encode('utf-8')

# You must encode your message before it is hashed.
message = b'This is a test of the emergency broadcast system; it is only a test.'
rd = make_digest(message)
print (rd)
```

```
C:\Program Files (x86)\Microsoft Visual Studio\Shared\Python37_64\python.exe                    —    □    ×
b'9c85c5c76d83a9d25990ea1d37446f6e452112aa934aa6067e6807ba1e1608f9'
Press any key to continue . . .
```

Figure 7.1: Binary digests

NIST Compliance

In the FIPS PUB 180-4 (Federal Information Processing Standards Publication), the National Institute of Science and Technology (NIST) outlines a secure hash standard that can be used to generate digests of messages and specifies secure hash algorithms: SHA-1, SHA-224, SHA-256, SHA-384, SHA-512, SHA-512/224, and SHA-512/256. Any change to a message results in a different message digest.

NIST provides a sample zip file that contains a file named HMAC.rsp. As you study the inner workings of hashing, you should know about a common practice with message authentication codes, which is to truncate the tag. In the NIST example, you may notice the TLen parameter, which is the number of bytes that the tag truncates. The truncating may benefit some applications that require a hash function with a message digest length different than those provided by the hash functions. In cases such as these, a truncated tag or digest should be used, whereby a hash function with a more considerable tag length is applied to the data to be hashed, and the resulting message digest is truncated by selecting an appropriate number of the leftmost bits. To learn more about the guidelines on choosing the length of the truncated message digest and information about its security implications for the cryptographic application that uses it, see SP 800-107.

```
import hashlib
hasher = hashlib.md5()
# from http://csrc.nist.gov/groups/STM/cavp/documents/mac/
hmactestvectors.zip
with open('hmactestvectors.zip', 'rb') as afile:
    buf = afile.read()
    hasher.update(buf)
print(hasher.hexdigest())
```

The preceding Python should produce the following HMAC:

```
054d8addf01353605068508266eb2f19
```

To examine a NIST-supported SHA256 hash, review the following. It has many similarities, but this example incorporates a BLOCKSIZE:

```
import hashlib

BLOCKSIZE = 65536
hasher = hashlib.sha256()
with open('hmactestvectors.zip', 'rb') as afile:
    buf = afile.read(65536)
    while len(buf) > 0:
        hasher.update(buf)
        buf = afile.read(BLOCKSIZE)
print(hasher.hexdigest())
```

The second example will produce the following HMAC:

```
418c3837d38f249d6668146bd0090db24dd3c02d2e6797e3de33860a387ae4bd
```

CBC-MAC

The cipher block chaining message authentication code (CBC-MAC) is used in cryptography to construct a MAC from a block cipher. The initial message gets encrypted with a block cipher algorithm in CBC mode. The CBC mode creates a chain of blocks such that each block depends on the proper encryption of the previous block. CBC sets up an interdependence that ensures that a change to any portion of the plaintext bit causes the last block to be encrypted in a way that cannot be predicted or counteracted without knowing the key to the block cipher. The CBC-MAC encryption process is shown in Figure 7.2.

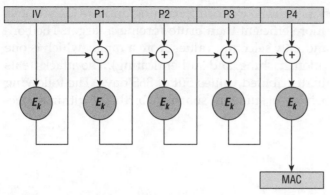

Figure 7.2: CBC-MAC example

There are some security issues related to CBC-MAC; if the block cipher used is secure, the CBC-MAC is secure for the fixed-length message. It should be noted that CBC-MAC by itself is not a secured option for variable-length messages. A single key must be used for messages of a fixed length; this is because an attacker who knows the correct message-tag (i.e., CBC-MAC) pairs for two messages can generate a third message whose CBC-MAC would be the same as the produced tag. This weakness can be exploited by XORing the first block of m' with t and then concatenating m with the modified m'. One solution is to include the length of the message in the first block.

Additionally, encrypting the last block has the advantage of not needing to know the length of the message until the end of the computation. One standard error is to reuse the same key k for CBC encryption and CBC-MAC. Reusing the same key for different purposes is a poor practice in general; in this particular case, the mistake leads to attacks against the encryption mode.

CBC-MAC is similar to the CBC mode for encryption with a few differences. The first difference is that the initialization vector (IV) is a fixed value. Secondly, the CBC-MAC only outputs the last block of the ciphertext. Additionally, CBC-MAC can support a random IV but requires you to know the IV. If you had a safe place to store the IV, one could argue your message would be safe there as well. If nefarious users can change the CBC-MAC IV, they can also change the first block of the MAC message to produce a tag that would match the original hash. The attack can be made because one of the first steps to CBC-MAC is to XOR the IV with the message.

Birthday Attacks

The birthday attack is based on the observation that finding equal random values is significantly more manageable when you check all pairs and do not preselect one value. When it comes to exploring hashing and MACs, you end up with an attack that is more efficient than brute-forcing a target. The context is when someone is randomly selecting values from a range (which is one way of interpreting encryption, hashing, and authenticating). The attack treats our birthdays as uniformly distributed values out of 365 days. The following Python calculates the probability of students' sharing a birthday within a specified class size:

```python
import random
import decimal
classSize = 23
numTrials = 1000
dupeCount = 0

for trial in range(numTrials):
    year = [0]*365
    foundDupe = False
    for i in range(classSize):
        newBDay = random.randrange(365)
        year[newBDay] = year[newBDay] + 1
        if year[newBDay] > 1:
            foundDupe = True

    if foundDupe == True:
        dupeCount = dupeCount + 1

prob = float(dupeCount / (numTrials * 1.0))
print('The probability of a shared birthday in a class of', classSize,
'is', prob)
```

The probability of a shared birthday in a class of 23 is 0.481.

You can import itertools and get a more condensed version. In the following Python script, you see that 35 students would offer closer to an 80% chance of a birthday collision:

```python
import itertools
from functools import reduce
def alldifferent(k,n):
    '''The probability that k random selections from n possibilities
    are all different.'''
    assert(k<=n)
    nums = range(n,n-k,-1)
    dens = itertools.repeat(n)
    fracs = map(lambda x,y: float(x)/y, nums,dens)
    return reduce(float.__mul__, fracs)

def collide(k,n):
```

```
    '''The probability that, in k random selections from n
possibilities,
    at least two selections collide.'''
    return 1 - alldifferent(k,n)


print(collide(35,365))
```

Crafting Forgeries

The biggest failure of a MAC scheme is that a nefarious user can generate a
false message that the recipient accepts as authentic. These failures are made
possible due to the CBC-MAC/birthday paradox.

Given a particular message, how many other messages would you expect to
create message tags for before finding a collision? Imagine that you have found
two messages m1, m2 such that MAC K (m1) = MAC K (m2); then MAC K (m1 +
x) = MAC K (m2 + x). To prove that the vulnerabilities exist, a team at Google
released the first concrete collision attack against SHA-1. The team has produced
two files, shattered-1.pdf and shattered-2.pdf, that produce the same SHA-1
tag. To learn more about the attack, review shattered.io.

The Length Extension Attack

Now that you have a little insight on how collisions happen, let's examine the
SHA-1 digest in a little more detail and then define a Python forgery for it. The
Secure Hash Algorithms are a family of cryptographic hash functions published
by the National Institute of Standards and Technology (NIST) as a U.S. Federal
Information Processing Standard (FIPS), including SHA-0, SHA-1, SHA-2, and
SHA-3. The SHA-1 is a 160-bit hash function, which is like the MD5 algorithm.
The algorithm was designed by the NSA (National Security Agency) back in the
early 1990s. All hashing algorithms, including SHA-1, produce a fixed-length
message digest. The output for SHA-1 is 20 characters no matter how long the
message was that was hashed.

In general, you should use MACs such as HMAC-SHA-256 over those that
are not cryptographically secure such as MD5 and SHA-1. One of the primary
reasons is that the plain hash functions are susceptible to length extension
attacks. Many common hash functions use the Merkle-Damgård construction,
which are built using a compression function, f, and preserve an internal state,
s, which is initialized to a defined constant. Messages are produced by applying
a compression function to the current block and current state to compute an
updated internal state; the blocks are generated in fixed-sized blocks; i.e.,
$s_{i+1} = f(s_i, b_i)$. One of the consequences of this design, which allows us to exploit
it, is that if you know the hash of an n-block message, you may be able to find
the hash of longer messages by applying the compression function for each

block that we want to add $(b_{n+1}, b_{n+2}, \ldots)$. This type of attack is known as length extensions and it can be applied to many applications of hash functions.

The hashing process in this case, MD5, produces a message in 512-bit blocks. This means, internally, the hash function pads the message, m, to a multiple of that length. The padding consists of the bit 1 followed by as many 0 bits as needed. The padding is then followed by a 64-bit count of the number of bits in the unpadded message. If the padding will not fit in the current block, the system adds an additional block. You can use the function `padding(count)` in the pymd5 module to compute the padding that will be added to a `count-bit` message.

Some of the code we will use as you explore this attack can be downloaded in an MD5 Python module known as pymd5. As of this writing, the project is available at `pypi.org/project/pymd5/`; the module is used by many universities to help cryptography students play with hashing functions. It was originally developed in 1991 by RSA Data Security. You can install it using a `pip install pymd5`, but your experience will be different. The module allows for a more condensed md5 call and exposes two low-level methods named `md5 _ compress()` and `padding()`.

Depending on what you need, you may find the HashPump tool easier for your research. HashPump is a free tool that can be used to exploit the hash length extension attack on a number of algorithms including MD5, SHA-1, SHA-256, and SHA-512. You can install it using the following syntax to set it up on Debian or Ubuntu Linux distributions:

```
$ git clone https://github.com/bwall/HashPump.git
$ apt-get install g++ libssl-dev
$ cd HashPump
$ make
$ make install
```

Setting Up a Secure Channel

So far, you have explored only dealing with MACs in plaintext. Having a secure channel of communication that is secret and tamper-free would be ideal but as you are learning, secure communications can be tricky. If you wish to both encrypt data and authenticate the recipient, you must be careful. There are three possible ways to achieve this:

Encrypt and Authenticate   To encrypt and authenticate, you would compute $c = ENC_k(M)$ and $t = MAC_{k2}(M)$ and send (c,t); on the other side of the conversation, the recipient must compute $M = DEC_k(c)$ then check $t == VRFY_{k2}(M)$ once they know M. The problem with this method is that most MACs are deterministic. There are some flaws with this method.

First, when you send the same message many times, any potential eavesdropper has the advantage. Additionally, the MAC is not designed for secrecy; there is no assurance that the upper byte of t isn't identical to the first byte of M.

Authenticate Then Decrypt   In this world you compute $t = MAC(M)$ then $c = ENC(M||t)$. Your receiver computes $M||t = DEC(c)$, then checks that $t == VRFY(M)$. This next model is a bit stronger, but there is a bit of debate on the authenticate-then-decrypt model. Johnathan Katz recommends against this model while Bruce Schneier recommends it. Katz enjoys proofs of security and would recommend the next method.

Encrypt Then Authenticate   This is the recommended approach. First, $c = ENC_k (M)$, then $t = MAC_{k2}(c)$ and send (c,t). On the other side, verify $t == VRFY_{k2} (c)$ and if that computes, calculate $M = DEC_k$. If the MAC is cryptographically secure, then we are CCA-secure and unforgeable, provided the keys are random and independent.

Communication Channels

There are additional attacks that the security practitioner should be aware of, but they tend to border more on the network security side than cryptography best practices. In general, you should always encrypt the entire message. Ideally, you need to set up a channel for encrypted and authenticated messages between the two parties despite any malicious middlemen. Your crypto system cannot mitigate threats that are related to someone else controlling the network between the communicating parties. These attacks include the replay attack, the reordering attack, and the reflection attack.

- **Replay attack:** Occurs when a middleman captures the encrypted message and then has the ability to send it at a later time.

- **Reordering attack:** Occurs when an adversary takes encrypted messages and sends them out of order.

- **Reflection attack:** Occurs when a message is sent back to the sender and not passed along to the recipient.

None of these attacks would lead to a failure, and the messages would be decrypted correctly. To fight against reflection and replay attacks, you should include more than just the message in your MACs. In this case, you solve these problems by including some extra data with the encrypted messages, a message counter, and a direction bit (0 for A to B and 1 for B to A). Then both parties can maintain state and reject messages that don't match up. Our next goal is to explore opening up a socket using Python in order to deliver a message that cannot be successfully read from an unauthorized user. This will be the basis of exploring secured sockets after we examine certificates in the next chapter.

Sending Secure Messages Over IP Networks

Sockets are used to send messages across various networks that can be logical, local, or external. Sockets were introduced back in 1971 with the birth of ARPANET and then later became the Berkeley sockets, which is an API in the Berkeley Software Distribution OS that was released in 1983. Network programming started to boom in the 1990s as the use of the internet increased; the use of client-server applications of many types became widespread. The socket API in Python provides an interface to the Berkley sockets.

There are two types of sockets that you can experiment with. The first is a Transmission Control Protocol (TCP). TCP is used to produce reliability and has an in-order data delivery system. The second type of socket is the User Datagram Protocol (UDP). These sockets lack reliability and their data can be out of order; in fact, there is no guarantee that your data will reach the destination. Depending on the type of data you are sending, one type of socket will have advantages over the other. In the next two code samples provided, you will use Python to create a server listening for UDP communications and create a client server that will communicate with it.

Create a Server Socket

The following Python code will allow you to create a server that is listening on port 13000. Once this code executes, it will launch a command window that states *Waiting to receive message. . . .* See Figure 7.3.

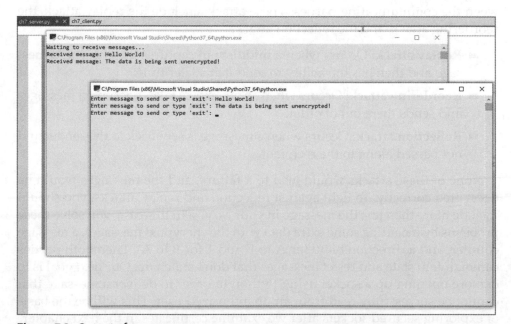

Figure 7.3: Output of `Server.py`

```
# Save as server.py
# Message Receiver
import os
from socket import *
host = ""
port = 13000
buf = 1024
addr = (host, port)
UDPSock = socket(AF_INET, SOCK_DGRAM)
UDPSock.bind(addr)
print ("Waiting to receive messages...")
while True:
    (data, addr) = UDPSock.recvfrom(buf)
    print ("Received message: " + str(data,'utf-8'))
    if data == "exit":
        break
UDPSock.close()
os._exit(0)
```

Create a Client Socket

The next Python code will create the client that will send messages to the server over port 13000. Once the code executes, it will launch a command window that states *Enter message to send or type 'exit'*. Messages entered here will be sent unencrypted to the server. We will explore how to encrypt and decrypt these messages using symmetric encryption. Once you complete the following script, you will be able to send messages from the client to the server, as shown in Figure 7.4.

```
# Save as client.py
# Message Sender
import os
from socket import *
host = "127.0.0.1" # set to IP address of target computer
port = 13000
addr = (host, port)
UDPSock = socket(AF_INET, SOCK_DGRAM)
while True:
    data = input("Enter message to send or type 'exit': ").encode()
    UDPSock.sendto(data, addr)
    if data == "exit":
        break
UDPSock.close()
os._exit(0)
```

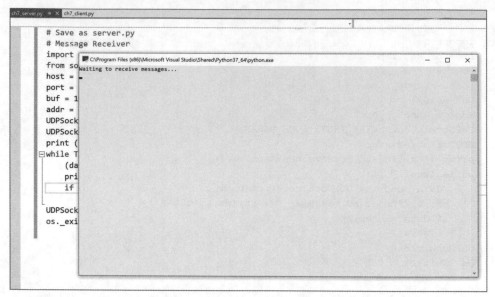

Figure 7.4: Messages entered here will be sent unencrypted to the server.

Create a Threaded Server with TCP

You can expand on your socket knowledge by examining the next code listing. The following script will create a server that you can send messages to via TCP. This example, just like the previous communications, sends data unencrypted from one application to another:

```
import socket
import sys
from _thread import *

host = 'localhost'
port = 5555
print (host, port)

s = socket.socket(socket.AF_INET, socket.SOCK_STREAM)

try:
    s.bind((host, port))
except socket.error as e:
    print(str(e))

s.listen(5)

def threaded_client(conn):
    conn.send(str.encode('Welcome, type your info\n'))
```

```
    while True:
        data = conn.recv(2048)
        reply = 'Server output: '+ data.decode('utf-8')
        if not data:
            break
        conn.sendall(str.encode(reply))
    conn.close()


while True:
    conn, addr = s.accept()
    print('connected to: ' +addr[0] + ':' + str(addr[1]))

    start_new_thread(threaded_client, (conn,))
```

Adding Symmetric Encryption

There is nothing new here; we are now combining elements we learned in this chapter to send data from one application to another. Unlike our previous examples, we will use the Cryptography module's Fernet implementation:

```
# Save as server.py
# Message Receiver
import hashlib
import random
import os
from socket import *
from cryptography.fernet import Fernet

key = Fernet.generate_key()
f = Fernet(key)

print ("The key is :", str(key, 'utf-8'))

host = ""
port = 8080
buf = 1024
addr = (host, port)
UDPSock = socket(AF_INET, SOCK_DGRAM)
UDPSock.bind(addr)
print ("Waiting to receive messages...")

def decrypt(ciphertext):
    try:
        msg = f.decrypt(ciphertext)
    except:
        msg = ciphertext
    return msg
```

```
while True:
    (data, addr) = UDPSock.recvfrom(buf)
    h = hashlib.md5(data)

    plaintext = decrypt(data)
    msg = str(plaintext, 'utf-8')
    print ("Received message: " + msg)
    if msg == "exit":
        break
    if msg == 'newkey':
        key = Fernet.generate_key()
        f = Fernet(key)
        print ("The key is :", str(key, 'utf-8'))

UDPSock.close()
os._exit(0)
```

The preceding code sample should generate a key for the session, as shown in Figure 7.5.

Figure 7.5: `server.py`

The previous implementation will present you with a key. To get both the client and server communicating with each other, you will need to copy and paste the provided key to the client window, as shown in Figure 7.5:

```
# Save as client.py
# Message Sender
import os
from socket import *
from cryptography.fernet import Fernet


host = "127.0.0.1" # set to IP address of target computer
port = 8080
addr = (host, port)
UDPSock = socket(AF_INET, SOCK_DGRAM)
```

```
key = input("Enter the secret key: ")
f = Fernet(key)

def encrypt(plaintext):
    msg = f.encrypt(plaintext)
    return msg

while True:
    data = str(input("Enter message to send or type 'exit': ")).encode()
    ciphertext = encrypt(data)
    UDPSock.sendto(ciphertext, addr)
    if data == b'exit':
        break
    if data == b'newkey':
        key = input("Enter the secret key: ")
        f = Fernet(key)
UDPSock.close()
os._exit(0)
```

The preceding client code should open up a terminal window, as shown in Figure 7.6. Once you paste the server key, you will be able to communicate securely between the two applications.

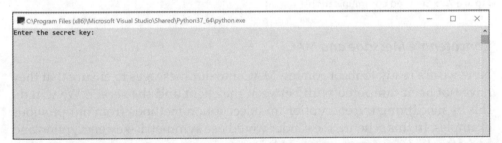

Figure 7.6: `client.py`

Once the correct key is entered, messages from the client will be encrypted and then passed over an unsecured socket; the key is used to encrypt and decrypt the message and must be the same on both sides. The server will attempt to decrypt the message. If the key is wrong, the message will remain encrypted. As a special feature to this code, you can type **newkey** in the client. This will allow you to update the encryption key. Once you have the same key, the communications can be recovered, as shown in Figure 7.7.

We now have a system that is more secure even though it is using an insecure network connection. In the next section, we will concatenate the message and the MAC to improve our system.

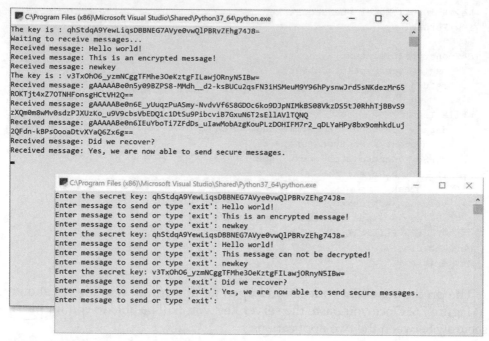

Figure 7.7: Secured communications

Concatenate Message and MAC

Now we are ready to incorporate a MAC into our messages to ensure that they have not been tampered with between the client and the server. We will do this by modifying the encryption and decryption methods from our previous examples. In this scheme, the sender would use symmetric-key encryption and concatenate the message and its MAC to form a composite message that is then encrypted and sent to the recipient. The receiver then decrypts the message using the symmetric key and separates the message and the MAC. The MAC would then provide the authentication, and the encryption provides the confidentiality. This example builds on top of the previous one.

This particular implementation modifies the `decrypt()` function to decrypt the original message and message digest and then strips off the message digest; the next step is to hash the message and compare the message digests to ensure that the message is both secure and proven not to have been tampered with. In these two examples, I am using the MD5 hash, but if you feel like adding HMAC, it will help secure your implementation even further:

```
# Save as server.py
# Message Receiver
```

```
import hashlib
import random
import os
from socket import *
from cryptography.fernet import Fernet

key = Fernet.generate_key()
f = Fernet(key)

print ("The key is :", str(key, 'utf-8'))

host = ""
port = 8080
buf = 1024
addr = (host, port)
UDPSock = socket(AF_INET, SOCK_DGRAM)
UDPSock.bind(addr)
print ("Waiting to receive messages...")

def decrypt(ciphertext):
    try:
        mmac = f.decrypt(ciphertext)
        mlen = len(mmac)
        m = (mmac[0:mlen - 32])
        h = (mmac[-32:])
        msg = m,h
    except:
        msg = ciphertext
    return msg

while True:
    (data, addr) = UDPSock.recvfrom(buf)

    plaintext = decrypt(data)

    h = hashlib.md5(plaintext[0])
    msg = str(plaintext[0], 'utf-8')
    hash = str(plaintext[1], 'utf-8')
    print ("Received message: " + msg)
    print ("Received digest: " + hash)
    print ("Calculated digest: " + h.hexdigest())

    if msg == "exit":
        break
    if msg == 'newkey':
        key = Fernet.generate_key()
        f = Fernet(key)
```

```
        print ("The key is :", str(key, 'utf-8'))

UDPSock.close()
os._exit(0)
```

The preceding code should produce a server that will give you a secret key that can be used in your text client. The difference between the previous examples and this one is that this program will extract the message hash that is received and then generate its own hash to confirm message integrity, as shown in Figure 7.8.

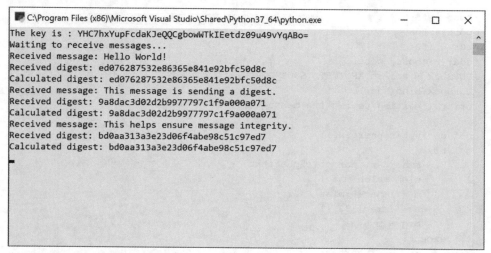

Figure 7.8: Message and MAC server

The client implementation modifies the encrypt function and concatenates the original message digest to the message. The message hash is then displayed on the screen so that you can verify that the hash is making it through the system and is being evaluated correctly:

```
# Save as client.py
# Message Sender
import os
import hashlib
from socket import *
from cryptography.fernet import Fernet


host = "127.0.0.1" # set to IP address of target computer
port = 8080
addr = (host, port)
UDPSock = socket(AF_INET, SOCK_DGRAM)
key = input("Enter the secret key: ")
```

```
    f = Fernet(key)

def encrypt(plaintext):
    h = hashlib.md5(plaintext).hexdigest()

    print("Message hash: " + h)

    mmac = str(str(plaintext,'utf-8') + h).encode()
    msg = f.encrypt(mmac)
    return msg

while True:
    data = str(input("Enter message to send or type 'exit': ")).encode()
    ciphertext = encrypt(data)
    UDPSock.sendto(ciphertext, addr)
    if data == b'exit':
        break
    if data == b'newkey':
        key = input("Enter the secret key: ")
        f = Fernet(key)
UDPSock.close()
os._exit(0)
```

The preceding code sample will generate the message digest and send it to the server so that the server can determine if the received message has been tampered with. Your result should appear similar to Figure 7.9.

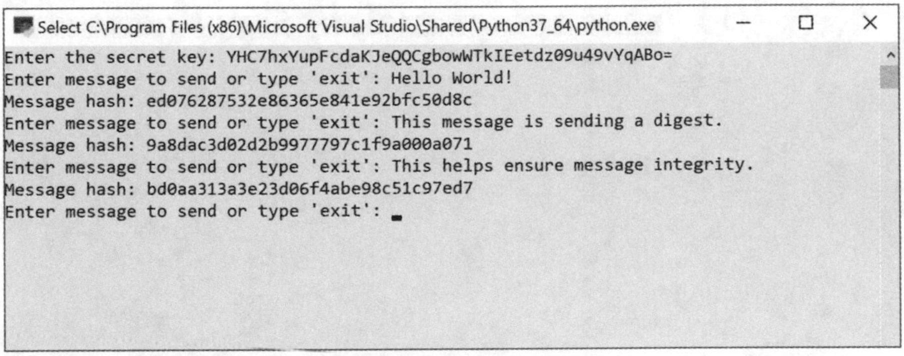

```
Select C:\Program Files (x86)\Microsoft Visual Studio\Shared\Python37_64\python.exe      —   □   ×
Enter the secret key: YHC7hxYupFcdaKJeQQCgbowWTkIEetdz09u49vYqABo=
Enter message to send or type 'exit': Hello World!
Message hash: ed076287532e86365e841e92bfc50d8c
Enter message to send or type 'exit': This message is sending a digest.
Message hash: 9a8dac3d02d2b9977797c1f9a000a071
Enter message to send or type 'exit': This helps ensure message integrity.
Message hash: bd0aa313a3e23d06f4abe98c51c97ed7
Enter message to send or type 'exit': _
```

Figure 7.9: Message and MAC client

Summary

In this chapter, we continued our exploration of hashing algorithms using Python. Hopefully, you understand how to effectively use message digests to protect the integrity of your messages. Algorithms such as SHA1 and MD5 have proven to be victims of birthday attacks and the length extension attack. One of the best ways to improve the security of your messages is to concatenate the message and the message digest in an encrypted form that the recipient can decrypt and verify the message integrity. The implementations in this chapter will help improve the successful tamper-free delivery of your message. In the next chapter, you will gain an understanding of the PKI infrastructure and will use it to add an additional layer of security beyond the network itself.

References

NIST. Aug. 2015. FIPS PUB 180-4. `nvlpubs.nist.gov/nistpubs/FIPS/NIST.FIPS.180-4.pdf`

Secure Hash Standard (shs) - Nist. (n.d.). Retrieved from `nvlpubs.nist.gov/nistpubs/FIPS/NIST.FIPS.180-4.pdf`

## CHAPTER 8

Cryptographic Applications and PKI

Encryption experts are pressed to find ever more effective encryption methods, measured by their security and performance, because the threats presented by hackers are increasingly greater. This is partly because the hackers have become more sophisticated in their attacks, but also because the fallout from an attack gets more severe as our use of data grows. In the previous chapter, we learned how to build a system to encrypt data and send it over an unsecured network. On the other side, a recipient can decrypt the data and verify that the message was not altered and that it was delivered in a secure manner. We will now expand our Python code by introducing public-key infrastructure or, as it is more commonly known, PKI. But what is PKI?

You have a highly classified letter that you need to send to a person on the other side of the world. You believe that the note can be intercepted, so you put the letter in a box, and you padlock it shut. Locking the letter in the box is essentially the same as encrypting the letter; it is another way to protect it. You can now send the letter on its way, but you still have the key. You also need to find a way to get the key to the other side of the world without it being compromised. This is known as the *key distribution problem*, and it is the oldest problem in cryptography.

As you know, the key is the secret recipe for scrambling and unscrambling a secret message. By the 1960s, key distribution was costing a fortune; banks, governments, and big businesses used to pay heavily guarded couriers to travel around the world to deliver keys in person. By early 1970, it was clear that something had to be done, which led to the development of the holy grail of cryptography. In this chapter, you will learn about a secret code so ingenious that it would change the way we communicate forever. Through this chapter, you gain cryptographic knowledge as you:

- Gain an understanding of the importance of PKI
- Learn how to implement a PKI solution in Python
- Gain an understanding of RSA
- Learn how to implement ElGamal
- Gain an understanding of Elliptic Curve Cryptography
- Learn how to implement a key exchange using Diffie-Hellman

The Public-Key Transformation

In 1975, Martin Hellman, Whitfield Diffie, and Ralph Merkle were working in the electrical engineering department at Stanford University; unlike most cryptographers, they worked outside the classified world of military intelligence. The team proposed that, instead of the sender being responsible for encryption, the receiver of the message would be responsible. The proposal asks the receiver for their padlock to lock up the sender's message. The system works because the participants are exchanging padlocks and not the keys themselves. The keys are always with the receiver; this mitigates the keys falling into the wrong hands. Since it is not practical to send physical padlocks, the team had to invent a way to create a mathematical padlock; these are often referred to as *trapdoors*. The mathematical padlock had to be easy to lock but difficult to unlock without the key. Developing the mathematical padlock was not a trivial process since most operations are easy to do one way and easy to reverse. An example is taking a number and then doubling it; for this example, if $x = 20$, and $y = 2 * x$, then $y = 40$. To reverse the process, it is easy to find half of y: $x = y/2$. This is an example of two-way operation. To find the perfect mathematical padlock, it is necessary to find a one-way operation. Multiplication is the perfect tool. If you are given two four-digit numbers and asked to multiply the two numbers together, you can easily complete the task. However, if you are given the product and asked to work backward, that is a much harder problem to solve. To illustrate this example, let's assume you start with the number 3,261,611. Can you provide the two numbers used to produce the number (aka factoring)? Where would you start?

Multiplying two large integers together creates a mathematical lock, but it is also a lock without a key. As such, it is an operation that is irreversible unless you have the mathematical equivalent of a key. Enter Clifford Cocks; Cocks was a British mathematician and cryptographer. In 1973, while working with the GCHQ, the United Kingdom's Government Communication Headquarters, Cocks invented the algorithm that would later be adopted into the RSA algorithm. After arriving at GCHQ, Cocks learned of James Ellis's non-secret encryption idea, which was published in 1969 but never successfully implemented. While many other cryptographers attempted to find a one-way function that would serve as a mathematical lock, Cocks's background in number theory led him to a solution. Because he was at home and not in a classified environment, he was not allowed to write anything down; however, he developed a solution in his head in about 30 minutes:

$$C = M^e \,(\bmod\, N)$$

The function serves as both a mathematical padlock and a key. To gain an understanding of how it works, take two integers: $x = 11$; $y = 17$. These two numbers are your secret key. The numbers produce a product of 187, which you will use in the following equation, substituting 187 for N. This creates a mathematical padlock that is exclusive to you. You will need to keep the values 11 and 17 secret. They are your key, and you will need them later:

$$C = M^{13} \,(\bmod\, 187)$$

From this point, you can make the details of your mathematical padlock public:

From: You

To: Everyone

Subject: My public key example

Message: Please use this algorithm to send me secret messages:

M^{13} (mod 187) = C

To continue the example, assume that someone wants to send you a message. The message is simply the character x, which has an ASCII code of 88. Place 88 into the algorithm in place of M:

88^{13} (mod 187) = C

165 = C

You have encrypted the value of x to 165. You would send the 165 to the message receiver. If the message is intercepted, it is still safe because it was encrypted with Cocks's equation. To decrypt the message, you use the two integers you originally picked. Cocks developed another version of his equation that uses the two secret numbers, 11 and 17, to unlock the mathematical padlock:

$$C^{1/e} \bmod (p-1)\,(q-1) \bmod N = M$$

$$165^{1/13} \bmod (11-1)\,(17-1) = 88$$

With your algorithm being public, one could argue that someone can take the secret key and find the factors used to produce it. Remember, multiplying is a one-way operation, meaning it is difficult to go backward. Greater difficulty is introduced as the numbers become larger. It wouldn't take very long to find that 11 and 17 were the secret numbers when examining 187 since the only numbers that factor into 187 are 1, 11, 17, and 187.

If you come up with two larger numbers that are 300 digits long, then your padlock is secure. Factoring large numbers is hugely time-consuming. While the math can get tough, Cocks invented a super secure encryption system and, more importantly, he solved the key distribution problem. In the end, the Cocks equation was the most important breakthrough in the history of secret codes. The GCHQ was unable to implement the algorithm and classified it top secret, keeping it closely guarded. In fact, it would remain top secret for another 24 years, even though a similar algorithm was published by Rivest, Shamir, and Adleman in 1977.

Ron Rivest, Adi Shamir, and Leonard Adleman, researchers at the Massachusetts Institute of Technology (MIT), developed a similar equation to Cocks's algorithm four years after Cocks. Their breakthrough was also attributed to Rivest's knowledge of number theory. This time, the discovery was in the public arena. Knowing nothing about the British discovery, the team named their cipher Rivest, Shamir, Adleman, better known as RSA. RSA has become one of the most important ciphers ever introduced. Almost every time you transmit credit card details online, the data is encrypted using RSA, making RSA the cornerstone of a multi-billion-dollar e-commerce revolution. So, while the Americans were not the first to invent public-key cryptography, they were the first to bring it out into the public domain where anyone can use it. You can now communicate as privately as a nation-state. You can send messages that cannot be cracked even by the combined efforts of all the world's secret services. For the first time ever, you have access to unbreakable code. Cryptography may be the science of secrecy, but through your continued practice, it is no longer a secret science.

Exploring the Basics of RSA

This first example is a simple implementation of the RSA algorithm that can encrypt and decrypt a message. Note that the keys here are far too small to be of practical use since they are still relatively easy to factor:

```
import random
```

```python
#Euclid's algorithm - Chapter 4
def gcd(a, b):
    while b != 0:
        a, b = b, a % b
    return a

#Euclid's extended algorithm - Chapter 4
def multiplicative_inverse(e, phi):
    d = 0
    x1 = 0
    x2 = 1
    y1 = 1
    temp_phi = phi

    while e > 0:
        temp1 = temp_phi//e
        temp2 = temp_phi - temp1 * e
        temp_phi = e
        e = temp2

        x = x2- temp1* x1
        y = d - temp1 * y1

        x2 = x1
        x1 = x
        d = y1
        y1 = y

    if temp_phi == 1:
        return d + phi

# Verify the number is prime - Chapter 4
def is_prime(num):
    if num == 2:
        return True
    if num < 2 or num % 2 == 0:
        return False
    for n in range(3, int(num**0.5)+2, 2):
        if num % n == 0:
            return False
    return True

def generate_keypair(p, q):
    if not (is_prime(p) and is_prime(q)):
        raise ValueError('Both numbers must be prime.')
    elif p == q:
        raise ValueError('p and q cannot be equal')
    #n = pq
    n = p * q
```

```
        #Phi is the totient of n
        phi = (p-1) * (q-1)

        #Choose an integer e such that e and phi(n) are coprime
        e = random.randrange(1, phi)

        #Use Euclid's Algorithm to verify copprimes for e and phi(n)
        g = gcd(e, phi)
        while g != 1:
            e = random.randrange(1, phi)
            g = gcd(e, phi)

        #Use Extended Euclid's Algorithm to generate the private key
        d = multiplicative_inverse(e, phi)

        #Return public and private keypair
        #Public key is (e, n) and private key is (d, n)
        return ((e, n), (d, n))

def encrypt(pk, plaintext):
    key, n = pk
    #Convert each letter in the plaintext to numbers based on the
character using a^b mod m
    cipher = [(ord(char) ** key) % n for char in plaintext]
    #Return the array of bytes
    return cipher

def decrypt(pk, ciphertext):
    key, n = pk
    #Generate the plaintext based on the ciphertext and key using a^b
mod m
    plain = [chr((char ** key) % n) for char in ciphertext]
    #Return the array of bytes as a string
    return ''.join(plain)


if __name__ == '__main__':

    print ("Chapter 8 - Understanding RSA\n")
    # First 20 prime numbers include:
    # 2, 3, 5, 7, 11, 13, 17, 19, 23, 29, 31, 37, 41, 43, 47, 53, 59,
61, 67, 71
    p = int(input("Enter a prime number: "))
    q = int(input("Enter a second distinct prime number:"))
    print ("\nGenerating your public/private keypairs . . .")
    public, private = generate_keypair(p, q)
    print ("\nYour public key is {} and your private key is {}\n".
format(public, private))
    message = input("Enter a message to encrypt with your public key: ")
    encrypted_msg = encrypt(public, message)
    print ("Your encrypted message is: {}".format(''.join(map(lambda x:
str(x), encrypted_msg))))
```

```
    print ("\nDecrypting message with your personal private key ",
private ," . . .")
    print ("\nYour message is: {}\n\n".format(decrypt(private,
encrypted_msg)))
```

To produce the output in Figure 8.1, enter 11 as your first prime and 17 as your second.

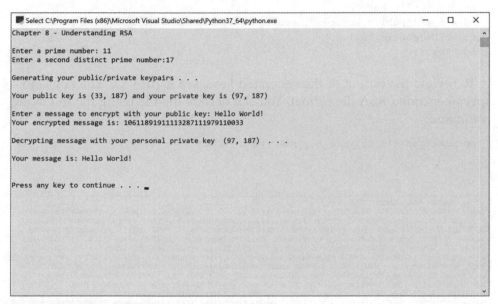

Figure 8.1: Understanding RSA

Generating RSA Certificates

For our next example, we will utilize the PyCrypto library and import the RSA module. In the next code listing, you will generate a new RSA key and then export the private and public aspects of the key into variables that are then saved as certificates to disk. The keys here are much larger than used in the previous example, which makes them much harder to crack. You may notice that this program is also much slower due to the increased time it takes to find the coprime key pair as the key size increases:

```
#ch8_Generate_RSA_Certs.py
from Crypto.PublicKey import RSA

#Generate a public/private key pair using 4096 bits key length (512
bytes)
new_key = RSA.generate(4096, e=65537)

#The private key in PEM format
private_key = new_key.exportKey("PEM")
```

```
#The public key in PEM Format
public_key = new_key.publickey().exportKey("PEM")

print (private_key)
fd = open("private_key.pem", "wb")
fd.write(private_key)
fd.close()

print (public_key)
fd = open("public_key.pem", "wb")
fd.write(public_key)
fd.close()
```

To review the output of the generated keys, see Figure 8.2. The key is in a special encoded RSA file format. You can decode the file using the following command:

```
openssl rsa -in private_key.pem -text -noout
```

```
b'-----BEGIN RSA PRIVATE KEY-----
\nMIIJKAIBAAKCAgEAnlVY+KmAB4T3dNs+jjjEumbBMP7tKR3+zlIlv4/7VL8PmtdT\n20810aOv+IDEtYVNg4KWIeUr6vKJ2
xU/CgRBOkxSA9w6gCcwxpPHKxfR+1rAVdug\n4k5gua+xBJPgenWz6V8rOBBvFoJkrAGrZ/i7J6Txg3q8bcTvuad3C55aeimJ
D6UF\nphCV7kZ9VRHCxp6nJYc+KFvHFoBC14yXy8hui/QkPaZm+muL+bOPm/k9kskhPw55\nMlyIBr4ViCuemfCP2H/VONnt5
zWXaGM//DFAcQX5Sm82s9H5dRWMSsxJEoUViuYr\nepSN0Ls1Z2VSIiWqdLjRi9VTCQS4AoVpmBku5UAlL3o+0qAwOqFEdmhi
rt1Hd7a7\n9pdxU4AaUukGHSHTBlFTaqDXtoQaoAb3zghFCt6gR9Z5H0XgSVkt0uXmZ9WYFOy2\nTV9mX/oe4FZ3OTwf+RQAm
/j0mzyQDNq0z5FisVHvN6IriPKzMCWAfgZm+Mgq9UhH\nJy8hPsowo8FIVNwCALxDAy+a23PZ6oG0bzTjBN9VuQs4kOgMk3vK
+vEk7VJG8CD1\nd/nX0FxlNvN13IsR2vtQcSNJ3I0/LH62Cvdo1PhdDpmjncGOkeoTVoQhKs0xi8Wm\n/4hIa4VTjeTLXm29b
QD7X9npQmJ0nmLwrJ9QCPEVfTK7bI2UFZNeezanG68CAwEA\nAQKCAgBUjjG4ghSsb1cToe5TV3/AKBXuC4Yt2iX0mywrlEHd
bTdxMqNG0Ira3Pah\n2Gq0od7WZ4uzyEZe722tgTgsKj+HWbDG/PqE6+kBc3P+0HbELB/g+ix+Duta3rfD\nQRG1dFxDOh7Dj
ws0UyheL3oRSWTxdAXCeG5elLiNRiCuJMAe00WuBCvzFpJrMFvI\nbXa+SYXr5cDNHs5Advi7UgrSulRHC3e7ML136K1VCY6c
9krqs9y8ZwdU5YqDR0oK\ncXj+rtiy/vn50hhZzGXySmamUMsgUNdj5+anu2/kFkDYxSYU7NunVOpNST4/BWKh\nSBvHvq08N
+M4MRFqFIoMVqEgp/pBfb/v4omMZOnvOcQchHlPGWoK4JzBjzVtbR32\nrJuTRxKOqwPkXX+f0QylqMPlTNY2i12BjVhnFaOl
0/9Q+EENRqiT3FW0QHJT4Bvb\npiluLFREp5tf0X+oacsrwKMiySDXxz2yo902iq3/zLa/U+A5davbcltfB0VmmMkx\nvE5Lq
qoiL5eCBjp+Ezgmu8fskBNbYHZoqsPgor0H2qqaKb6Cx9KAuH7kM0ypqKzG\nzNu6nWx65fIkL0vlwNCpufBte7V+Re+U12rR
2c6KHRSq9oGyTRrEHVmRu6MczbWZ\nfHhDwQrVjrOxVZE39Yj6adZpdkyoJxfEK1uAjn0JQIBSgv7naQKCAQEAt5tKixcY\nt
7tngNAr0HjorI/ePK8vCp7V+6x5Jg5IB3xxFBltyYAnDSUmhm6dGcy3ga0W3Y7K\nITCy/eeRXonrtPvoKYwi87n6+19sVlvM
fD1uj8cK9VMa3YGMvWnTL1J/G2hgEXEv\nSJpY/IOZWx18Ys16DCEhGxM143Q81c1J86MnVUP1IkvyLdx96DV9cG4CTKRFVZA
U\nKIHeC2erU/VmXa8ZyPKx1Hn51De+viL00HKPK5+NiljJE+f3inx5+ekvc2FabEBC\nhex90Wk/vWjKmwIdQSJ/OCbn7erz
oW3Lyx7AfzqMe2RzIQp72kUprFTaeC08K3JF\nobN4HyuBl4ylewKCAQEA3MMNap0FnfLQ3IlmINHhf1FVXAExK/Ech8p5wTI
3spGV\nZVmIRGiWFFHM4IM8leFjZGkOw3YcBEycijXi6V4263TqBoqtGaqXwSeKR7zF1aRv\nnDw3Dn8UYLEwOJDD48X0UlNQ6
81mvrSaJeZbvqmBCxAyJz61Jbs2If0gA7nqAZc3G\nnd5SsH5N5nqeTB8ssbf42R88W4Uy9GLy6bgHj9sxEAOEf4ixVgFhh94z
n11R4nQbw\nnryfjOn8Qjr9EJiynN815EO6440mV4EASea2bX0Q5Fj5QqpWjc0kW69n7rzR2tMyi\nPZ3rrkHiq4TkRjRVkncu
TG+Kfo0NmUNetMvp7BmaXQKCAQEAj2gnjQP5NmiVqzLt\nReNqOH4WYuehonX1RKGt719xOwejesNx0NTbq5S8xntXEXOoUQz
UszB4B/x1kYNx\nnM5oeFDo9V1YxZpR4yCX8BGenC9MfrAUXNg43CZPKTZd+b5PL26hmgLka6WZE4tYW\nzef142YCUb7+kJsg
GMwNFiEmNbnVWu+w5FzVR6TUYq6Ez2/dM+eKkA388Laeq+HJ\nG8assbe2OBH3e7Hzkj8IKJI9DSKtWLFCaDB4vaeM3Qnka6I
KgeAkNDDsxJW2n/3I\n3z2eK3w3RUygeUdKF7ZPnGKZrojSaY1ddHM8yS3bFty2c/fCu+L5ACY85NO8mvvs\nnoGaOSQKCAQAW
LaJTa6L800AYZ9VSxsMYv1sL+zKtb3OmULkap6jgz69qlywRc1Bg\nnijdC9uxHQnVxyPwqttrps6imWfOJ7mUmEoDQV248fd7
xEL/bpSNa60IdCQz2KB7d\nlGZ3TFQ2LpK6wPeLKx9zDcQR6w/41eLfP0M5EZDHCO8Fmn49dyEfGSUvLkh8g5xc\nTAmBZu/3
vOpHHI7343W73nn8QORbrvnF/NfvKPUOB9MPw6Am8CWN4PydHCy/27QW\nnIzD9hM7n1EStZs48R1A/TzCL+Nz7HSd/DJOeD5p
OIoui9itK1sJ2N3ilKABdaVEU\nnWil0wB04sbB9DVekjxcmppYFI9dEWO4hAoIBAG/KBvzRhXdNVLj/0bdQWhY4jZbt\nTa2Y
K/vtNao3MHgyDMlsX1ZrJlsE/UMgCsFgESWzTkTH/p7mvqdt0mDjwmMg8HOV\nnv0Z10LGzpebJwouwCoMVxRrdvafovMwNLum
MLfiN6GWlZBxpLTPdv0az1aQ4wJL9\nnby1heRWedG6q4BXn4SH7xvtXQj/uF9tcOh8kj+9B8rOF/gwWbnWIr9wyEI151T5\n
x91154MlQFmRpQ3KxqhT6sCPtJsiZo291V9u2PmdF9n7F1KEnkPjguf1zPQ3qx6K\nDMhSsF/Dek5XWuBBCM/posqa0H4Pk5X
PPJsUHZFk9F/c8mDBosQkL3jmpCI=\n-----END RSA PRIVATE KEY-----'
b'-----BEGIN PUBLIC KEY-----
\nMIICIjANBgkqhkiG9w0BAQEFAAOCAg8AMIICCgKCAgEAnlVY+KmAB4T3dNs+jjjE\numbBMP7tKR3+zlIlv4/7VL8PmtdT2
0810aOv+IDEtYVNg4KWIeUr6vKJ2xU/CgRB\nOkxSA9w6gCcwxpPHKxfR+1rAVdug4k5gua+xBJPgenWz6V8rOBBvFoJkrAGr
Z/i7\nnJ6Txg3q8bcTvuad3C55aeimJD6UFphCV7kZ9VRHCxp6nJYc+KFvHFoBC14yXy8hu\ni/QkPaZm+muL+bOPm/k9kskhP
w55MlyIBr4ViCuemfCP2H/VONnt5zWXaGM//DFA\ncQX5Sm82s9H5dRWMSsxJEoUViuYrepSN0Ls1Z2VSIiWqdLjRi9VTCQS4
AoVpmBku\n5UAlL3o+0qAwOqFEdmhirt1Hd7a79pdxU4AaUukGHSHTBlFTaqDXtoQaoAb3zghF\nnCt6gR9Z5H0XgSVkt0uXmZ
9WYFOy2TV9mX/oe4FZ3OTwf+RQAm/j0mzyQDNq0z5Fi\nnsVHvN6IriPKzMCWAfgZm+Mgq9UhHJy8hPsowo8FIVNwCALxDAy+a
23PZ6oG0bzTj\nBN9VuQs4kOgMk3vK+vEk7VJG8CD1d/nX0FxlNvN13IsR2vtQcSNJ3I0/LH62Cvdo\n1PhdDpmjncGOkeoTV
oQhKs0xi8Wm/4hIa4VTjeTLXm29bQD7X9npQmJ0nmLwrJ9Q\nCPEVfTK7bI2UFZNeezanG68CAwEAAQ==\n-----END
PUBLIC KEY-----'
```

Figure 8.2: Generating RSA certs

Constructing Simple Text Encryption and Decryption with RSA Certificates

In the next code listing, we'll use the RSA certificates we created in the previous section to encrypt and decrypt a simple message: *To be encrypted*. The module uses the RSA encryption protocol according to PKCS#1 OAEP, and the scheme is more properly known as RSAES-OAEP. At the receiver side, decryption can be done using the private part of the RSA key:

```
from Crypto.Cipher import PKCS1_OAEP
from Crypto.PublicKey import RSA

message = b'To be encrypted'
key = RSA.importKey(open('public_key.pem').read())
cipher = PKCS1_OAEP.new(key)
ciphertext = cipher.encrypt(message)

print (ciphertext)

key = RSA.importKey(open('private_key.pem').read())
cipher = PKCS1_OAEP.new(key)
plaintext = cipher.decrypt(ciphertext)

print (plaintext)
```

Figure 8.3 shows the results of the previous code. The message entered is "To be encrypted." You will see the RSA encrypted output followed by the decryption back to plaintext.

```
b'\x90f\xe4\xcb\xce\xffT\xf3Q\x1d\x1c\x9c+\xa3\x81M\xea\xc3\xac
\xd4\x13\x06\xfb1\x81\x93}\'\x93\xaa\xa2\x07\x9e*)y_\xf7}|\xe1%\xc9a\xf9\xf8n\xef
\xc0^\xf3\x17\xc9\x9d\x98\x89\x8a\xe8\x06\xd6\x03U\x90\xa4\xf8\xf0MX1\xea
\x11\xd27\xd51\x90\xdbz=\xb5K\xf9;\x88lQ\x8d\xc3M\x179\xec2C8\x94A\x1bp\xcdmIPS&
\x91h\x87\xe5\xd4\xf2\xd8\x8b\x9e\x89\xd6SB\xcd\x9d\xfbI\xa9\xaa\xe0\x0f]\xbd\xab
\xe4\xff\\^\xef\xb7\x0c\x0c\x0e\xbfL\x8fxP\x11e\xa0l\xb5\x8d\xd3\xf6\xaa\x1f\xc7i
\xae\xdf\x8d\xa5\x9d\x0f:\x11\r\x80\x9f\x1f\x10\xea\x11\xcetT
\x17\xa8\xb1\xde1\xc3\xd9J\x9ay\x92._X\xa2\x15\xbb\xd4\t\x95\xc5\xd1\x1cE#E
\xf4\xeb\xe5\x19\x94\x83\xc8.9\xd0\xe6t\xf0R]\xf5\r\x13?\xc6\xb4\xe1\x9c\x90\x08a:
\xa7\xbd\xb3s(e\x92\x1a\xcc"/\xd9\x1bD\x06^\xe8\xde>\x10\x0b(\xd9\x0f
\x04\xb5\x18\xd8\xa4\x1a\x8c\xf5jq\x96\xac\x94\x11\x0b\x18\x95wW\xafd\x1f\xb6R?
\xe1(\xd0\xe5\x0c/\xb0(\xb6YL\x83\x17\xd0g4\x19\xb1\x18\xd3\xc3\xda?@&
\x03\xf5\xa2\xde\xe6\x14b61\xd2@\xa9;v\xaaN\x90\xd9$5\xcc;r\xe3\x8f
\xe6\xc6`6\xb1\xf3\xf0\x85\xae>\xa3s\xc8\xe31\xca8\xa2\x0c-\x1e\xe9\x9b\x9b\xec
\x8f\xba\x82\xb6\xcb\x0b\x99\xcc\xa5\x9fx|\xb2\x90\xac\x83\xb7I\x93\xf0\xdf#
\x97\xbf~\xb8\xdfN\xc9\x063|\x12\xf3\xcc\xac\xa1?>-\x9fI+)\xbax$\x93k\xea\x9a
\xe9\x15f\xc7\'\\\xbb\xf4\xb7X|\xbe\x08(\x16i\x17\x8c6\xa4\x89\xbc\x91\xf8\xdc
\xd6\x0bA\xccB:\x87:\xb3\x95<X\xcdB\xf9op6`f\xf0P\xeb\xda5\xa6\xd4#\xb8\xcb~\xc0FD
\x9d7<ZT\xd2\n\x8b\x9d\x00\x89j\x96.,\xa9\x92\xdc\x1f_\xd1M&\xfb\x8d\xd4z^\xff
\x84\x9awi_q\x9c\xe7\xe6\x12\xf3\xda\xf6\x1d\x01\xd0T\x83\xc2E\x8c\xc8<'

b'To be encrypted'
```

Figure 8.3: RSA decrypt

If you try to encrypt larger messages, you will get an exception because the key length limits the maximum message length. In the next section, we will craft a more robust solution using the same concepts we just applied. Our next recipe will demonstrate how to encrypt and decrypt a wide variety of data using the PKI infrastructure.

Constructing BLOB Encryption and Decryption with RSA Certificates

In the previous section, you were able to encrypt and decrypt data using a PKI infrastructure, but the size of the message was limited. Examine the following Python demo, which will take an image and encrypt it using RSA and then decrypt it. It works with larger amounts of data by encrypting the image in key-size chunks. The resulting code will produce both an encrypted image and a decrypted image that should match the original:

```python
#ch8_RSA_blob.py
import zlib
import base64
from Crypto.PublicKey import RSA
from Crypto.Cipher import PKCS1_OAEP
from pathlib import Path

# Generate new key pair function
def generate_new_key_pair():
    # Generate a public/private key pair using 4096 bits key length
(512 bytes)
    new_key = RSA.generate(4096, e=65537)

    # The private key in PEM format
    private_key = new_key.exportKey("PEM")

    # The public key in PEM Format
    public_key = new_key.publickey().exportKey("PEM")

    private_key_path = Path('private.pem')
    private_key_path.touch(mode=0o600)
    private_key_path.write_bytes(private_key)

    public_key_path = Path('public.pem')
    public_key_path.touch(mode=0o664)
    public_key_path.write_bytes(public_key)


# RSA Encryption Function
def encrypt_blob(blob, public_key):
    #Import the public key and use for encryption using PKCS1_OAEP
    rsa_key = RSA.importKey(public_key)
    rsa_key = PKCS1_OAEP.new(rsa_key)
```

```
    #compress the data first
    blob = zlib.compress(blob)
    #In determining the chunk size, determine the private key length
used in bytes
    #and subtract 42 bytes (when using PKCS1_OAEP). The data will be
encrypted
    #in chunks
    chunk_size = 470
    offset = 0
    end_loop = False
    encrypted = bytearray()

    while not end_loop:
        #The chunk
        chunk = blob[offset:offset + chunk_size]

        #If the data chunk is less than the chunk size, then we need to
add
        #padding with " ". This indicates that we reached the end of the
file
        #so we end loop here
        if len(chunk) % chunk_size != 0:
            end_loop = True
            #chunk += b" " * (chunk_size - len(chunk))
            chunk += bytes(chunk_size - len(chunk))
        #Append the encrypted chunk to the overall encrypted file
        encrypted += rsa_key.encrypt(chunk)

        #Increase the offset by chunk size
        offset += chunk_size

    #Base 64 encode the encrypted file
    return base64.b64encode(encrypted)

# RSA Decryption Function
def decrypt_blob(encrypted_blob, private_key):

    # Import the private key and use for decryption using PKCS1_OAEP
    rsakey = RSA.importKey(private_key)
    rsakey = PKCS1_OAEP.new(rsakey)

    # Base 64 decode the data
    encrypted_blob = base64.b64decode(encrypted_blob)

    # In determining the chunk size, determine the private key length
used in bytes.
    # The data will be decrypted in chunks
    chunk_size = 512
    offset = 0
    decrypted = bytearray()
```

```
        # keep loop going as long as we have chunks to decrypt
        while offset < len(encrypted_blob):
            # The chunk
            chunk = encrypted_blob[offset: offset + chunk_size]

            # Append the decrypted chunk to the overall decrypted file
            decrypted += rsakey.decrypt(chunk)

            # Increase the offset by chunk size
            offset += chunk_size

    # return the decompressed decrypted data
    return zlib.decompress(decrypted)


# generate_new_key_pair() # run if you don't already have a key pair

print("This program is looking for an image named 'cloud.jpg'.")

private_key = open('private_key.pem').read()

print("The private key has been read.")

public_key = open('public_key.pem').read()

print("The public key has been read.")

unencrypted_file = Path('cloud.jpg')
encrypted_file = unencrypted_file.with_suffix('.dat')
encrypted_blob = encrypt_blob(unencrypted_file.read_bytes(), public_key)

print("The cloud has been encrypted.")

# Write the encrypted contents to a file
fd = open("e_cloud.jpg", "wb")
fd.write(encrypted_blob)
fd.close()

print("The encrypted image is named e_cloud.jpg")

# Our candidate file to be decrypted
fd = open("e_cloud.jpg", "r")
encrypted_blob = fd.read()
fd.close()

print()
print("The contents of the encrypted file is too long to print.")
print()

# Write the decrypted contents to a file
fd = open("d_cloud.jpg", "wb")
```

```
fd.write(decrypt_blob(encrypted_blob, private_key))
fd.close()

# Decrypt the encrypted blob
decrypt_blob(encrypted_blob, private_key)

print("The cloud has been decrypted. Examine the d_cloud.jpg file.")
```

Figure 8.4 shows the output for the RSA BLOB program.

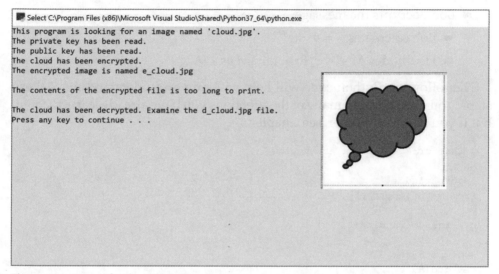

Figure 8.4: Output for the RSA BLOB program

The El-Gamal Cryptosystem

El-Gamal encryption is a public-key cryptosystem. As with the previous use of RSA, El-Gamal uses asymmetric key encryption for communicating between two parties and encrypting the message. This cryptosystem is based on the difficulty of finding a discrete logarithm in a cyclic group. That is, even if we know g^a and g^k, it is extremely difficult to compute g^{ak}. In this section, we will examine the basic idea of the cryptosystem with an example using cryptography's favorite couple: Alice and Bob.

Suppose Alice wants to communicate to Bob.

- Bob generates a public and a private key:
  - Bob chooses a very large number q and a cyclic group F_q.
  - From the cyclic group F_q, he chooses any element g and an element a such that $\gcd(a, q) = 1$.
  - Then he computes $h = g^a$.

- Bob publishes F, $h = g^a$, q, and g as his public key and retains a as his private key.
- Alice encrypts data using Bob's public key:
  - Alice selects an element k from cyclic group F such that $\gcd(k, q) = 1$.
  - Then she computes $p = g^k$ and $s = h^k = g^{ak}$.
  - She multiplies s with M.
  - Then she sends $(p, M{*}s) = (g^k, M{*}s)$.
- Bob decrypts the message:
  - Bob calculates $s' = p^a = g^{ak}$.
  - He divides $M{*}s$ by s' to obtain M as $s = s'$.

The following Python code will help you gain an understanding of these steps. You should notice many of the functions you have already learned about, but if you need a refresher, see Chapter 4.

```python
# Chapter 8 - ElGamal encryption

import random
from math import pow

a = random.randint(2, 10)

# Compute the GCD
def gcd(a, b):
    if a < b:
        return gcd(b, a)
    elif a % b == 0:
        return b;
    else:
        return gcd(b, a % b)

# Generating large random numbers
def gen_key(q):

    key = random.randint(pow(10, 20), q)
    while gcd(q, key) != 1:
        key = random.randint(pow(10, 20), q)

    return key

# Compute the power
def power(a, b, c):
    x = 1
    y = a

    while b > 0:
        if b % 2 == 0:
```

```
            x = (x * y) % c;
        y = (y * y) % c
        b = int(b / 2)


    return x % c

# Encrypt the message
def encrypt(msg, q, h, g):

    en_msg = []

    k = gen_key(q)# Private key for sender
    s = power(h, k, q)
    p = power(g, k, q)

    for i in range(0, len(msg)):
        en_msg.append(msg[i])

    print("g^k used : ", p)
    print("g^ak used : ", s)
    for i in range(0, len(en_msg)):
        en_msg[i] = s * ord(en_msg[i])

    return en_msg, p

# Decrypt the message
def decrypt(en_msg, p, key, q):

    dr_msg = []
    h = power(p, key, q)
    for i in range(0, len(en_msg)):
        dr_msg.append(chr(int(en_msg[i]/h)))

    return dr_msg


def main():

    msg = 'Please do not let the enemy know our position.'
    print("Original Message :", msg)
    print()

    q = random.randint(pow(10, 20), pow(10, 50))
    g = random.randint(2, q)

    key = gen_key(q)# Private key for receiver
    h = power(g, key, q)
    print("g used : ", g)
    print("g^a used : ", h)

    en_msg, p = encrypt(msg, q, h, g)
    dr_msg = decrypt(en_msg, p, key, q)
```

```
        dmsg = ''.join(dr_msg)
        print ()
        print ("The encrypted message :", en_msg)
        print ()
        print("Decrypted Message :", dmsg);
        print ()



if __name__ == '__main__':
    main()
```

The preceding recipe should take the message "Please do not let the enemy know our position." and generate an ElGamal key that is used to encrypt and decrypt the message. Examine Figure 8.5. The program displays the g^a and g^k that is produced along with the g^{ak}.

Figure 8.5: ElGamal key

Elliptic Curve Cryptography

Now that you have a better understanding of how the more traditional algorithms work using Python, we will examine an alternative approach that is considered a more efficient type of public-key cryptography: elliptic curve cryptography, or as it is more simply known, ECC. The security of the cryptosystem lies within the difficulty of solving discrete logarithms on the field defined by specific equations computed over a curve; the group of cryptographic algorithms were introduced in 1985 and were based on the esoteric branch of mathematics called *elliptic curves*. Although the system was introduced in the mid '80s, it took another twenty years for the cryptosystem to gain wide acceptance. Several factors are contributing to its increasing popularity. First, the security of 1024-bit RSA encryption is degrading due to faster computing and a better understanding and analysis of encryption methods. While brute force is still unlikely to crack 1024-bit RSA keys, other approaches, including highly intensive parallel computing in distributed computing arrays, are resulting in more sophisticated attacks. These attacks have reduced the effectiveness of this level of security. Even 2,048-bit encryption is estimated by the RSA Security to be effective only until 2030. A second factor that is contributing to the adoption of ECC is that many government entities have started to accept ECC as an encryption method. Third, the authentication speed of ECC is faster than RSA in terms of server authentication. Finally, certificate authorities have started embedding ECC algorithms into their SSL certificates.

ECC was independently suggested by Neal Koblitz (University of Washington) and Victor S. Miller (IBM) in 1985. After the introduction of Diffie-Hellman and RSA, cryptographers started exploring other mathematics-based cryptographic solutions looking for other algorithms that would offer easy one-way calculations that were hard to find an inverse for; these types of functions are referred to as trapdoors. A trapdoor function is a function that is easy to perform one way but has a secret that is required to perform the inverse calculation efficiently. That is, if f is a trapdoor function, then $y = f(x)$ is easy to compute, but $x = f - 1(y)$ is hard to compute without some special knowledge k. Unless you have a mathematical background, elliptic curves may be new to you; so what exactly is an elliptic curve and how does the elliptic curve trapdoor function work?

An elliptic curve is the set of points that satisfy a specific mathematical equation. The equation for an elliptic curve looks something like this:

$$y^2 = x^3 + ax + b$$

That graphs to something that looks like Figure 8.6.

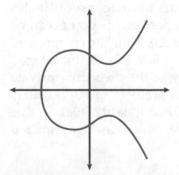

Figure 8.6: An elliptic curve

The most important takeaway for this section is that you understand that ECC produces encryption keys based on using points on a curve to define the public and private keys. An ECC key is very helpful for the current generation as more people are moving to the smartphone. As the utilization of smartphones continues to grow, there is an emerging need for a more flexible encryption for business to meet with increasing security requirements.

The elliptic curve cryptography certificates allow key size to remain small while providing a higher level of security. The ECC certificate key creation method is entirely different from previous algorithms, while relying on the use of a public key for encryption and a private key for decryption. By starting small and with a slow growth potential, ECC has a longer potential life span. Elliptic curves are likely to be the next generation of cryptographic algorithms, and we are seeing the beginning of their use now.

When you compare ECC with other algorithms like RSA, you will find the ECC key is significantly smaller yet offers the same level of security. One notable instance is that a 3,072-bit RSA key takes 768 bytes, whereas the equally strong NIST P-256 private key only takes 32 bytes (that is, 256 bits). PyCryptodome offers us an ECC module that provides mechanisms for generating new ECC keys, exporting and importing them using widely supported formats like PEM or DER. To install PyCryptodome, execute the following pip command:

```
pip install pycryptodome
```

If you're worried about ensuring the highest level of security while maintaining performance, it makes sense to adopt ECC.

Generating ECC Keys

ECC private keys are integers that represent the curve's field size; the typical size is 256 bits. A 256-bit private key would look like the following:

```
0x51897b64e85c3f714bba707e867914295a1377a7463a9dae8ea6a8b914246319
```

Generating an ECC key requires generating a random integer within a specified range.

The public keys in the ECC are EC points—pairs of integer coordinates {x, y}, lying on the curve. Due to their special properties, EC points can be compressed to just one coordinate + 1 bit (odd or even). Thus the compressed public key, corresponding to a 256-bit ECC private key, is a 257-bit integer. An example of an ECC public key (corresponding to the preceding private key, encoded in the Ethereum format, as hex with prefix 02 or 03) is 0x02f5 4ba86dc1ccb5bed0224d23f01ed87e4a443c47fc690d7797a13d41d2340e1. In this format, the public key takes 33 bytes (66 hex digits), which can be optimized to exactly 257 bits.

The following example demonstrates how to generate a new ECC key, export it, and reload it back into your program. The code uses the NIST P-256 algorithm, which is the most-used elliptic curve, and there are no reasons to believe it's insecure:

```
from Crypto.PublicKey import ECC
key = ECC.generate(curve='P-256')
f = open('myprivatekey.pem','wt')
f.write(key.export_key(format='PEM'))
f.close()
f = open('myprivatekey.pem','rt')
key = ECC.import_key(f.read())
print (key)
```

The key generated will look similar to the following:

```
EccKey(curve='NIST P-256',
point_x=855113179251930915915380005554467283386311991513737248626228047210
0045098335773,
point_y=628340279585450803474544915532061331165702608792911648142249285993
82610602892,
d=206364178669833714313004378849899155839757351483697034158227768943776816
06808)
```

Key Lengths and Curves

The ECC algorithms have many strengths, including the variety of elliptic curves that can be used; each curve offers different levels of security, which extends a variable of cryptographic strength. Each type of curve also presents a variety of performance and key lengths. The ECC curves that are provided in our libraries provide the ability to have named curves such as Curve25519 or Secp256k1.

Curve25519 provides 128 bits of security and is designed for use with the Elliptic Curve Diffie-Hellman key scheme; it is considered one of the fastest ECC curves and is publicly available. Secp256k1 is an elliptic curve that is used in Bitcoin's public-key cryptography and is defined in the Standards of Efficient Cryptography (SEC). Another benefit to Secp256k1 is that unlike the popular NIST curves, Secp256k1's constants were selected in a predictable way, which significantly reduces the possibility that the curve's creator inserted any sort of backdoor into the curve. ECC keys have length, which directly depends on the underlying curve. Following is a list of common ECC named curves and their key lengths:

- **secp192r1:** 192-bit
- **sect233k1:** 233-bit
- **secp224k1:** 224-bit
- **secp256k1:** 256-bit

- **NIST P-256:** 256-bit
- **Curve25519:** 256-bit
- **sect283k1:** 283-bit
- **p384:** 384-bit
- **secp384r1:** 384-bit
- **sect409r1:** 409-bit
- **Curve41417:** 414-bit
- **Curve448-Goldilocks:** 448-bit
- **M-511:** 511-bit
- **P-521:** 521-bit
- **sect571k1:** 571-bit

Diffie-Hellman Key Exchange

The history of cryptography can be split into two eras: the classical era and the modern era. The turning point between the two occurred in 1977, when both the RSA algorithm and the Diffie-Hellman key exchange algorithm were introduced. These new algorithms were revolutionary because they represented the first viable cryptographic schemes where security was based on the theory of numbers; they were the first to enable secure communication between two parties without a shared secret. Cryptography went from being about securely transporting secret codebooks around the world to being able to have provably secure communication between any two parties without worrying about someone listening in on the key exchange.

The Diffie-Hellman algorithm was developed to create secure communications over a public network using ECC to generate points on the curve and get the secret key using parameters; for our exploration we will consider four variables that include P, G, A, B:

P: One prime number; publicly available.

G: A primitive root of P. You may remember that a primitive root of a prime is an integer such that the modulus has multiplicative order; publicly available.

A: A user (Alice) picks private values for A and B and use them to generate a key to exchange publicly with a second user (Bob).

B: The second user (Bob), receives the key from Alice and uses it to generate a secret key; this gives both users the same secret key to encrypt.

Examine Figure 8.7x to see how the points intersect with the ECC.

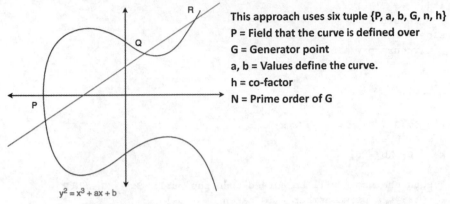

This approach uses six tuple {P, a, b, G, n, h}
P = Field that the curve is defined over
G = Generator point
a, b = Values define the curve.
h = co-factor
N = Prime order of G

$y^2 = x^3 + ax + b$

Figure 8.7: Point intersection of ECC curve

To get a better understanding, review the following five steps:

1. Alice and Bob get public numbers $P = 23$, $G = 9$.
2. Each user selects a private key:
   - Alice selected a private key $a = 4$
   - Bob selected a private key $b = 3$
3. Each user computes public values:
   - Alice: $x = (9{\wedge}4 \bmod 23) = (6561 \bmod 23) = 6$
   - Bob: $y = (9{\wedge}3 \bmod 23) = (729 \bmod 23) = 16$
4. Alice and Bob exchange public numbers:
   - Alice receives public key $y = 16$
   - Bob receives public key $x = 6$
5. Alice and Bob compute symmetric keys:
   - Alice: $ka = y{\wedge}a \bmod p = 65536 \bmod 23 = 9$
   - Bob: $kb = x{\wedge}b \bmod p = 216 \bmod 23 = 9$

The completed process generates 9, which is the shared secret. Notice this value was never shared between the two parties. Review the following code to see how to implement Diffie-Hellman in Python:

```python
def power(a, b, p):
    if (b == 1):
        return a;
    else:
        return pow(a,b,p)


def main():

    P = 0; G = 0; x = 0; a = x;
    y = 0; b = 0;
    ka = 0; kb = 0;

    # Both the users will be agreed upon the public keys G and P
    P = 23; # A prime number P is taken
    print("The value of P:", P);

    G = 9; # A primitive root for P, G is taken
    print("The value of G:", G);

    # Alice will choose the private key a
    a = 4; # a is the chosen private key
    print("The private key a for Alice:", a);
    x = power(G, a, P); # gets the generated key

    # Bob will choose the private key b
    b = 3; # b is the chosen private key
    print("The private key b for Bob:", b);
    y = power(G, b, P); # gets the generated key

    # Generating the secret key after the exchange of keys
    ka = power(y, a, P); # Secret key for Alice
    kb = power(x, b, P); # Secret key for Bob

    print("Secret key for the Alice is:", ka);
    print("Secret Key for the Bob is:", kb);


if __name__ == '__main__':
    main()
```

Your results should look like those shown in Figure 8.8.

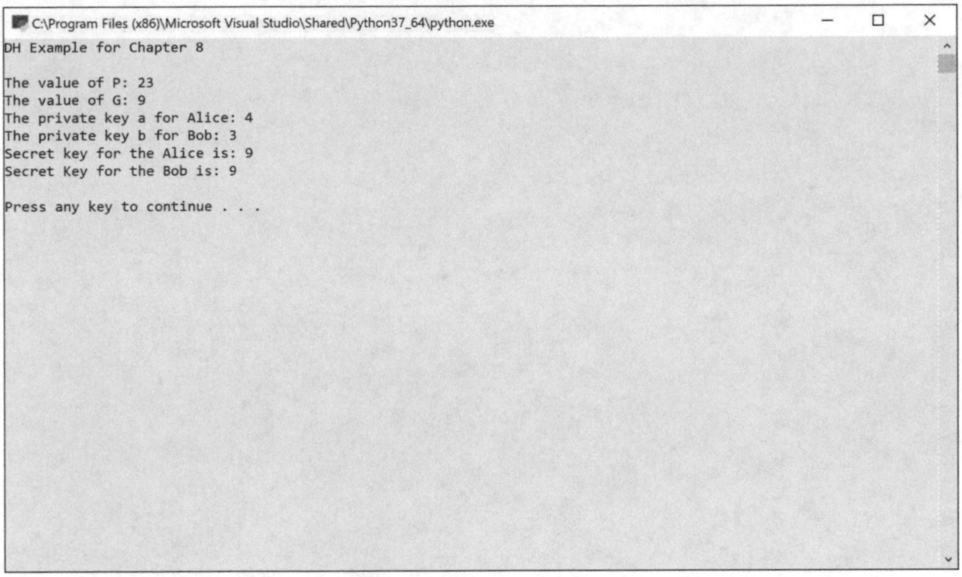

Figure 8.8: Diffie-Hellman exchange example

Summary

In this chapter, you were able to expand on your knowledge of working with a public-key infrastructure using Python. The biggest secrets in our government and business entities are largely protected by two simple mathematical equations:

- $C = M^e \pmod{N}$
- $C^{1/e} \bmod (p - 1)\ (q - 1) \bmod N = M$

These equations provide the basis of creating very large keys that are easy to generate but difficult to crack, essentially creating mathematical locks or trapdoors.

After gaining an understanding of how PKI works, we then explored how to implement ElGamal, which is a cryptosystem based on the difficulty of finding a discrete logarithm in a cyclic group.

The use of large keys in cryptography could have limitations as the world moves to smaller mobile devices. You also learned about the elliptic curve cryptography encryption system, which provides an alternative and more efficient type of public-key cryptography. The use of ECC is critical to how we implement key exchanges using the Diffie-Hellman algorithms.

In the next chapter, you will create a chat application that will incorporate many of the recipes and styles you have learned in this book.

Summary

Mastering Cryptography Using Python

The time has come to put all you have learned into action; you should now understand the concepts you need to secure communications between two parties. The chapter will focus on building an application that can send messages in plaintext, or encrypted using asymmetric public key infrastructure (PKI) and using the symmetric key method with an Elliptic Curve Diffie-Hellman key exchange. Implementing these techniques between two applications over an insecure UDP connection will help you think through how to send messages securely and ensure that they have not been tampered with. We will use Wireshark, a popular network analyzer, to verify that the messages are encrypted and cannot be distinguished from random noise. We will highlight using AES (Advanced Encryption Standard) in Counter (CTR) and Galouis/Counter (GCM) modes. We covered CTR in Chapter 5, and while the implementation of GCM is quite similar, it requires some special consideration as we design our encryption protocol. Our first task will be to build a small working application for plaintext communications, then adding the other cryptographic components to the mix. Throughout this chapter, you gain cryptographic experience as you:

- Construct an application that communicates in plaintext
- Install Wireshark and examine the communication traffic
- Implement a PKI into the application
- Implement RSA Digital Certificates

- Encrypt the message using ECC
- Implement the Elliptic Curve Diffie-Hellman exchange

Constructing a Plaintext Communications Application

Our first task is to revisit the construction of a threaded server with unencrypted traffic, which was introduced in Chapter 7. In addition to building a server and client Python file, we will create a helper file here that will support the coding additions we will implement as we are building our Python solution.

The architecture for the application includes a server file (`crypto _ server _ a. py`), a client file (`crypto _ client _ a.py`), and a helper file that will be used by both the client and server since they share many of the same components. One side encrypts, and the other one decrypts. For the sake of keeping this example simple, we will only do one-way communication. The same techniques used in this chapter can be used between any applications that transmit data over UDP.

Creating a Server

Our first step is to create an application that will use UDP sockets to accept packets from other programs. For our example we can use the localhost so that you can use the client application to send plaintext messages to the server. The server will then display the text as received.

Here's the Python code:

```python
# Message Receiver - crypto_chat_server.py
import hashlib, random, os, time
from binascii import hexlify
from socket import *
import Chapter9.ch9_crypto_chat as ct

def get_dh_sharedsecret():
    return

def get_dh_sharedkey():
    return

def decrypt(ciphertext, usePKI, useDH, serverSecret):
    #msg = ct.decrypt(ciphertext, usePKI, useDH, serverSecret)
    try:
        msg = ct.decrypt(ciphertext, usePKI, useDH, serverSecret)
    except:
        msg = ciphertext
    return msg
```

```python
def main():
    # set variables used to determine scheme
    useClientPKI = False;
    useDHKey = False;
    serverSecret = 0

    # set the variables used for the server components
    key = ""
    host = ""
    port = 8080
    buf = 1024 * 2
    addr = (host, port)
    UDPSock = socket(AF_INET, SOCK_DGRAM)
    UDPSock.bind(addr)

    # welcome to the server message
    print ("Waiting to receive messages...")

    # listening loop
    while True:
        # read the data sent from the client
        (data, addr) = UDPSock.recvfrom(buf)

        # send the data packet for decryption
        plaintext = decrypt(data, useClientPKI, useDHKey, serverSecret)

        # check to see if the user typed a special command such as
addPKI or addDH
        result = ct.check_server_command(plaintext)

        if result == 10: # encryption has been disabled so no message
            plaintext = b'PKI Encryption disabled!'
        elif result == 11: # encryption enabled
            plaintext = b'PKI Encryption enabled!'
        elif result == 20: # dh enabled
            clientKey = plaintext
            plaintext = b'Diffie-Hellman disabled!'
        elif result == 21: # encryption enabled
            plaintext = b'Diffie-Hellman enabled!'

        # messages are received encoded so you must decode the message
for processing
        msg = str(plaintext, 'utf-8')

        # process any client special commands
        if result == 0:
            # no encryption
            break
```

```
        # if any encryption is used, change the message to 'secure'
message
        if useClientPKI == True or useDHKey == True:
            print ("Received secured message: " + msg)
        else:
            print ("Received message: " + msg)


    UDPSock.close()
    os._exit(0)

if __name__ == '__main__':
    main()
```

Creating the Client

The client file will largely stay the same as its original counterpart in Chapter 7. One of the main modifications added here is an encrypt method that is used to call the helper file.

Here's the Python code:

```
# Message Sender - crypto_chat_client.py
import hashlib, random, os, time
from binascii import hexlify
from socket import *
import ch9_crypto_chat as ct


def get_dh_sharedsecret():
    return

def get_dh_sharedkey():
    return

def encrypt(plaintext, usePKI, useDH, clientSecret):
    msg = ct.encrypt(plaintext, usePKI, useDH, clientSecret)
    return msg

def main():
    host = "127.0.0.1" # set to IP address of target computer
    port = 8080
    addr = (host, port)
    UDPSock = socket(AF_INET, SOCK_DGRAM)

    # initiate the encryption variables
    sendUsingPrivate = False;
    sendUsingDH = False;
    skipEncryption = False;
```

```python
    # no matter what, get the ECC shared key, only use it if the user
enables
    clientSecret = get_dh_sharedkey()

    print ("Welcome to Crypto-Chat! \n")
    print ()

    # sending loop
    while True:
        if sendUsingPrivate == True or sendUsingDH == True:
            data = str(input("Enter secure message to send or type
'exit': ")).encode()
        else:
            data = str(input("Enter message to send or type 'exit': ")).
encode()

        # determine if the user initiated a special command
        result = ct.check_client_command(data)

        # handle any custom commands
        if data == b'exit':
            break
        if result == 0:
            break


        ciphertext = encrypt(data, sendUsingPrivate, sendUsingDH,
clientSecret)
        if skipEncryption:
            ciphertext = data;
            skipEncryption = False;

        # send the packet over UDP
        UDPSock.sendto(ciphertext, addr)

    # close UDP connection
    UDPSock.close()
    os._exit(0)

if __name__ == '__main__':
    main()
```

Creating the Helper File

To keep the code as consistent as possible between each step in our design, I will include various hooks that will be used later but, in this version, will not be cryptographically functional. The helper file will be the primary focus on most of our development tasks. Be sure to name this file ch9 _ crypto.py so that the client and server files created earlier can find it. I will attempt to keep it as clear and concise as possible, so keep in mind that the code represented here is intended to be readable as opposed to using some Python shorthand:

```python
# Chat Encryption Helper - ch9_crypto_chat.py
import os, base64, json
from Crypto.Cipher import PKCS1_OAEP, AES
from Crypto.PublicKey import RSA, ECC
from binascii import hexlify, unhexlify
from base64 import b64encode, b64decode

# encryption method used by all calls
def encrypt(message, usePKI, useDH, dhSecret):
    return message

# decryption method used by all calls
def decrypt(message, usePKI, useDH, dhSecret):
    return message

# decrypt using RSA
def decrypt_rsa(ciphertext):
    return ciphertext

# encrypt using RSA
def encrypt_rsa(message):
    return message

# check client commands
def check_client_command(data):
    return 1

# check server commands
def check_server_command(data):
    return 1
```

Execution

To execute this example, you can run the Python server and client in any order. This will hold true for the other implementations as well but in this example, you can start and stop either one and the program will continue to work once you put the missing component back in service. This will not always be true in the other examples if you have initiated encryption because the certificates get regenerated each time the files are executed. Your initial view should look similar to Figure 9.1.

Figure 9.1: Plaintext messaging

Installing and Testing Wireshark

Packet capture can provide a security professional or network administrator with information about individual packets such as transmit time, source, destination, protocol type, and header data. Wireshark is an open-source tool for analyzing packets and profiling network traffic. These types of tools are often referred to as a network analyzer, a network protocol analyzer, or a sniffer. We will be using Wireshark to examine the content that is sent between the client and server applications; the tool is designed to examine the details of traffic at a variety of levels, ranging from connection-level information to the bits that make up a single packet. This information can be useful for evaluating security events and troubleshooting network security device issues. For our example, you will ensure that the various modes of the client/server application are working correctly.

Wireshark will typically display information in three panels (see Figure 9.2). The top panel lists frames individually with key data on a single line. Any single frame selected in the top pane is further explained in the tool's middle panel. In this section of the display, the tool shows packet details, illustrating how various aspects of the frame can be understood as belonging to the data link layer, network layer, transport layer, or application layer. Lastly, Wireshark's bottom pane displays the raw frame, with a hexadecimal rendition on the left and the corresponding ASCII values on the right.

Because Wireshark can also be used for eavesdropping, an organization using the tool should make sure it has a clearly defined privacy policy that spells out the rights of individuals using its network, grants permission to sniff traffic for security and troubleshooting issues, and states the organization's policies for obtaining, analyzing, and retaining network traffic samples.

You can download Wireshark for free from www.wireshark.org for Windows and macOS. Wireshark is also likely available for Linux in your Linux distribution

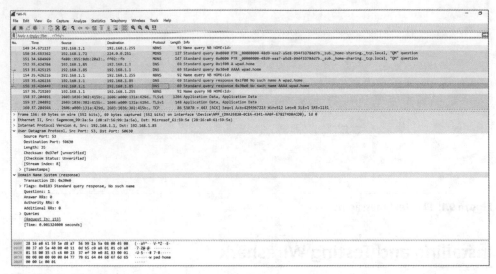

Figure 9.2: Wireshark overview

package manager. As your installation requirements will be different for each OS, check out the Wireshark site for any specifics.

Once you have it installed, you can turn on the packet capture. If you have any web browsers or other network-intensive applications open, you may want to close them or disable capturing those packets. You can filter traffic to show only packets to a specific destination IP, from a specific source IP, and even to and from an entire subnet; as an example, if you want to filter out data except that which has a source or destination of 192.168.2.11, type `ip.addr == 192.168.2.11` in the filter bar. Once you are ready for a test, execute the following steps:

1. Start Wireshark.

2. Execute the server file.

3. Execute the client file.

4. Click the blue shark fin on the command bar to start capture.

5. In the client command window, type **Hello World!**

6. Click the stop button on the command bar to stop capture.

7. Examine the UDP packet. You should notice that the length of the packet is 12 bytes. The only time you should see a result that equals 12 is when the data is being submitted in plaintext.

8. Examine the bottom pane; you should see your plaintext message. The middle frame tells you the protocol (UDP), src port, and destination port (8080), along with the number of bytes (12).

If you have everything set up correctly, you should see the plaintext message appear within your Wireshark capture, as shown in Figure 9.3.

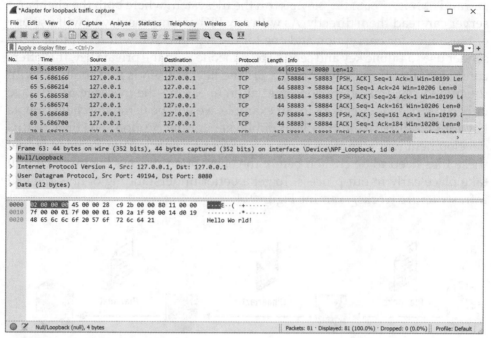

Figure 9.3: Wireshark traffic

Once you have your packet capture working, it is time to encrypt the data so that you can communicate securely. We will implement a PKI solution in the next section.

Implementing PKI in the Application Using RSA Certificates

You should have a working solution that sends a plaintext message over a port using the UDP protocol from a client application to a server application. If you have Wireshark configured, you should be able to confirm that the message being sent is readable in plaintext. Since we are looking to encrypt the data, we will now implement public-key infrastructure algorithms to secure the data. As you will recall, this type of infrastructure requires the use of public and private keys. Usually the *infrastructure* in public-key infrastructure implies some sort of shared key server where clients and servers can share public keys. For the sake of our example, this will simply be a shared file called `client _ public _ key.` `pem` on the filesystem.

We will be using the PyCrypto library to generate `client _ private _ key.` `pem` and `client _ public _ key.pem` on the filesystem where both the client and server can read them directly. As with any PKI arrangement, you will use one of these files for encryption and one for decryption. You will recall that if the sender uses a public key and sends it to someone with the private key, this offers confidentiality. If the sender uses a private key and sends it to someone with the public key, this offers nonrepudiation (meaning the message could have only come from the sender). In our example, we will be using the client private key for encryption and the client public key for decryption. The bulk of this development will take place in the `ch9 _ crypto _ chat.py` file. Remember that these files need to be created before the encryption process begins, so it will take place early in our process. To get a better understanding of how the PKI infrastructure works, examine Figure 9.4.

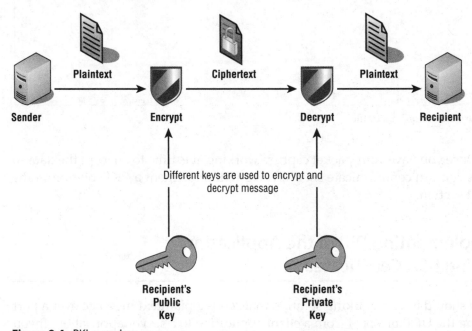

Figure 9.4: PKI overview

Modifying the Server

The primary change to the server file (`ch9 _ crypto _ chat _ server.py`) will be in constructing and utilizing the `check _ server _ command()` method to examine the plaintext and to modify the command sent with a result message.

The command being used in this example is `addPKI`:

```
# send the data packet for decryption
plaintext = decrypt(data, useClientPKI, useDHKey, serverSecret)

# check to see if the user typed a special command such as addPKI or
addDH
result = ct.check_server_command(plaintext)

if result == 10: # encryption has been disabled so no message
    plaintext = b'PKI Encryption disabled!'
elif result == 11: # encryption enabled
    plaintext = b'PKI Encryption enabled!'


# messages are received encoded so you must decode the message for
processing
msg = str(plaintext, 'utf-8')

# process any client special commands
if result == 0:
    # no encryption
    break
if result == 10:
    # turn off the use of PKI
    useClientPKI = False;
if result == 11:
    # turn on the use of PKI
    useClientPKI = True;
    # let the user know PKI is certs are found
    print ("Client certificate found ...")
```

Modifying the Client

The primary modifications to the client file capture the user commands, such as `addPKI` or `addDH`, and then configure the communications accordingly. Once we know which encryption method the user wants (plain, PKI, ECC), we pass the data, the type of encryption, and the required key or client secret. The client file will pass the heavy lifting over to the helper file:

```
# handle any custom commands
if data == b'exit':
    break
if result == 0:
    break
if result == 10:
    sendUsingPrivate = False;
if result == 11:
    sendUsingPrivate = True;
    skipEncryption = True;
```

Modifying the Helper File

The helper file will be growing quite a bit now. In addition to using it to create the private and public key files, we also use it for reading the key files and performing our encryption and decryption process. You've seen code examples of this in a number of chapters, but if you would like to review the topic again, check out Chapter 5.

PyCrypto is being used in this example to expose the PKCS1_OAEP module. The only difference between the encryption and decryption methods is the use of specific keys:

```python
# Chat Encryption Helper - ch9_crypto_chat.py
import os, base64, json
from Crypto.Cipher import PKCS1_OAEP, AES
from Crypto.PublicKey import RSA, ECC
from binascii import hexlify, unhexlify
from base64 import b64encode, b64decode

# encryption method used by all calls
def encrypt(message, usePKI, useDH, dhSecret):
    if usePKI == True:
        message = encrypt_rsa(message)
    return message

# decryption method used by all calls
def ch9_decrypt(message, usePKI, useDH, dhSecret):
    if usePKI == True:
        message = ch9_decrypt_rsa(message)
    return message


# generate RSA certs
def gen_rsa_certs():
    #ch8_Generate_RSA_Certs.py
    from Crypto.PublicKey import RSA

    #Generate a public/private key pair using 4096 bits key length (512
bytes)
    new_key = RSA.generate(4096, e=65537)

    #The private key in PEM format
    private_key = new_key.exportKey("PEM")

    #The public key in PEM Format
    public_key = new_key.publickey().exportKey("PEM")

    fd = open("client_private_key.pem", "wb")
    fd.write(private_key)
    fd.close()
```

```
        fd = open("client_public_key.pem", "wb")
        fd.write(public_key)
        fd.close()


# decrypt using RSA
def decrypt_rsa(ciphertext):
    key = RSA.importKey(open('client_private_key.pem').read())
    cipher = PKCS1_OAEP.new(key)
    plaintext = cipher.decrypt(ciphertext)
    return plaintext


# encrypt using RSA
def encrypt_rsa(message):
    key = RSA.importKey(open('client_public_key.pem').read())
    cipher = PKCS1_OAEP.new(key)
    ciphertext = cipher.encrypt(message)

    plaintext = decrypt_rsa(ciphertext)

    return ciphertext



# check client commands
def check_client_command(data):
    if data == b'addPKI':
        gen_rsa_certs()
        return 11
    elif data == b'removePKI':
        usePKI = False
        return 10
    return 1


# check server commands
def check_server_command(data):
    if data == b'addPKI':
        return 11
    if data == b'removePKI':
        useDH = False
        return 10

    return 1
```

Execution

The execution of the PKI solution will appear to work just as the original version did. Once you type addPKI, the client sends the message to the server unencrypted and then modifies the data to state "PKI Encryption enabled!" This should pop up in the command window for the server, as shown in Figure 9.5.

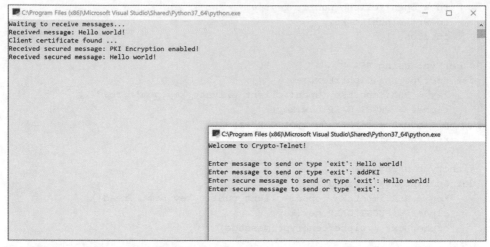

Figure 9.5: PKI Encryption enabled

In addition, Wireshark should encrypt `addPKI` using the client private key. This will convert the message to 512 bytes. While you will be able to find the UDP packet just as you did in the previous section, this time, the data going over the wire is encrypted; your Wireshark output should look similar to Figure 9.6.

Figure 9.6: Wireshark output

The server file will then receive the encrypted message and then decrypt it using the client public key. If all works according to plan, instead of seeing the decrypted message of addPKI, you should see the enabled notification. You can turn off the use of PKI by typing **removePKI**. This should then produce readable traffic in Wireshark again. Play with this a few times to ensure that you can switch back and forth.

Implementing Diffie-Hellman Key Exchange

In Chapter 7, you learned about the concepts of hashing and how it can be utilized to ensure message integrity. AES-GCM was designed to preserve the integrity and the confidentiality of the message. This holds true even if the same nonce is used for each message. The function used for the encryption utilizes the nonce, the plaintext message, and optional associated data. If you elect to use the same nonce, nothing will be revealed except in the case that the same message is encrypted multiple times with the same nonce. When that happens, an eavesdropper (in our case, Wireshark) will be able to observe repeated encryptions in the message traffic. Beyond that, no further information will be available. In our example here, we will not use the same nonce for different messages, but this requires us to also send it over the wire to the server.

One obstacle identified with creating the client/server application that sends text encryption is that you will need to concatenate the nonce and possibly a message authentication tag. Because the UDP protocol does not specify anything regarding message format, one solution is to use Python's JSON encoder and decoder to structure our messages. JSON, which stands for JavaScript Object Notation, is a lightweight data interchange protocol supported by many different applications and programming languages. We will use the json.dumps method to build a string that contains the nonce and message for a CTR example, and the nonce, message, and authentication tag for the GCM example. On the server side, the json module is used to extract the data using json.loads. Once we have the message and nonce on the server side, we can convert the data back to binary and decrypt the message. The use of the json module for both encryption and decryption is shown in Figure 9.7.

As you examine the helper file content, you will notice that the tag is passed into the decrypt_and_verify() method. This method checks the integrity of the message as well as the confidentiality. We will examine the data that is being sent from the client in the "Execution" section.

If you do not need message integrity, you can use the AES_CTR methods. These methods also use the JSON interchange to pass the nonce and the message. The authentication tag would not be required.

```python
    # encrypt using AES-GCM
⊟def encrypt_AES_GCM(msg, secretKey):
    aesCipher = AES.new(secretKey, AES.MODE_GCM)
    ct, authTag = aesCipher.encrypt_and_digest(msg)

    ct = hexlify(ct)
    ct = ct.decode('utf-8')
    authTag = hexlify(authTag)
    authTag = authTag.decode('utf-8')
    noncea = hexlify(aesCipher.nonce)
    nonce = noncea.decode('utf-8')

    ciphertext = json.dumps({'nonce':nonce, 'ciphertext':

    return ciphertext

    # decrypt using AES-GCM
⊟def decrypt_AES_GCM(encryptedMsg, secretKey):

    b64 = json.loads(encryptedMsg)

    nonce = str(b64['nonce'])
    nonce = nonce.encode()
    nonce = unhexlify(nonce)
```

Figure 9.7: `json` module

Modifying the Server File

Our goal now is to add the functionality we need to implement the Diffie-Hellman exchange. While it may not be completely obvious at first, the bulk of this is the creation of the Diffie-Hellman certificates for both the server and client. The server will call the `gen_server_DH()` method to generate the certificates when the application starts up. The certificates need to be in place prior to the client requiring them, which takes place when the user types `addDH` on the client.

In addition to the Diffie-Hellman certificates that get created, we also need to implement the Diffie-Hellman methods to examine the client's public key and use it to create a shared secret using the server's private key. The same process happens on the client.

The new code from this module should look like the following:

```python
serverDH = crypto.gen_server_DH()
serverSecret = 0;

def get_dh_sharedsecret():
    key = int(open('client_public_dh_key.pem').read())
    serverDH.generateSharedKey(key)
    serverDH.getSharedKey()
```

```
        serverDH.generateSharedKey(key)

        #serverDH.displayParameters()
        #serverDH.displayShared()

        return  (serverDH.sharedSecret)

def get_dh_sharedkey():
    key = int(open('client_public_dh_key.pem').read())
    serverDH.generateSharedKey(key)
    serverDH.getSharedKey()

    serverDH.generateSharedKey(key)

    #serverDH.displayParameters()
    #serverDH.displayShared()

    private_key = serverDH.key

    return  private_key
```

In the main method, you will also need to update the examination of the results so that you can set the correct Boolean operators:

```
# check to see if the user typed a special command such as addPKI or
addDH
result = crypto.check_server_command(plaintext)

if result == 10: # encryption has been disabled so no message
    plaintext = b'PKI Encryption disabled!'
elif result == 11: # encryption enabled
    plaintext = b'PKI Encryption enabled!'
elif result == 20: # dh enabled
    clientKey = plaintext
    plaintext = b'Diffie-Hellman disabled!'
elif result == 21: # encryption enabled
    plaintext = b'Diffie-Hellman enabled!'

# messages are received encoded so you must decode the message for
processing
msg = str(plaintext, 'utf-8')

# process any client special commands
if result == 0:
    # no encryption
    break
if result == 10:
    # turn off the use of PKI
    useClientPKI = False;
if result == 11:
```

```
        # turn on the use of PKI
        useClientPKI = True;
        # let the user know PKI certs are found
        print ("Client certificate found ...")
    if result == 20:
        # turn off Diffie-Hellman
        useDHKey = False;
    if result == 21:
        # turn on Diffie-Hellman
        useDHKey = True;
        print ("DH Key Exchange ...")
        serverSecret = get_dh_sharedkey()

    # if any encryption is used, change the message to 'secure' message
    if useClientPKI == True or useDHKey == True:
        print ("Received secured message: " + msg)
    else:
        print ("Received message: " + msg)
```

Modifying the Client File

The client will call the `gen_client_DH()` method to generate the certificates when the application starts up. The certificates need to be in place prior to the client requiring them, which takes place when the user types `addDH` on the client.

In addition to the Diffie-Hellman certificates that get created, we also need to implement the Diffie-Hellman methods to examine the server's public key and use it to create a shared secret using the client's private key. The same process happens on the server.

The following code was added to the client file:

```
import Chapter9.ch9_crypto_chat as ct

clientDH = clientDH = ct.gen_client_DH()
clientSecret = 0;

def get_dh_sharedsecret():
    key = int(open('server_public_dh_key.pem').read())
    clientDH.generateSharedKey(key)
    clientDH.getSharedKey()

    clientDH.generateSharedKey(key)

    shared_key = clientDH.sharedSecret

    return (shared_key)
```

```
def get_dh_sharedkey():
    key = int(open('server_public_dh_key.pem').read())
    clientDH.generateSharedKey(key)
    clientDH.getSharedKey()

    clientDH.generateSharedKey(key)

    private_key = clientDH.key

    return private_key
```

As with the server file, the client file needs to address the results determined by the message sent over UDP:

```
# determine if the user initiated a special command
result = ct.check_client_command(data)

# handle any custom commands
if data == b'exit':
    break
if result == 0:
    break
if result == 10:
    sendUsingPrivate = False;
if result == 11:
    sendUsingPrivate = True;
    skipEncryption = True;
if result == 20:
    sendUsingDH = False;
if result == 21:
    sendUsingDH = True;
    skipEncryption = True;
```

Prior to going into the loop, you will need to get the client secret by calling the `get_dh_sharedkey()` method:

```
# no matter what, get the ECC shared key, only use it if the user
enables
clientSecret = get_dh_sharedkey()

print ("Welcome to Crypto-Chat! \n")
print ("    Enable PKI: type 'addPKI'")
print ("    Disable PKI: type 'removePKI'")
print ("    Enable Diffie-Hellman: type 'addDH'")
print ("    Disable Diffie-Hellman: type 'removeDH'")
print ()
```

We also make a number of changes to the client screen to show the user the special commands. These are nothing more than just `print()` calls. The final version should look similar to Figure 9.8.

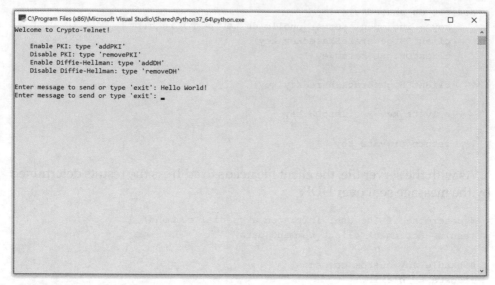

Figure 9.8: Final version

Modifying the Helper File

Now that you understand how the Diffie-Hellman protocol works, it is time to implement the processes into the helper file. Examine the helper file that you have created and implement the following code:

```
# encryption method used by all calls
def encrypt(message, usePKI, useDH, dhSecret):
    if usePKI == True:
        message = encrypt_rsa(message)
    if useDH == True:
        message = encrypt_dh(message, dhSecret)
    return message


# decryption method used by all calls
def decrypt(message, usePKI, useDH, dhSecret):
    if useDH == True:
        message = decrypt_dh(message, dhSecret)
    if usePKI == True:
        message = decrypt_rsa(message)
    return message


# delete all generated DH certs
def remove_dh_certs():
    try:
        os.remove("client_private_dh_key.pem")
        os.remove("client_public_dh_key.pem")
        os.remove("server_private_dh_key.pem")
        os.remove("server_public_dh_key.pem")
```

```python
    except:
        return 0


# generate Diffie-Hellman certificates for client
def gen_client_DH():
    clientDH =  dh.DiffieHellman(2,17,1024)

    privateKey = str(clientDH.privateKey).encode()
    fd = open("client_private_dh_key.pem", "wb")
    fd.write(privateKey)
    fd.close()

    publicKey = str(clientDH.publicKey).encode()
    fd = open("client_public_dh_key.pem", "wb")
    fd.write(publicKey)
    fd.close()

    clientDHSet = clientDH
    return clientDH

# generate Diffie-Hellman certificates for server
def gen_server_DH():
    svrDH =  dh.DiffieHellman(2,17,1024)

    privateKey = str(svrDH.privateKey).encode()
    fd = open("server_private_dh_key.pem", "wb")
    fd.write(privateKey)
    fd.close()

    publicKey = str(svrDH.publicKey).encode()
    fd = open("server_public_dh_key.pem", "wb")
    fd.write(publicKey)
    fd.close()

    key = (open('server_public_dh_key.pem').read())

    serverDHSet = svrDH
    return svrDH


# encrypt using Diffie-Hellman - ECC
def encrypt_dh(plaintext, dhSecret):
    # encrypt using the shared secret from Client (Private) and Server
(Public)
    ciphertext = encrypt_AES_GCM(plaintext,dhSecret)
    ciphertext = ciphertext.encode()
    #reverse = decrypt_AES_GCM(ciphertext, dhSecret)
    return ciphertext
```

```python
# decrypt using Diffie-Hellman - ECC
def decrypt_dh(ciphertext, dhSecret):
    # decrypt using the shared secret from Client (Private) and Server
(Public)
    ciphertext = ciphertext.decode('utf-8')
    plaintext = decrypt_AES_GCM(ciphertext,dhSecret)
    #reverse = encrypt_AES_GCM(ciphertext, dhSecret)
    return plaintext


# generate ECC certs
def gen_ecc_certs():
    key = ECC.generate(curve='P-256')
    f = open('myprivatekey.pem','wt')
    f.write(key.export_key(format='PEM'))
    f.close()
    f = open('myprivatekey.pem','rt')
    key = ECC.import_key(f.read())
    print (key)


# encrypt using AES-GCM
def encrypt_AES_GCM(msg, secretKey):
    aesCipher = AES.new(secretKey, AES.MODE_GCM)
    ct, authTag = aesCipher.encrypt_and_digest(msg)

    ct = hexlify(ct)
    ct = ct.decode('utf-8')
    authTag = hexlify(authTag)
    authTag = authTag.decode('utf-8')
    noncea = hexlify(aesCipher.nonce)
    nonce = noncea.decode('utf-8')

    ciphertext = json.dumps({'nonce':nonce, 'ciphertext':ct,
'tag':authTag})

    return ciphertext

# decrypt using AES-GCM
def decrypt_AES_GCM(encryptedMsg, secretKey):

    b64 = json.loads(encryptedMsg)

    nonce = str(b64['nonce'])
    nonce = nonce.encode()
    nonce = unhexlify(nonce)

    ct = str(b64['ciphertext'])
    ct = ct.encode()
    ct = unhexlify(ct)
```

```
        authTag = str(b64['tag'])
        authTag = authTag.encode()
        authTag = unhexlify(authTag)

        aesCipher = AES.new(secretKey, AES.MODE_GCM, nonce)
        nonce = b64encode(aesCipher.nonce).decode('utf-8')
        plaintext = aesCipher.decrypt_and_verify(ct, authTag)
        return plaintext

# encrypt using AES-CTR
def encrypt_AES_CTR(msg, secretKey):
        cipher = AES.new(secretKey, AES.MODE_CTR)
        ct_bytes = cipher.encrypt(msg)
        nonce = b64encode(cipher.nonce).decode('utf-8')
        ct = b64encode(ct_bytes).decode('utf-8')
        ciphertext = json.dumps({'nonce':nonce, 'ciphertext':ct})
        return ciphertext

# decrypt using AES-CTR
def decrypt_AES_CTR(msg, secretKey):
        b64 = json.loads(msg)
        nonce = b64decode(b64['nonce'])
        ct = b64decode(b64['ciphertext'])
        cipher = AES.new(secretKey, AES.MODE_CTR, nonce=nonce)
        plaintext = cipher.decrypt(ct)
        return plaintext

# check client commands
def check_client_command(data):
        if data == b'addPKI':
            gen_rsa_certs()
            return 11
        elif data == b'removePKI':
            usePKI = False
            return 10
        elif data == b'addDH':
            return 21
        elif data == b'removeDH':
            usePKI = False
            return 20
        return 1

# check server commands
def check_server_command(data):
        if data == b'addPKI':
            return 11
        if data == b'removePKI':
            useDH = False
            return 10
        if data == b'addDH':
            return 21
```

```
        if data == b'removeDH':
            useDH = False
            return 20
    return 1
```

Creating the Diffie-Hellman Class File

There are many cryptographic libraries that will handle the Diffie-Hellman exchange for you, and the DH primes listed in this section are a bit brutal to type; the code listed in this section is presented more to help you understand how the protocol works. This code, like all of the code in this book, is available on the book's website. This section is mostly for students who need to understand how to generate the Diffie-Hellman exchange in other languages that may not have libraries for it or for those of you in academia:

```python
import hashlib
from binascii import hexlify

try:
    #Preferably using urandom (more secure)
    import os
    random_function = os.urandom
    random_provider = "OS random"
except (AttributeError, ImportError):
    import ssl
    random_function = ssl.RAND_bytes
    random_provider = "Python SSL"


class DiffieHellman():
    """
    Using standard primes from RFC 3526 MODP Groups 17 and 18.
    Both are sufficient to generate AES 256 keys with a 540+ bit
exponent.
    https://datatracker.ietf.org/doc/rfc3526/
    """

    def __init__ (self, generator = 2, group = 17, keyLength=2048):
        """
        Generate the public and private keys
        """

        #Length in bits
        min_keyLength = 1024
        default_keyLength = 2024

        default_generator = 2
        valid_generators = [2, 3, 7] #Must be primes
```

```python
        # Sanity check for generator
        if (generator not in valid_generators):
            print ("Error: Invalid generator. Default (2) will be used
instead.")
            self.generator = default_generator
        else:
            self.generator = generator

        # Sanity check for keyLength
        if (keyLength < min_keyLength):
            print ("Error: keyLength is too small. Setting to minimum
(",min_keyLength,").")
            self.keyLength = min_keyLength
        else:
            self.keyLength = keyLength

        #Getting prime
        self.prime = self.getPrime(group)

        #Generating Keys
        self.privateKey = self.generatePrivateKey(self.keyLength)
        self.publicKey = self.generatePublicKey()


    def getPrime(self, group = 17):
        """
        Returns the correspondent prime.
        To explore more primes: https://github.com/
RedHatProductSecurity/Diffie-Hellman-Primes
        """

        default_group = 17

        primes = {
            17:
0xFFFFFFFFFFFFFFFFC90FDAA22168C234C4C6628B80DC1CD129024E088A67CC74020BBE
A63B139B22514A08798E3404DDEF9519B3CD3A431B302B0A6DF25F14374FE1356D6D51C2
45E485B576625E7EC6F44C42E9A637ED6B0BFF5CB6F406B7EDEE386BFB5A899FA5AE9F24
117C4B1FE649286651ECE45B3DC2007CB8A163BF0598DA48361C55D39A69163FA8FD24CF
5F83655D23DCA3AD961C62F356208552BB9ED529077096966D670C354E4ABC9804F1746C
08CA18217C32905E462E36CE3BE39E772C180E86039B2783A2EC07A28FB5C55DF06F4C52
C9DE2BCBF6955817183995497CEA956AE515D2261898FA051015728E5A8AAAC42DAD3317
0D04507A33A85521ABDF1CBA64ECFB850458DBEF0A8AEA71575D060C7DB3970F85A6E1E4
C7ABF5AE8CDB0933D71E8C94E04A25619DCEE3D2261AD2EE6BF12FFA06D98A0864D87602
733EC86A64521F2B18177B200CBBE117577A615D6C770988C0BAD946E208E24FA074E5AB
3143DB5BFCE0FD108E4B82D120A92108011A723C12A787E6D788719A10BDBA5B2699C327
186AF4E23C1A946834B6150BDA2583E9CA2AD44CE8DBBBC2DB04DE8EF92E8EFC141FBECA
A6287C59474E6BC05D99B2964FA090C3A2233BA186515BE7ED1F612970CEE2D7AFB81BDD
762170481CD0069127D5B05AA993B4EA988D8FDDC186FFB7DC90A6C08F4DF435C9340284
9236C3FAB4D27C7026C1D4DCB2602646DEC9751E763DBA37BDF8FF9406AD9E530EE5DB38
```

```
2F413001AEB06A53ED9027D831179727B0865A8918DA3EDBEBCF9B14ED44CE6CBACED4BB
1BDB7F1447E6CC254B332051512BD7AF426FB8F401378CD2BF5983CA01C64B92ECF032EA
15D1721D03F482D7CE6E74FEF6D55E702F46980C82B5A84031900B1C9E59E7C97FBEC7E8
F323A97A7E36CC88BE0F1D45B7FF585AC54BD407B22B4154AACC8F6D7EBF48E1D814CC5E
D20F8037E0A79715EEF29BE32806A1D58BB7C5DA76F550AA3D8A1FBFF0EB19CCB1A313D5
5CDA56C9EC2EF29632387FE8D76E3C0468043E8F663F4860EE12BF2D5B0B7474D6E694F9
1E6DCC4024FFFFFFFFFFFFFFFF,
            18:
0xFFFFFFFFFFFFFFFFC90FDAA22168C234C4C6628B80DC1CD129024E088A67CC74020BBE
A63B139B22514A08798E3404DDEF9519B3CD3A431B302B0A6DF25F14374FE1356D6D51C2
45E485B576625E7EC6F44C42E9A637ED6B0BFF5CB6F406B7EDEE386BFB5A899FA5AE9F24
117C4B1FE649286651ECE45B3DC2007CB8A163BF0598DA48361C55D39A69163FA8FD24CF
5F83655D23DCA3AD961C62F356208552BB9ED529077096966D670C354E4ABC9804F1746C
08CA18217C32905E462E36CE3BE39E772C180E86039B2783A2EC07A28FB5C55DF06F4C52
C9DE2BCBF6955817183995497CEA956AE515D2261898FA051015728E5A8AAAC42DAD3317
0D04507A33A85521ABDF1CBA64ECFB850458DBEF0A8AEA71575D060C7DB3970F85A6E1E4
C7ABF5AE8CDB0933D71E8C94E04A25619DCEE3D2261AD2EE6BF12FFA06D98A0864D87602
733EC86A64521F2B18177B200CBBE117577A615D6C770988C0BAD946E208E24FA074E5AB
3143DB5BFCE0FD108E4B82D120A92108011A723C12A787E6D788719A10BDBA5B2699C327
186AF4E23C1A946834B6150BDA2583E9CA2AD44CE8DBBBC2DB04DE8EF92E8EFC141FBECA
A6287C59474E6BC05D99B2964FA090C3A2233BA186515BE7ED1F612970CEE2D7AFB81BDD
762170481CD0069127D5B05AA993B4EA988D8FDDC186FFB7DC90A6C08F4DF435C9340284
9236C3FAB4D27C7026C1D4DCB2602646DEC9751E763DBA37BDF8FF9406AD9E530EE5DB38
2F413001AEB06A53ED9027D831179727B0865A8918DA3EDBEBCF9B14ED44CE6CBACED4BB
1BDB7F1447E6CC254B332051512BD7AF426FB8F401378CD2BF5983CA01C64B92ECF032EA
15D1721D03F482D7CE6E74FEF6D55E702F46980C82B5A84031900B1C9E59E7C97FBEC7E8
F323A97A7E36CC88BE0F1D45B7FF585AC54BD407B22B4154AACC8F6D7EBF48E1D814CC5E
D20F8037E0A79715EEF29BE32806A1D58BB7C5DA76F550AA3D8A1FBFF0EB19CCB1A313D5
5CDA56C9EC2EF29632387FE8D76E3C0468043E8F663F4860EE12BF2D5B0B7474D6E694F9
1E6DBE115974A3926F12FEE5E438777CB6A932DF8CD8BEC4D073B931BA3BC832B68D9DD3
00741FA7BF8AFC47ED2576F6936BA424663AAB639C5AE4F5683423B4742BF1C978238F16
CBE39D652DE3FDB8BEFC848AD922222E04A4037C0713EB57A81A23F0C73473FC646CEA30
6B4BCBC8862F8385DDFA9D4B7FA2C087E879683303ED5BDD3A062B3CF5B3A278A66D2A13
F83F44F82DDF310EE074AB6A364597E899A0255DC164F31CC50846851DF9AB48195DED7E
A1B1D510BD7EE74D73FAF36BC31ECFA268359046F4EB879F924009438B481C6CD7889A00
2ED5EE382BC9190DA6FC026E479558E4475677E9AA9E3050E2765694DFC81F56E880B96E
7160C980DD98EDD3DFFFFFFFFFFFFFFFF
    }

    if group in primes.keys():
        return primes[group]
    else:
        print("Error: No prime with group",group,"Using
default,",default_group,".")
        return primes[default_group]


def generateRandomNumber(self, bits):
    """
    Generate a random number with the specified number of bits
```

```
(https://en.wikipedia.org/wiki/Cryptographically_secure_pseudorandom_
number_generator)
        """

        randomNumber = 0
        _bytes = bits // 8 + 8

        while (randomNumber.bit_length() < bits):
            randomNumber = int.from_bytes(random_function(_bytes),
byteorder='big')

        return randomNumber


    def generatePrivateKey(self, bits):
        """
        Generate the private key
        """

        return self.generateRandomNumber(bits)


    def generatePublicKey(self):
        """
        Generate public key with generator ** privateKey % prime
        """
        return pow(self.generator, self.privateKey, self.prime)


    def testReceiverPublicKey (self, receiverPublicKey):
        """
        Checks receiver Public Key to make sure it's valid.
        Since a safe prime is used, verify that the Euler's Criterion
for the Legendre Symbol == 1
        Not super trustworthy tho, it has its limitations.
        (https://en.wikipedia.org/wiki/Legendre_symbol)
(https://www.youtube.com/watch?v=o23itWTcEYw)
        """

        if (receiverPublicKey > 2 and receiverPublicKey < self.prime - 1):
            if(pow(receiverPublicKey, (self.prime - 1)//2, self.prime) == 1):
                #if it's a quadratic residue
                return True
        return False
```

```python
    def generateSharedSecret(self, privateKey, receiverPublicKey):
        """
        Generates the shared secret after checking if receiverPublicKey
is valid.
        """

        if (self.testReceiverPublicKey(receiverPublicKey) == True):
            sharedSecret = pow (receiverPublicKey, privateKey, self.
prime)
            return sharedSecret
        else:
            raise Exception ("Invalid public key.")


    def generateSharedKey (self, receiverPublicKey):
        """
        Gets shared secret, then hash it to obtain the shared key.
        """

        self.sharedSecret = self.generateSharedSecret(self.privateKey,
receiverPublicKey)

        try:
            _sharedSecretBytes = self.sharedSecret.to_bytes(self.
sharedSecret.bit_length() // 8 + 1, byteorder="big")
        except AttributeError:
            _sharedSecretBytes = str(self.sharedSecret)

        shared = hashlib.sha256()
        shared.update(bytes(_sharedSecretBytes))
        self.key = shared.digest()


    def getSharedKey (self):
        """
        Return shared secret Key
        """
        return self.key


    def displayParameters (self):
        """
        Display parameters used on the DH agreement.
        """

        print(">>>>>>> Parameters:")
        print("Prime[{0}]: {1}\n".format(self.prime.bit_length(), self.
prime))
        print("Generator:", self.generator, "\n")
```

```
        print("Private Key[{0} bits]: {1}\n".format(self.privateKey.bit_
length(), self.privateKey))
        print("Public Key[{0} bits]: {1}\n".format(self.publicKey.bit_
length(), self.publicKey))


    def displayShared (self):
        """
        Display the results of the exchange.
        """
        print(">>>>>>> Results:")
        print("Shared Secret[{0}]: {1}\n".format(self.sharedSecret.bit_
length(), self.sharedSecret))
        print("Shared Key [{0}]: {1}\n".format(len(self.key),
hexlify(self.key)))
```

Execution

Prior to typing your nonencrypted message, turn on Wireshark so that you can
verify the unencrypted traffic. Once you type addDH, the client sends an unencrypted command to the server that will initiate the encryption synchronization
on both sides. Once this is triggered, the server will know that the next message
sent will be using a shared secret that was created using Diffie-Hellman key
exchange. In the real world, these certificates, as with the RSA ones too, should
be on different systems. The certificates are left on the same computer to keep the
concept easy for you to test without having to have multiple computers. With the
changes made to the client file, you should see something similar to Figure 9.9
when you execute the server file and the client file on the same machine.

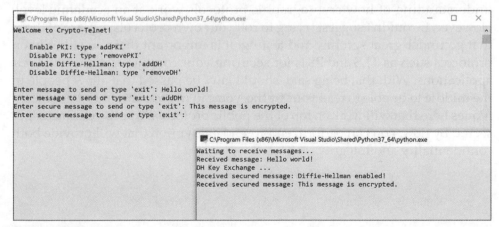

Figure 9.9: Diffie-Hellman Exchange chat

The message will be encrypted and passed over UDP along with the nonce and authentication tag; you will see those data labels in the UDP packet but will only see the encrypted versions. As you will see in Figure 9.10, the shared key is not passed over the connection.

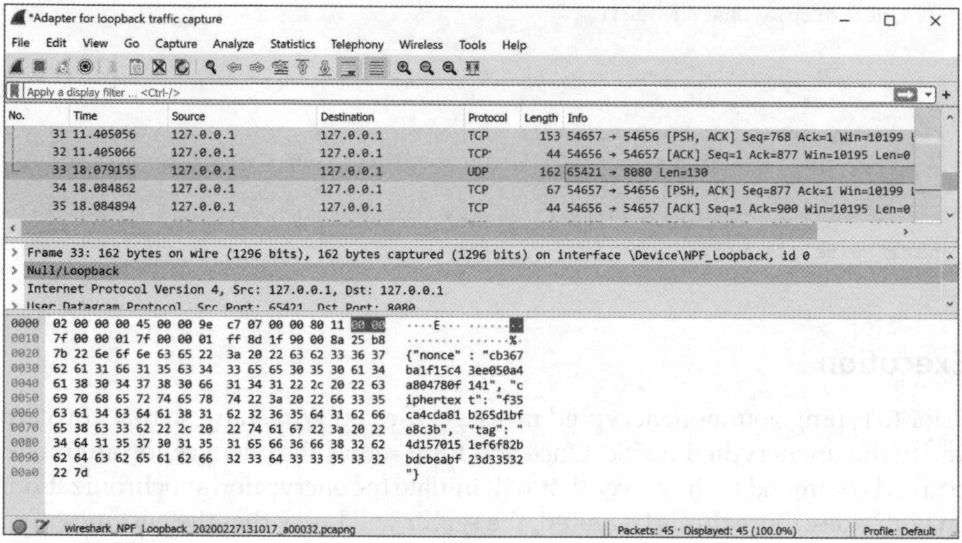

Figure 9.10: Shared key not passed

Wrapping Up

You should now have a working Python application that sends encrypted messages over an unsecure network. Hopefully, this book has provided you a better understanding of how cryptographic protocols work at an academic level; However, I wouldn't suggest trying to roll your own protocols in place of those that go under great scrutiny and testing. It is important that you still rely on protocols such as TLS and PKIs for securing your communications and your applications. With that being said, should laws be passed that allow people in the middle to be able to read your traffic, you can implement a number of techniques here that will work on top of the public protocols to keep your messages secret. By now, you can perform end-to-end encryption that will provide both confidentiality and integrity.

Index